REVOLUTION OR RECONCILIATION?

The struggle in the Church in South Africa

Rachel Tingle

Christian Studies Centre

ACKNOWLEDGEMENTS

I would like to thank the many Christians who did so much to help me during research trips to South Africa in Autumn 1989 and Summer 1991, and those who have kept me constantly informed of developments since then. This study is dedicated to them.

BIOGRAPHICAL NOTES

Rachel Tingle, an economist and journalist, is the founder director of the Christian Studies Centre. Her articles on religious topics have appeared in *The Daily Telegraph, The Church of England Newspaper, Catholic Herald, The Modern Churchman, Churchman, Crossway, and Prophecy Today* and she has contributed a regular column on Church affairs to *Free Nation/Freedom Today* since 1977. Her previous publications include *Gay Lessons: How Public Funds are used to Promote Homosexuality among Children and Young People* (Pickwick Books, 1986) and *Another Gospel? An account of the growing involvement of the Anglican Church in secular politics* (Christian Studies Centre, 1988).

Rt. Rev. B. B. Burnett was Archbishop of Cape Town (primate of the Church of the Province of South Africa) from 1974-1981. He was general secretary of the South African Council of Churches from 1967-1969 and also served on the Central Committee of the World Council of Churches during the 1960s.

© 1992   Rachel Tingle

Published by the Christian Studies Centre
8, Victoria Square,
London SW1W OQY
071-834-6473

ISBN 0 9513721 1 4

CONTENTS

FOREWORD 2

INTRODUCTION 3

CHAPTER

    1. THE INFLUENCE OF THE WORLD COUNCIL OF CHURCHES 10

    2. RADICAL THEOLOGY 53

    3. FROM RADICAL THEOLOGY TO ACTION 88

    4. THE CHURCH AS A 'SITE OF STRUGGLE' 134

    5. WHO PAYS FOR THE STRUGGLE? 166

    SUMMARY AND CONCLUSION 192

APPENDIX

    1. Main Political Groups and Recent Political Events in South Africa 198
    2. The Reform Process 235
    3. WCC Grants to 'Organisations Combating Racism' 240
    4. Ecumenical Association of Third World Theologians 242
    5. Grants Received by the Institute for Contextual Theology 246
    6. The Harare Declaration 247
    7. The Lusaka Statement 249
    8. South African Council of Churches: Income and Expenditure 256
    9. South African Council of Churches: Grants and Donations 258

INDEX 265

FOREWORD

Anyone who knows anything about contextual/liberation theology will realise how important and timely Rachel Tingle's book is.

The Scriptures handed down to us begin with the affirmation: "In the beginning God created the Heaven and the Earth." In the fullness of time, He gave us a Saviour, Jesus Christ our Lord, to deliver us from darkness into His light, and to lead us into all Truth. This truth is not man's truth, but God's Truth. But now we are confronted with another 'truth' called contextual or liberation Theology, which says "In the beginning, Man!" Here it is not God, but man, who determines what is to be done. This is Humanism and not Theology at all. What we see now is the Cuckoo's Nest syndrome - the false has neatly ensconsed itself within the Church and has been nurtured to such an extent that it is now replacing the true teaching of the Church.

Isaiah prophesied (Isaiah 30: 1-3) "Woe to the rebellious children, who carry out a plan, but not mine; and who make a league, but not of my Spirit, that they may add sin to sin." This is what this book talks about. It shows the influence of a false 'gospel' in which there is little personal evangelism and key Christian concepts are replaced with political concepts which then become paramount. In South Africa, this counterfeit form of Christianity has depended on funds from outside agencies.

Christians need to be alert to what is happening in the Church. This important book will enlighten you.

>   Rt. Rev. B. B. Burnett
>   (formerly Anglican Archbishop
>   of Cape Town)

INTRODUCTION

Since President De Klerk took office in 1989, the South African government has taken enormous steps to dismantle the country's highly complex and racially discriminatory apartheid legislation whereby almost every facet of peoples' lives had been governed by the colour of their skin. At the same time as this reform process has been going on, however, the country has continued to be shaken by appallingly high levels of political violence. According to the authoritative South African Institute of Race Relations (SAIRR),[1] 1990 and 1991 were the two worst years for political violence South Africa has ever experienced, with 3,699 fatalities in 1990 and 2,672 in 1991. It is estimated that, up to the end of 1991, a total of 11,910 people had been killed in such violence since it took off in September 1984.[2] The vast majority of these deaths were caused by black people killing other black people within the townships and in rural areas of Natal. In many cases,

---

1. The South African Institute of Race Relations was founded in 1929 as a multi-racial organisation to promote racial goodwill. It is not affiliated to any political body and, over the years, it has built up an international reputation for objective and detailed research. It has been a firm critic of apartheid and was amongst the first organisations to call for the ban on the African National Congress, the Pan African Congress, and other political organisations to be lifted, and for Nelson Mandela and other political prisoners to be released.
2. All these figures were provided by the SAIRR in a press release issued on 29 January, 1992.

the nature of the killings was almost indescribably horrible.

This situation has obviously caused great alarm within South Africa and many explanations have been advanced as to who is mainly to blame - the African National Congress? its chief political rival, Inkatha? or members of the security forces attempting to derail the negotiating process to a non-racial South Africa? One thing is clear: there is now a distressing *climate* of violence in the country, which seems to be continuing in the early months of 1992 in spite of recent attempts to establish a Peace Accord between most of the political parties.

In February 1991, John Kane-Berman, the executive director of the SAIRR, put forward his own apparently surprising explanation for this climate of violence. He argued that the Christian leadership in South Africa "has helped to legitimate violence as an instrument of liberation" and he maintained therefore that "black people in the townships are reaping a whirlwind of violence that the churches have helped to sow."[3]

Kane-Berman's remarks were widely reported in the South African press, so it was to be expected that they would provoke a reaction from the Churches. Frank Chikane, General Secretary of the South African Council of Churches (SACC), for instance, immediately declared, that "we are disgusted by the vicious and unwarranted attack on

---

3. For further details of his speech see SAIRR press release, 4 February 1991.

the Churches by Mr John Kane-Berman" and went on to say that "we have always believed and still believe the apartheid system is the primary cause of violence in our country."[4] To this Kane-Berman responded by arguing that his remarks were merely a continuation of his institute's tradition of even-handed research. It was, he said, precisely because the SAIRR had "played a leading role down the years in condemning state violence" that their experience and track record not only equipped but also compelled them to "speak out fearlessly against malpractices committed in the name of liberation."[5]

Since John Kane-Berman made his remarks, Frank Chikane and other Church leaders like Peter Storey, the Methodist bishop of the south-eastern Transvaal, and the Anglican Archbishop Tutu, have expressed their concern about the political violence sweeping South Africa.[6] So far, however, neither they nor any other Churchman in South Africa have been able to refute his allegations about the role played by the Church in helping to *sow* this violence. **The contention of this study is that this is because Kane-Berman was essentially correct.** In their understandable desire to see an end to apartheid, sections of the Church in South Africa, aided and supported by sections of the Church overseas, have sympathised with the 'liberation' movements - especially the African National Congress (ANC) - to

---

4. SACC press release, 5 April 1991.
5. *Race Relations News* (Instutute of Race Relations, April 1991.)
6. Chikane, *Sunday Star* (SA), 10 February 1991; Storey, *Citizen* (SA), 7 June 1991; Tutu, *Saturday Star* (SA), 30 March 1991.

such an extent that they have either simply turned a blind eye to the methods such organisations have been prepared to employ to gain political power, or have developed a theology which actually justifies violence. This has been confirmed, at least in part, by the ANC Youth League which, in a response to Kane-Berman's remarks, stated that "the church advocated the use of organised violence employed by a disciplined liberation movement to advance the cause of liberation...".[7] At the same time, as we shall see, the liberation movements have themselves initiated attempts to win Christians to their cause.

The effect of these developments has been to distort the traditional teaching of the Christian Church to a quite extraordinary degree. For any Christian this is cause for concern in itself. But at this stage in South Africa's history it is a particular cause for concern. An estimated 77% of the country's population describe themselves as Christian, and the level of genuine commitment and belief is far higher than in virtually any European country. Because of this, what the Churches do and say is of immense importance for South African society. At this time of rapid change, many people are looking to the Churches to provide the shared values amongst the races on which to build the 'New South Africa.'

Therefore, given the high hopes invested in the Churches, it is all the more tragic that there are some Church organisations (funded mainly by European Church groups and aid agencies) which have become so closely identified with the liberation

---

7. *The Citizen* (SA), 6 February 1991.

movements and their programmes, that they are continuing to perpetuate the divisions and conflicts in South African society. In this they are making a mistake similar to that of the Dutch Reformed Church (DRC) which, not only broadly supported the apartheid policies of the ruling National Party, but helped provide theological justification for them. The Dutch Reformed Church has now recognised and publicly admitted that this was wrong and that it should have "distanced itself much earlier" from policies of forced separation and division of peoples.[8]

---

8. The DRC began to move away from its support for apartheid in the 1980s. In its *Church and Society* report, adopted by its 1986 Synod, it declared that "racism is a sin" which "must be rejected and opposed in all its manifestations because it leads to oppression and exploitation." This prompted the break-away of 8,245 of the more conservative of the DRC's estimated 1.4 million members. The 1990 *Church and Society* report went further and declared that "Any system which in practice functions in this way (i.e. as apartheid had done), is unacceptable in the light of Scripture and the Christian conscience and must be rejected as sinful. Any attempt by a church to try to defend such a system biblically and ethically, must be seen as a serious fallacy, that is to say it is in conflict with the Bible." DRC delegates (including Moderator, Pieter Potgeiter, and former Moderator, Prof. Johan Heyns) also supported the declaration of the National Conference of Churches held at Rustenburg in November 1990 which stated that, "we denounce apartheid in its intention, its implementation and its consequences, as an evil policy. The practice and defence of apartheid as though it were biblically and theologically legitimate is an act of disobedience to God, a denial of the Gospel of Jesus Christ and a sin against our unity in the Holy Spirit." These decisions by the (white) DRC had, however, been preceded by the (coloured) Dutch Reformed Mission Church which in 1982 had adopted a statement, the *Belhar Confession,* which had declared that apartheid was a "sin" and a "theological heresy". For this reason it had accused the DRC of "theological heresy and idolatry".

Those who have used the Church as an arm of the 'liberation struggle', and have provided theological justification for revolutionary violence, should likewise admit that their stance has also been wrong.

It is to be hoped that all the Churches in the country will return to preaching the true Gospel of Jesus Christ - including His command to show unconditional love and forgiveness to one's enemies. This may well be the only hope of bringing about the reconciliation between people of all races and political factions which is imperative if South Africa is to avoid plunging into a full-scale civil war and emerge as a genuine multi-racial, free and stable democracy.

The first chapter of this study describes how changes in thinking within the World Council of Churches led to an increasing legitimisation of the activities of the South African liberation movements, including their readiness to use violence. The second chapter explains what is meant by contextual theology and how it differs significantly from orthodox Biblical theology. It describes, from the early 1970s onwards, how forms of contextual theology began to grow up in South Africa and their links with various radical political movements. Chapter 3 discusses how the development and spread of contextual theology in South Africa was greatly assisted by the establishment of an Institute for Contextual Theology (ICT), and how the ICT and related organisations drew on the concepts of contextual theology to demand that the Church should become involved in the liberation struggle. Chapter 4 deals with the way in which the ANC has itself attempted to draw the Churches into the struggle and how, as a result of this and the spread of contextual theology, the Church in South Africa has now become deeply divided. Chapter 5 describes the sources of funding of the radicalised Church in South Africa. Appendices 1 and 2 attempt to provide an objective description of the main political parties and political developments up to early April 1992 as a background to understanding what has been going on in the Church. The other appendices provide detailed supporting material to the main text.

1. THE INFLUENCE OF THE WORLD COUNCIL OF CHURCHES

The story of how sections of the Church came to side with the 'liberation' movements in South Africa and legitimise violence is a complicated one and it is not possible here to study all the people or organisations involved, particularly in the early years of this development.[1] Undoubtedly one of the most significant continuing influences, however, has been that of the World Council of Churches (WCC), and particularly its highly controversial Programme to Combat Racism (PCR). This chapter will discuss how the PCR came to be established and something of its impact on the world-wide Church.

Early Anti-Racist Initiatives of the WCC

Throughout the 1950s, the WCC watched with growing concern the gradual implementation of apartheid legislation in South Africa, and the increasing injustice and suffering it brought in its wake. It attempted to overcome this by example, persuasion, and international diplomacy.[2] Thus it

---

1. For some information see John de Gruchy, *The Church Struggle in South Africa* (Collins, 1986), and Peter Walshe, *Church Versus State in South Africa: The Case of the Christian Institute* (Orbis Books, 1983).
2. For a full discussion of this, see Darril Hudson, *The World Council of Churches in International Affairs* (The Royal Institute of International Affairs, 1977), pp. 61-90.

tried to persuade its member Churches to eradicate any racial discrimination in their own structures and, at the same time, sought to influence wider society through public statements. At its 1954 General Assembly in Evanston, for instance, the WCC declared that "any form of segregation based on race, colour, or ethnic origin is contrary to the gospel, and incompatible with the Christian doctrine of man and with the nature of the Church of Christ." Member Churches were urged to renounce "all forms of segregation or discrimination and to work for their abolition within their own life and within society."[3]

During the ensuing years, the WCC also tried to keep open the channels of communication and influence with its member Churches in South Africa. This was of great importance, for members included not only some of the English-speaking Churches which had publicly denounced apartheid,[4] but also the Cape and Transvaal Synods of the Dutch Reformed Church (DRC). Closely associated as it was with the Afrikaner people, the DRC had largely accepted and, indeed, had provided some theological justification for the apartheid policies of the ruling

---

3. W. A. Visser 't Hooft (ed.), *The Evanston Report* (WCC, 1955), p. 158.
4. For instance, both the (Anglican) Church of the Province of South African and the Methodist Church of South Africa issued statements in 1953 condemning apartheid.

National Party.[5] In fact, the Dutch Reformed family of Churches had itself long been divided along racial lines into the white 'parent' DRC, and its 'daughter' Churches which had been created as a result of missionary activity amongst other races - the Dutch Reformed Church in Africa for blacks (NGK in Afrika); the Dutch Reformed Mission Church (NGSK) for coloureds, and the Reformed Church in Africa for Indians.[6]

This approach by the WCC reached a high-point in 1960 when, in the wake of the Sharpeville tragedy, it convened a consultation of its South African member Churches at Cottesloe, near Johannesburg, in order to discuss race relations in the country. This eventually resulted in a statement which rejected all unjust discrimination in the Church and in society and drew attention to the disastrous consequences of aspects of the implementation of apartheid. The triumph for the WCC was the fact that

---

5. It has been argued that the theological justification for the apartheid ideas of the National Party as they first began to emerge in the 1930s, came not from the main DRC, but from the much smaller *Gereformeerde Kerk*, influenced by the neo-Calvinist ideas of Abraham Kuyper - see de Gruchy, *op. cit.*, pp. 31-34. Once the National Party took power, however, the DRC largely accepted apartheid and, indeed, it may have been the recommendations of a DRC missionary conference in 1950, advocating territorial apartheid, which led to the Group Areas' Act and the homelands policy.

6. This division in the Dutch Reformed Church dates back to 1857 when it decided that, although not desirable or scriptural, due to the weakness of some (whites) it was permissable to hold separate services for whites and blacks. There are also some smaller white members of the Dutch Reformed Church family created because of doctrinal differences. For more details see de Gruchy, *op. cit.*

it was not only the English-speaking Churches who endorsed the statement, but the DRC delegates also gave it their support. Sadly, however, as a result of direct pressure from then Prime Minister, Dr. Verwoerd, and also its own grassroots members, the DRC subsequently issued a statement defending apartheid and, as a result, decided to leave the WCC.[7]

Critics of the WCC's approach over this period may claim that it did not have much apparent success in reversing the apartheid policies of the South African regime. This does not mean, however, that the WCC had been wrong in its approach - nor does it indicate what might have happened if it had persisted with it. Starting in the mid-1960s, however, the WCC adopted a radically different stance.

Towards a More Radical Stance

Church and Society Conference (1966)

The WCC again condemned apartheid at its 1961 General Assembly in New Dehli, calling upon the Churches to strive actively for racial justice by all means short of violence.[8] However, some WCC officials were disappointed with the Assembly's inability, as they saw it, to come to grips with the theological and political implications of rapid change in the Third World, and they set about organising a semi-autonomous conference, held in Geneva in 1966, on the theme "Christians in the Technical and Social Revolutions of Our Time". This was concerned

---

7. For a useful summary of the events surrounding the Cottesloe Consultation see de Gruchy *op. cit.,* and Walshe, *op. cit.*
8. Hudson, *op. cit.,* p. 88.

with such questions as: "What is the calling of the Church in a modern society?" and "How can the Church make a positive contribution towards peace and freedom in a community plagued by poverty, injustice and other forms of social distress?"

As it turned out, the conference was to prove a watershed in WCC thinking. Rather than considering the power of the Christian Gospel to change *people,* platform speakers considered these questions in almost entirely secular terms, focussing their attention instead on the ways in which the Church might work to change society by socio-economic means.[9]

The most significant and radical lecture along these lines was given by an American theologian and fomer Latin American missionary, Richard Shaull.[10] According to him, one of the major features of modern society was the revolutionary process taking place in the Third World. Because the avowed end of this process was the establishment of a 'just social order' and also because (he maintained) Christ was a socio-political revolutionary, Shaull argued that the Church should no longer support the status quo but should involve itself in this revolution. This, he said, necessitated the adoption by the Church of an effective analysis of society which, he argued, had to be based on Marxism because, unlike Conservatism

---

9. For a description of this conference see Ernest Lefever, *Amsterdam to Nairobi: The World Council of Churches and the Third World* (Ethics and Public Policy Center, Georgetown University, USA, 1979).
10. Whilst in Latin America Shaull was responsible for organising a number of discussions on Christian-Marxist dialogue

or Liberalism which seek change through gradual evolutionary processes, Marxism demands a radical change in society through revolutionary means. He thus concluded that theology cannot be anything else than a social theory, drawing on Marxism, with the strategy of revolutionary change as a major component.[11]

Shaull's analysis can be criticised on a number of points. For instance, he accepted at face value the Marxist claim that a revolution would establish a better, more just social order, without quoting any supporting historical evidence. The evidence from Eastern Europe, the former Soviet Union, and also parts of Africa, tends, in fact, to prove quite the opposite. Shaull also made no attempt to distinguish between the different circumstances which might give rise to revolutions in order to consider when a revolution might be justified and when it might not; and he displayed an irrational preference for revolution as opposed to gradual political reform. Nor did he consider the *methods* to be used in revolutions in order to judge whether a Christian could, in good conscience, support them.

Of equal, if not of even greater importance, was Shaull's view of the Church. He referred to Christ as a socio-political revolutionary (in contrast to

---

11. Shaull "Revolutionary Change in Theological Perspective" in Bennett (ed.), *Christian Social Ethics in a Changing World* (SCM Press, 1966). For other theologians developing similar ideas at about the same time, see the collection of papers based on a colloquium organised by the Catholic organisation, IDOC International, *Christianisme et revolution* (Paris, Editions La Lettre, 1968).

the orthodox Christian view that Christ is the Son of God who died on the Cross that we might receive forgiveness for our sins); regarded theology as primarily a social theory (rather than our knowledge about God); and let the transient affairs of this world set the agenda for the Church (rather than stressing that the values of the Church are unchanging and should influence the world in every age). All these ideas amounted to a complete departure from the traditional teaching of the Church. Indeed, it needs emphasising that Shaull's views were so incompatible with orthodox Christianity that logically they could not both be true. Either Shaull was right and the Church had been wrong in its teaching for the previous two thousand years; or the traditional teaching of the Church was correct, in which case Shaull's ideas (although dressed up in Christian language) amounted to a major attack on the Church.

The weakness of Shaull's arguments (and those of similar theologians who put forward what came to be known as a 'theology of revolution') have been summed up by the French sociologist, Jacques Ellul, as follows:[12]

> "He is convinced, on the one hand, that the work of God in Christ is a work of humanization; and, on the other, that the objective of revolution is humanization. Thus revolution is inserted into the category of the humanizing activity of God. And, almost inevitably the conclusion follows that it is God

---

12. Jacques Ellul, *Violence: Reflections from a Christian Perspective* (Mowbrays, 1978).

himself who is demolishing the old structures in order to create a more human existence. In other words, God is at the center of the struggle led by revolutionaries ... (these theologians) do not consider even for a second that forces other than God might be at work, that, very likely the Prince of this World also has a finger in revolutions."

It was Shaull, however, who set the direction for the whole Church and Society conference. Other speakers, like H. D. Wendland, for instance, argued that the mission of the Church in the world must, of necessity, result in revolutionary social action, and concluded that "the Church itself becomes the source of constant revolutionary changes in State and society."[13] In a similar vein, Bola Ige, a lawyer and former leader of the Nigerian Student Christian Movement, criticised all who advocated gradual reform, and called instead for a world revolution to "knock out all existing suffocating constitutions, systems and the powers that keep them going."[14]

Such views influenced the Church and Society Conference report, which stated:[15]

"As Christians we are committed to work for the transformation of society. In the past we have usually done this through quiet efforts a social renewal, working in and through the

---

13. H. D. Wendland, "The Church and revolution" in *The Ecumenical Review*, October 1966.
14. *Official Report: World Conference on Church and Society* (World Council of Churches, Geneva, 1967), p. 18.
15. *Ibid.*, p. 49.

established institutions according to their rules. Today, a significant number of those who are dedicated to the service of Christ and their neighbour assume a more radical and revolutionary position."

The Conference also considered the use of violence. In doing so it drew on the concept, first put forward by Marx and further refined in the 1960s and 1970s by new-Left thinkers like Herbert Marcuse, of 'institutional violence' - that is the idea that social structures like restrictive laws, the police, and even the existence of private property, may be a form of 'violence' which in turn justifies the use of revolutionary 'counterviolence' such as bomb attacks, arson, etc. to overturn these structures and set up new ones in their place. The obvious danger of this idea is the fact that, since all societies need some sort of legal system and police force to maintain order, 'institutionalised violence' may be used to justify terrorism in any society - not just those where political and civil liberties are highly restricted, but even the most liberal and democratic. Ignoring this, the Conference report stated:

"Violence is very much a reality in our world, both the overt use of force to oppress and the invisible violence perpetrated on people who by the millions have been or still are the victims of repression and unjust social systems. Therefore the question often emerges today whether the violence which sheds the blood in planned revolutions may not be a lesser evil than the violence which, though bloodless, condemns whole populations to perennial despair."

It then reached the conclusion:

> "It cannot be said that the only possible position for the Christian is one of absolute non-violence ... Wherever small elites rule at the expense of the welfare of the majority, political change towards achieving a more just order as quickly as possible, should be actively promoted and supported ... in cases where such political changes are needed ... the use by Christians of revolutionary methods - by which is meant violent overthrow of existing political order - cannot be excluded a priori."

This was obviously a highly significant statement, but the report ignored many crucial political and theological questions implicit within it. Who, for instance, was to determine which situations were so oppressive as to justify revolution? Were there to be any constraints or limits on the kinds of revolutionary violence used? Was any judgement to be made about the political order to be installed in place of the old one? And what was to be the role of the Church on the ground during the violence and terror of a revolution?

Uppsala General Assembly (1968)

Whilst the 1966 Church and Society Conference only had the authority to speak *to* the Churches and the WCC and not *for* them, it largely set the agenda for the fourth General Assembly of the WCC, held in Uppsala in 1968, four of the six sessions of which were devoted to a discussion of the problems of rapid social change.[16] The Assembly supported the idea of revolutions in the Third World - although it was more cautious and ambiguous than the Church and Society Conference had been as to whether the use of violence was justified or not. A committee from the Church and Society Conference also made recommendations for a 'post assembly programme', the priority of which was to be the elimination of racism, especially white racism which, it said, was firmly embedded in developed Western countries. This proposal was adopted by the Assembly and, as a first step in this direction, the WCC organised an international consultation on racism in May 1969 which would be able to make recommendations to the WCC Central Committee later in the year.

Consultation on Racism (1969)

The terms of reference of the Consultation on Racism,[17] and its choice of setting - Notting Hill, London (the scene in 1958 of Britain's worst race riots to date) - meant that the discussion concentrated almost entirely on white racism, to the neglect of other forms of racism in the world. This was

---

16. For accounts of this Assembly see Norman Goodall (ed.), *The Uppsala Report, 1968* (WCC, 1968), and Kenneth Slack, *Uppsala Report* (SCM Press, 1968). For a critical summary see Lefever, *op. cit.*, pp. 27-29.

17. These were: "to explore the nature, causes and consequences of racism, especially white racism, and to evaluate present church positions and their theological and social bases, so that an ecumenical programme of education and action could be proposed" - see Elisabeth Adler, *A Small Beginning: An assessment of the first five years of the Programme to Combat Racism* (WCC, 1974), p. 11.

reinforced by the presence of a strong delegation of American Black Power activists and some black British delegates who had also adopted the ideas and tactics of the American Black Power movement. Most significant from a South African perspective, however, was the presence of two members of the ANC - Joseph Matthews and ANC Chairman, Oliver Tambo. At this time the ANC was a banned organisation within South Africa but was operating in exile from various bases with the objective of securing a transfer of power within South Africa by revolutionary means (see Appendix 1).

Rather than discussing in any detail which societies were the most racially prejudiced and for what reason, or dealing with concrete proposals to attempt to change attitudes, the Conference discussions tended to lay the blame for white racism on political structures. Using highly simplistic and essentially Marxist economic analysis, it was argued that the relative wealth of Western societies compared with the rest of the world had come about as a result of exploitation and thus Western wealth was proof of extensive white racism.[18] The final Statement produced by the Consultation declared:[19]

---

18. For a discussion and refutation of this view see, for instance, Brian Griffiths, *Morality and the Market Place* (Hodder and Stoughton, 1982); P. T. Bauer, *Equality, The Third World and Economic Delusion* (Methuen, 1981); and Thomas Sowell, *The Economics and Politics of Race* (William Morrow, New York, 1983).
19. *Statement of the WCC Consultation on Racism* (WCC, 1969), p. 14.

"The developed Western and so-called Christian countries of the world have obtained their wealth from centuries of exploitation of the newly independent and developing countries."

From such claims it is but a short step to the assertion that the only way to destroy racism is by the destruction of Western economic and political systems. This point was, in fact, made forcibly by Oliver Tambo. Speaking of a "world-wide revolution involving the great majority of the peoples of the world, aimed at replacing the old order of human society with a new order", he declared: "you call them communists, I don't. I call them the true leaders of the crusade for a world community ... volunteers who have freely answered the call to rid mankind of the scourge of racism, colonialism and imperialism."[20] He proceeded to demand that WCC member Churches should individually and collectively "throw their moral and material resources" behind those working for such a revolution.[21]

The Rev. Channing Phillips of the United Church of Christ, Washington, DC, spoke in similar terms in a speech particularly worth noting because of his understanding of the role which the Church should play in helping to bring about 'reconciliation'. Reconciliation is, of course, an important concept in the Bible. The Bible tells us that, no matter what sins we may have committed, Christ's death upon the Cross offers to us all a means of reconciliation with

---

20. See John Vincent, *The Race Race* (SCM, 1970), p. 6.
21. *Ibid.*, p. 61.

God. It also teaches us that we should forgive those who have hurt us - thus opening up the possibility of reconciliation with our enemies. The Rev. Channing Phillips, however, grossly distorted this Biblical understanding of reconciliation by declaring:[22]

> "..if the church is to take its mission of reconciliation seriously, if it is to attack racism significantly, then it must be willing to be not only an institution of love, but an institution of power, making economic and political inputs into societies to effect new equilibria of power. And where a society does not permit restructuring power that produces justice through economic and political manoeuvres, the church ought not to shy away from aiding and abetting the development of the only power available - the power of violence."

Not all those present at the consultation supported such sentiments, and even amongst those who favoured radical political and economic change, there were some who preferred the sort of non-violent methods which had been advocated by Dr. Martin Luther King in the early days of the American civil rights movement. Nevertheless, the majority were persuaded by the argument that those in more favoured positions had no right to counsel those who had suffered 'institutional violence' not to use violence in return. The consultation thus urged the WCC both to support members of resistance and liberation movements in Latin America and also to act as a "co-ordinating centre for the implementation

---

22. *Ibid.*, pp. 52-53.

of multiple strategies for the struggle against racism in Southern Africa."[23]

Apart from perceiving a need for radical political and economic change, achieved by revolutionary means if need be, the consultation took up two other major themes. The first was the inauguration of an educational programme against racism by the Churches and in the seminaries, and the other was the idea that white Churches should make reparations for previous injustices inflicted by the white population against black people. This second demand had first surfaced in the USA the previous month and had received a not unfavourable response from the American National Council of Churches. Encouraged by this, four uninvited American Black Power activists used the Notting Hill Consultation as an opportunity for pressing their point further, demanding a total of £60 million in reparations, £30 million of which was to go to various African liberation movements then involved in guerilla activities against white regimes.[24]

Although in the end it did not agree to all these demands, the Consultation took them wholly seriously, and decided after much debate to accept the principle of reparations by the Churches for white racism. It also agreed that in order to avoid any

---

24. Demands were also made for £20 million to establish an international printing house to be dedicated to Malcolm X, Che Guevara and Eduardo Mondlane of FRELIMO, and £5 million for a Defence Fund for named 'political prisoners', most of whom had been prominent in the American Black Power movement and had been arrested for various violent crimes.

possible charge of paternalism, money paid in reparations should be given without strings as to how it should be spent. Thus, amongst the Consultation's more radical recommendations to the WCC were the following:[25]

> • that the World Council of Churches ... serves as the co-ordinating centre for the implementation of multiple strategies for the struggle against racism in Southern Africa by the churches;
> • that the World Council of Churches and its member churches do support and encourage the principle of 'reparations' to exploited peoples and countries to the end of producing a more favourable balance of economic power throughout the world;
> • that all else failing, the Church and churches support resistance movements, including revolutions, which are aimed at the elimination of political or economic tyranny which makes racism possible.

If the WCC were to take up these proposals it would, of course, affect the Churches in South Africa. In August 1969, the executive of the South African Council of Churches (SACC) - a corporate body to which most of the English-speaking mainline Churches belong, and an associated council of the WCC - responded critically. This was not because the SACC had any desire to defend apartheid, or disputed that maintenace of the existing social order depended

---

25. Vincent, *op. cit.,* p. 98.

on the use of force. Rather, the SACC said that it was:[26]

> "disturbed by the way in which the Churches and the World Council ... are called upon to initiate the use of means usually associated with the civil power in the struggle against racism. These are the weapons of the world rather than the Church."

Bishop Bill Burnett, then General Secretary of the SACC, made an appeal to this effect to the subsequent WCC Central Committee meeting, but with no apparent result.

The Programme to Combat Racism

Although the 1969 Consultation was in no way binding on the WCC, it had a profound influence on the Central Committee meeting held in Canterbury in August of that year. This Committee admitted that racism takes other forms than white racism, but stated that it was the "accumulation of wealth and power in the hands of the white peoples ... which is the reason for a focus on the various forms of white racism."[27] Although some members criticised the reparations proposal and thought that insufficient attention had

---

26. "Comments by the South African Council of Churches' Executive on the Statement of the WCC Consultation on Racism", a mimeographed letter, 6 August 1969, quoted in de Gruchy, *op. cit.*
27. "Statement from the Central Committee Canterbury" reprinted in Ans van der Brent, *World Council of Churches Statements and Actions on Racism: 1948-1979* (World Council of Churches, 1980).

been given to the role of non-violent methods of achieving political change, these objections were eventually overcome (largely by the intervention of a caucus of newly-elected radical black American ministers and laymen). Thus, in a historic decision, the Central Committee called on the Churches to:[28]

> "move beyond charity, grants and traditional programming ... to become agents for the radical reconstruction of society."

It then went on to declare that:

> "There can be no justice in our world without a transfer of economic resources to undergird the redistribution of political power and to make cultural self-determination meaningful. In this transfer of resources a corporate act by the ecumenical fellowship of churches can provide a significant moral lead."

To this end, the Central Committee proposed the establishment of an ecumenical Programme to Combat Racism (PCR), which would be worldwide in scope and involve all departments and divisions of the WCC. Part of the work envisaged for the PCR (which was clearly derived both from the Notting Hill Consultation's reparations proposal, and also from the commitment to transfer economic resources to undergird a redistribution of political power), was the establishment of a Special Fund from which grants would be distributed to groups apparently working to overcome racism.

---

28. *Ibid.*

It is interesting to note that a measure of the WCC's commitment to the Programme was that the Central Committee decided quite specifically to make it a co-ordinated effort of the *whole* Council and that, until the WCC was restructured in 1971, the Programme was a direct responsibility of the General Secretary.[29] This centrality of the PCR in the work of the WCC was confirmed by its initial funding: the PCR administrative budget was drawn from the three basic budgets of the WCC - the General Reserve, the Service Programme of the Division of Inter-Church Aid, Refugee and World Service (DICARWS), and the Division of World Mission and Evangelism (DWME). The Special Fund was created by drawing $200,000 from these three sources, supplemented by an appeal to member churches for another $300,000.[30] Since the General Reserve had been built up from contributions from member Churches, DICARWS received its funds mainly from aid and relief organisations (like Christian Aid in the UK), and the DWME was funded by missionary societies, this meant that the initial funding of an intentionally highly-political programme came from money which donors had believed would be used for very different purposes.[31] Although subsequently the Special Fund was financed solely by special appeal and not by general contributions from

29. This is made clear in David Johnson (ed.), *Uppsala to Nairobi: Report of the Central Committee to the Fifth Assembly of the World Council of Churches* (WCC/SPCK, 1975), p.154.
30. See Ecumenical Press Service (EPS), No. 26, 21 September 1972.
31. Some member Churches, like the Presbyterian Church in Ireland (which later suspended its membership of the WCC) protested about this. See "The WCC Programme to Combat Racism: A Statement by the Presbyterian Church in Ireland, 1978" which is reproduced as Appendix H in Lefever, *op. cit.*

member Churches, the running costs continued to be met from the general funds of the WCC up to around 1975. It still appears that whenever the PCR is unable to meet its administrative costs in full, the deficits are met by other WCC departments.

The Special Fund

The first grants from the Special Fund of the PCR were made on the recommendation of a newly-established Advisory Committee (which later became the PCR Commission) and approved by the WCC Executive Committee meeting in Arnoldsheim, West Germany, in September 1970. The Committee decided to disburse a total of $200,000, $120,000 of which was to go to liberation movements in Southern Africa prepared to use violence to achieve their goals. These were: the People's Movement for the Liberation of Angola (MPLA); its rivals, the Revolutionary Government of Angola in Exile (GRAE) and the National Union for the Total Independence of Angola (UNITA); the Mozambique Liberation Front (FRELIMO), and the African Independence Party of Guinea and Cape Verde Islands (PAIGC) - all of which were fighting against Portuguese colonial authorities. The Patriotic Front fighting against Ian Smith's regime in Rhodesia, and the South West People's Organization (SWAPO) and the ANC fighting for a transfer of power in South West Africa (Namibia) and South Africa, respectively, also received grants.

Most people, including Church leaders, first learnt of the grants through press reports. In South Africa the news caused an uproar and, after much soul-searching, Church leaders there adopted a position similar to that taken by the SACC after the Notting Hill Consultation - that is, whilst opposing racism, they wanted to promote non-violent means of change and so were deeply unhappy about grants going to the liberation movements. Indeed, although all South African member churches eventually decided to remain within the WCC, some came very close to leaving, and most decided to make a protest about the grants by withholding their annual WCC contributions.[32]

In Europe, particularly in Britain, many ordinary churchgoers were shocked by the grants and the editorials of the leading newspapers condemned them,[33] but this had little effect on the policy of the WCC, probably because hardly any protest came from its member Churches.[34] Indeed, over the next few years, the WCC became even more committed to this new Programme. The 1971 Central Committee, for instance, urged member Churches to support the PCR fully, and initiated a new appeal to support the original $500,000 Special Fund appeal established at

---

32. See de Gruchy, *op. cit.*, pp. 128-132.
33. *The Times, Guardian, Daily Telegraph,* and *Sunday Times* all carried editorials about the grants. *The Times,* 15 September 1970, stated that "...Christian authorities have no business to support organisations which are engaged in the use of terror, whatever their grievances and however sincere they may be."
34. Whilst the Archbishop of Canterbury denounced the grants in an address to the General Synod of the Church of England in February 1971, Anglican reaction was subsequently muted after the first meeting of the Anglican Consultative Council (essentially a steering committee for the international Anglican Communion) held in Kenya in 1971 supported the grants.

Canterbury.[35] This was increased at the Central Committee meeting the following year to a minimum of $1 million.[36] The PCR had originally been set up for an initial period of five years, but the 1974 Central Committee meeting both resolved to continue the Programme and to further encourage "cooperation with racially oppressed groups".[37] The 1975 WCC General Assembly again recommended the PCR to member Churches and asked for further support in terms of increased commitment, prayer and finance.

Even when guerillas belonging to the Rhodesian Patriotic Front attacked a lonely mission station near the Mozambique border in June 1978, brutally murdering eight British Pentecostal missionaries and their four children, the WCC continued with the Programme, causing a major outcry in the British press and from the grassroots of the Churches with its announcement of an $85,000 grant to the Front barely three weeks later. The outcry grew when the news was announced in September of that year that members of the Patriotic Front had shot down a Rhodesian civilian aircraft, killing thirty-four passengers in the crash and subsequently bayonetting and shooting to death ten of

---

35. Van der Brent, *op. cit.*, p. 32.
36. *Ibid.*, p. 34.
37. *Ibid.*, p. 37.

the eighteen survivors.[38] As a result of these events, the Salvation Army and the Presbyterian Church of Ireland immediately suspended their membership of the WCC and the following year the Presbyterian Church of Ireland formally withdrew from the WCC.[39] At the 1979 Central Committee, the Irish Anglican, Canon Elliott, provided an explanation for this decision, particularly worth noting in the context of this study. He said, "we in Ireland feel that violence is undesirable ... The WCC is in danger of making the same mistake we made in Ireland when we identified ourselves with one political movement."[40] In 1981 the Salvation Army also

---

38. Indeed, the reaction from the grassroots of the Church of England was such that an emergency debate had to be held by General Synod. The motion finally passed, however, merely *noted* that the grant had "caused controversy in certain areas of the Church of England", and that "certain aspects of the PCR have political and theological implications which urgently call for further discussions...". The Standing Committee of Synod was instructed to appoint a delegation to take up these matters with the General Secretary and other officers of the WCC - for full details of the debate see *Report of Proceedings,* General Synod Group of Session 1978, Vol. 9, No. 3, pp. 1071-1100 and also George Austin, *World Council of Churches' Programme to Combat Racism* (The Institute for the Study of Conflict, London, 1979). Consequently in March 1979 a delegation from the Church of England visited the WCC headquarters in Geneva. However their recommendation was that the Church of England should have "fuller participation" in the WCC and make "increased financial contributions." Thus, in a quite extraordinary way, a debate which had been initiated because of disatisfaction with WCC activities, led to a call for the Church of England to be more closely involved in it.

39. For details of these incidents and their aftermath, see Bernard Smith, *The Fraudulent Gospel: Politics and the World Council of Churches* (Foreign Affairs Publishing Co., London, 1979) and J. A. Emerson Vermaat, *The World Council of Churches and Politics* (Freedom House, New York, 1989).

40. Quoted by Emerson Vermaat, *op. cit.*, p. 69.

withdrew from full membership of the WCC, stressing its unhappiness with the political nature of WCC actions.[41]

This response to the grant to the Patriotic Front, however, did nothing to halt the Programme. In his report to the Central Committee in 1979, the then General Secretary of the WCC, Philip Potter, whilst acknowledging the furore caused by the grants in some quarters, renewed his commitment to the PCR. He urged the Central Committee to set up a process of consultation both to review what had been done during the first ten years of the PCR and to consider how the Churches might be involved in combatting racism in the 1980s.[42] As a result, a conference on racism involving 300 Churches from six continents - by far the largest such conference to date - was held in Holland in June 1980. This resulted in an expansion of the PCR and an even greater

---

41. The Salvation Army stated: "Our gravaman has to do with the issuance by the World Council of Churches of statements, the developing of policies and the carrying out of actions which we regard as political, and which, as such endanger the non-political nature of the Army, the preservation of which is basic to the Movement's effectiveness in a number of countries. Refusal to identify with political factions, as distinct from deep social concern for the needy people of all lands regardless of creed, colour, or political persuasion, has been the essence of the Army's life and endeavour from its very beginning. Indeed, we see clearly that any such political identification would inevitably cut us off from large numbers of those very people we seek to succour. The Salvation Army's foundation belief is that the only real hope for the transformation of society lies in personal salvation through faith in the redemptive grace of Christ." See EPS, 3 September 1981.
42. Van der Brent, *op. cit.*, p. viii.

commitment to the liberation movements. Indeed, it has become more and more obvious that it has been the liberation movements themselves which have to a large extent determined WCC policy. For instance, at the Conference, Oliver Tambo, declared that:[43]

> "The church that the oppressed people of our country demand is one that openly, publicly and actively fights for the political, economic and social liberation of man, as part of the world forces engaged in the process of bringing into being a new world order...".

He concluded, in what must be regarded as a travesty of the Beatitudes:

> "When those who worship Christ shall have, in pursuit of just peace taken up arms against those who hold the majority in subjection by force of arms, then shall it truly be said of such worshippers also: blessed are the peacemakers, for they shall be called the sons of God."

He demanded that the world Christian community should:

- increase moral and material support to the ANC
- sever all political, economic and cultural links with the South African regime
- ensure strict observance of the UN arms embargo against South Africa
- urge all WCC member Churches to withdraw investments from South Africa

---

43. Quoted in the ANC Magazine, *Sechaba,* November 1980.

- educate and activate every single Christian throughout the world to raise their level of personal and collective involvement in the struggle to eradicate racism
- encourage the Church in South Africa to be fully involved in all aspects of the struggle against apartheid.

The 1980 WCC Central Committee meeting, in its acceptance of the recommendations from this consultation, called for comprehensive sanctions against South Africa and, in an echo of Tambo's demands, further invited member Churches to:

- listen to the racially oppressed*; they define the direction of the struggle;
- support organisations of the racially oppressed*, respecting their self reliance and making available money, land, resources, and publicity;
- mobilize people in the churches, helping them to be effectively active rather than guiltily passive in their opposition to racism;
- internationalise the issue, encouraging learning about and linking up with others combating racism in other regions and the global level.

(* It is important to be aware that this use of the term 'racially oppressed' by the WCC virtually always means one or other of the organised liberation movements - never politically moderate black people).

Total grant allocations

Although the Special Fund grants no longer hit the headlines as they once did, they have been made in every year since 1970 bar 1972. As Appendix 3 shows, up to and including 1991, the WCC distributed a total of $9,749,500 to various 'groups of the racially oppressed' and their 'support groups' (mainly anti-apartheid groups) around the world. Groups in Africa have received $4,873,000 and, apart from $20,000 to the Africa 2000 Congress in Zambia and $110,000 to the South African Congress of Trade Unions (which, in any case, were very closely linked to the liberation movements),[44] all of this money went to groups prepared to use revolutionary violence to wrest power from white regimes. As the MPLA, FRELIMO and the Patriotic Front achieved their aims in Angola, Mozambique and Rhodesia/Zimbabwe respectively, so the PCR was able to direct more of its funds to SWAPO in South West Africa/Namibia and to the ANC and Pan Africanist Congress (PAC) in South Africa. Since the independence of Namibia in 1989, the PCR has confined its attention in Africa solely to South Africa. In both 1990 and 1991, the PCR made grants of $141,000 to the ANC and $94,000 to the PAC, which together accounted for 43% of total grants made throughout the world in 1990 and 46.5% in 1991. Since 1970, the Programme to Combat Racism has given a total of $726,500 to the PAC and $1,351,500

---

44. The Africa 2,000 Congress conducted 'conscientisation' campaigns in Zambia in order to increase the level of support for the liberation movements. SACTU was the trade union wing of the ANC.

to the ANC.[45]

The Special Fund has by no means been the only source of aid from the WCC to African liberation movements - a number of other departments have also provided them with assistance. Since the WCC does not make this information public, it is impossible to assess the scale of such support, but nuggets of information may be obtained from time to time. A WCC press release issued on 21 September 1972 stated, for instance, that "recently the Commission on the Churches' Participation in Development (CCPD) made a grant of $150,000 to the Mozambique Institute of FRELIMO". Another press release issued on 12 December 1974 stated that the Commission on Inter-Church Aid, Refugee and World Service had given $1.2 million in agricultural equipment, medical help and educational supplies to liberation movements in Angola, Guinea-Bissau and Mozambique since 1972 and had agreed to continue its support for such movements and "to explore ways of extending help to other liberation movements in southern Africa."

---

45. Apart from the first year (1970) when, as we have seen, Special Fund grants were made from WCC reserves, these grants have been funded by a special appeal which resulted in gifts from member Churches, church organisations, individuals, and governments. Details of donors are not usually publicly disclosed, but according to an internal PCR paper, from 1970 to 1986 the principal European donor countries were: West Germany ($1,500,000), Sweden ($847,576), Norway ($303,186), The Netherlands ($233,594), Switzerland ($204,178) and Britain ($85,474). The main British donor has been the Methodist Church, with smaller amounts coming from the British Council of Churches, the Methodist Missionary Society, and the Iona Community.

The question of violence

Most of the controversy surrounding the Special Fund grants has arisen because of the liberation movements' readiness to use violence in pursuit of their aims. Since the WCC has appeared to be inconsistent in its views on violence, and since the issue of violence is central to this study, the WCC stance needs to be examined carefully.

We have already seen that both the 1966 Church and Society Conference and the 1969 Consultation on Racism were prepared to sanction Church support for revolutionary violence, but that although both of these conferences were organised by the WCC, they did not have the authority of the WCC itself. Indeed, the 1968 WCC General Assembly at Uppsala had not been clear on this issue, and the 1969 Central Committee meeting, which set up the Programme to Combat Racism and to which the Consultation on Racism made its recommendations, did not accept the Consultation's specific recommendation concerning Church support for revolutionary violence. When the first grants were announced by the 1970 Executive Committee meeting in Arnoldsheim, however, the following criteria regarding the Special Fund were laid down:[46]

> "1. The proceeds of the Fund shall be used to support organisations that combat racism, rather than welfare organisations that alleviate the effects of racism, which would normally be eligible for support of other units in the World Council of Churches.

---

46. Van der Brent, *op. cit.,* p. 31.

2.(a) The focus of the grants should be on raising the level of awareness and on strengthening the organisational capability of racially oppressed people.

(b) In addition we recognize the need to support organisations that align themselves with the victims of racial injustice and pursue the same objectives.

While these grants are made without control of the manner in which they are spent, they are at the same time a commitment of the Programme to Combat Racism to the causes the organisations themselves are fighting for.

3.(a) The situation in Southern Africa is recognized as a priority due to the overt and intensive nature of white racism and the increasing awareness on the part of the oppressed in their struggle for liberation.

(b) In the selection of other areas we have taken account of those places where the struggle is most intensive and where a grant might make a substantial contribution to the process of liberation particularly where racial groups are in imminent danger of being physically or culturally exterminated.

(c) In considering applications from organisations in countries of white and affluent majorities we have taken note only of those cases where political involvement precludes help from other sources.

4. Grants should be made with due regard to where they can have maximum effect; token grants should not be made unless there is a possibility of their eliciting a substantial response from other organisations."

Thus the WCC Executive Committee made it quite clear that the Special Fund would not be used to help welfare organisations attempting to alleviate the suffering of victims of oppression nor, by implication, would it be used to support politically moderate groups seeking to eliminate racism through gradualist reform. Rather, it would support groups committed to bringing about major changes in the whole structure of their societies, and nothing in the criteria precluded those who were prepared to use revolutionary violence and terror to achieve this end. In other words, although neither the WCC General Assembly nor its Central Committee had explicitly supported the use of violence, the initial criteria for the Special Fund grants clearly allowed them to be made to groups using violence, and this was borne out by the groups which actually received the grants over the years.

Following the adverse publicity surrounding the initial grants, and in an attempt to diffuse criticism, the WCC argued (and has maintained ever since) that the grants had been given for humanitarian purposes. Indeed, the 1971 Central Committee meeting subsequently modified the criteria for the grants to contain a new first clause[47] which stated that:

---

47. The last part of the original clause 2 (which now formed clause 4) was also reworded as follows: "The grants are made without control of the manner in which they are spent, and are intended as an expression of commitment by PCR in the cause of economic, social and political justice, which these organisations promote."

> "The purpose of the organisations must not be in conflict with the general purposes of the WCC and its units, and the grants are to be used for humanitarian activities, i.e. social, health and educational, legal aid, etc."

What should we conclude from this? Firstly, whilst it is *possible* that the liberation movements have used grants received from the WCC for purely humanitarian purposes, there is simply no way of discovering this since the WCC has always refused to exercise any control over the use of the grants.[48] Although in 1974 Dr Philip Potter rejected accusations that any money donated to African liberation movements was spent on arms,[49] Dr Eugene Carson Blake, his predecessor as secretary general of the WCC, had in 1970 warned that it was impossible to guarantee that the money might not be used in this way.[50] In any case, as many critics have pointed out over the years, even if the liberation movements did use the WCC grants for humanitarian purposes, this would only have freed funds from their total budgets which could then have been used to buy weapons.

Secondly, and more importantly, it can be argued that the *use* the liberation movements made of

---

48. The Presbyterian Church of Ireland stated, when it decided to suspend its membership of the WCC, that "to make payments without provision for accountability, such as we would apply strictly to ourselves and seek in all our sister Churches, when these happen to be grants to 'Anti-Racist' organisations appears simply as an example of Racism in reverse." See Lefever, *op. cit.,* Appendix H.
49. *Catholic Herald,* 1 March 1974.
50. *Church Times,* 13 November 1970.

the grants is not the real issue. Rather, simply by making the grants, the WCC appeared to be endorsing both the objectives and the methods of the liberation movements. This view is borne out by decisions taken by the 1971 Central Committee of the WCC, which stated that although it did not identify with any particular political movement,[51]

> "nor does it pass judgement on those victims of racism who are driven to violence as the only way left to them to redress grievances and so open the way for a new and more just social order."

The real point at issue then is whether the WCC should have given such unequivocal support to politically partisan organisations prepared to overthrow existing regimes through the use of violence and, in the main, to establish in their place societies based on the principles of Marxism-Leninism.

In their discussion of this question the WCC, and others, have often presented the issue as a simple choice between violence and absolute non-violence. They argue that since the Church has often justified violence in times of war, there is no reason why churchgoers should object to the WCC helping organisations which are "driven to violence" in what they regard as a war situation.

---

51. See "Statement from the Central Committee, Addis Ababa" in van der Brent, *op. cit.,* p. 32.

Presenting the question in these terms, however, leaves many vitally important ethical questions unanswered. For whilst it is true that down the ages the Church has said that it is not wrong to take up arms in times of war, it has argued that this is on the condition that it is a *just* war.[52] By the extension of established 'just war' principles, therefore, it might be argued that a revolution (and hence revolutionary violence) is only justified if the cause is just; if all other possibilities for change have been exhausted; if there is widespread support for the revolution; if there are reasonable expectations that such violence will achieve the ends desired; if the methods used are just; and if the new political order is better than the one it replaces.

Although the WCC itself both commissioned and commended a study which outlined the principles for a just revolution,[53] there is no indication that it has ever applied these principles to its own actions. It does not appear to have considered carefully the methods the liberation movements have been prepared to use to obtain their ends; nor asked if their objectives could have been achieved in other, less violent ways. Furthermore, the WCC does not appear to have investigated the degree to which the liberation

---

52. Some of these ideas have been put forward and debated in, for instance, Oliver Barclay (ed.), *Pacifism and War* (Inter-Varsity Press, Leicester, 1984); and T. E. Utley and Edward Norman, *Ethics and Nuclear Arms* (Institute for European Defence and Strategic Studies, London, 1983).
53. See *Violence, Nonviolence and the Struggle for Social Justice* (WCC, 1973). This was commissioned by its Central Committee in 1971 and commended by its 1973 Central Committee.

movements enjoyed genuinely popular support, as opposed to support gained through the use of terror and intimidation of other black people; and, crucially, in the case of those who attained their objectives during the early years of the PCR (as was the case with the MPLA in Angola and FRELIMO in Mozambique), the WCC has never published any studies looking at the nature of the regimes established by the liberation movements so that they might be judged against the regimes they replaced.

The MPLA and FRELIMO (like the ANC today) said they were fighting for economic, social and political justice, but what has been their record in power? Did they, for instance, establish an independent judiciary? Freedom of speech? Freedom of religion? Were they able to feed the people? In order to assess the impact of the Programme to Combat Racism, the WCC should have looked carefully at all these factors. It did not. From non-WCC sources, however, a sorry picture emerges. According to the human-rights monitoring organisation, Freedom House, which produces an annual table rating political rights and civil liberties in all countries on a scale from 1 (most free) to 7 (least free), Angola and Mozambique consistently scored 7 for political rights and civil liberties after the liberation movements took power. In other words, their regimes were amongst the most repressive in the world.[54] Detailed and harrowing descriptions exist of

---

54. The 1991 Freedom House assessment gave Angola ratings of 7 for both political rights and civil liberties, and Mozambique 6 for both political rights and civil liberties - see *Freedom Review,* Vol. 22, No. 1, 1991. In Freedom House terminology, both

the establishment by FRELIMO of a Mozambican 'Gulag' of forced re-education camps; of the mass deportation of Mozambican youth to Cuba, Eastern Europe, and the Soviet Union; and of the brutal repression of religion in Mozambique during the late 1970s and early to mid-1980s.[55] Furthermore, it is widely recognised within Africa and by the large international agencies working in Africa that, compared with pre-revolutionary days, the economies of Angola and Mozambique literally collapsed, largely as a result of ideologically-inspired programmes of nationalisation and the forced collectivisation of agriculture.[56]

---

countries were "not free". Liberalisation in Angola and Mozambique during 1991 meant that the Freedom House ratings for both these two countries for 1992 improved to 6 for political rights and 4 for civil liberties - the countries are now be judged to be "partly free". Throughout most of the 1980s and 1990s, South Africa has been regarded as "partly free". Its ratings for 1992 are 5 for political rights and 4 for civil liberties - see *Freedom Review*, Vol. 23, No. 1, 1992.
55. See David Hoile, *Mozambique: a nation in crisis* (The Claridge Press, London, 1989), and Rodney and Ellie Hein, *Mozambique: The Cross and The Crown* (Christ for The Nations, Dallas, 1989). In 1988 Freedom House summarised civil liberties in Mozambique as follows: "All media are rigidly controlled. Rights of assembly and foreign travel do not exist. There are no private lawyers. Secret police are powerful; thousands are in reeducation camps, and executions occur. Police brutality is common. Unions are prohibited. Pressure has been put on several religious groups, especially the Catholic clergy and Jehovah's Witnesses, although there has been some recent relaxation. Villagers are being forced into communes, leading to revolts in some areas...". See Raymond Gastil, *Freedom in the World: Political Rights and Civil Liberties* (Freedom House, New York, 1988).
56. This is a common experience of virtually all black African countries. See *Sub-Saharan Africa: From Crisis to Sustainable Growth* (World Bank, November 1989).

In a 1991 WCC publication, former director of the PCR, Baldwin Sjollema, described the PCR as "one of the ecumenical success stories." Referring to its aid to liberation movements like FRELIMO and the MPLA, Sjollema stated that "some of these movements are now legitimate governments, and the WCC and PCR's vision and commitment have been vindicated."[57] This is an extraordinary statement given, as we have just seen, the appalling record of these movements in power. Indeed, it is difficult to escape the conclusion that the real reason for the WCC grants has had little or nothing to do with humanitarian purposes or Christian principles. Rather, they should be seen as politically inspired, designed to express support for the Marxist ideology of the liberation movements. As a British Council of Churches information leaflet stated, "the grants are small, but they are intended to express solidarity with the struggle of the oppressed". Again, a PCR paper produced in 1980 stated, "the importance of the grants was not their size but the symbolic value of an ecumenical act of solidarity and the educational aspect for the churches themselves."[58]

Educating the Churches

This idea of the "educational aspect for the churches" is particularly important and from this perspective the enormous press coverage surrounding the grants can, paradoxically, be regarded as an aspect of their effectiveness. As the WCC itself has put it,

---

57. See *Dictionary of the Ecumenical Movement* (WCC, Council of Churches for Britain and Ireland, and Eerdmans, Grand Rapids, 1991), pp. 825-7.
58. *PCR Information,* 1980/No. 4.

because of the initial criticism of the grants and the ensuing debate, the liberation movements "had an unusual opportunity - often denied to them - through PCR and other media, to explain their goals, expectations and methods of work." The PCR published a series of profiles about the organisations and these were reprinted by the United Nations and many secular and Church publications in different parts of the world.[59] In other words, the storm about the grants provided the liberation movements with excellent opportunities for self-publicity which they would not otherwise have obtained.

As a result of such publicity, an increasing number of Christians have come to think of the cause of the liberation movements as 'just' and have therefore sided with them - at least emotionally - despite there being a good chance of eradicating racism and other forms of political injustice through more moderate organisations and through reformist governments. Equally important, the action of the PCR has to some extent accustomed Christians to blatantly partisan political activity by the Church and this in turn has helped to radically change the way in which the mission of the Church in the world is viewed. As the WCC itself has said, the debate about the Special Fund grants:[60]

> "produced much more than a reconsideration of the Churches' struggle to contribute to the social and political process of liberation. Its own identity, its theology and its mission have to be reconsidered."

---

59. EPS, No. 26, 21 September 1972, p. 8.
60. *Ibid.*

As far as the liberation movements themselves were concerned, the Special Fund grants were of great importance even though they were relatively small. They gave the movements publicity, lent moral credence to their cause, and thus enabled them to raise more money from elsewhere. As the WCC has stated:[61]

> "There is no doubt that in several cases the grants did act as a leverage particularly in Southern Africa. The humanitarian programmes of liberation movements such as FRELIMO, PAIGC and MPLA have received grants - in some cases very considerable ones - from governments (eg. The Netherlands, Sweden, Denmark, Norway). These governments have been directly or indirectly influenced by the WCC decision ... In the UK, the Joseph Rowntree Trust decided to support liberation movements after consultation with a member of the PCR Commission. Furthermore, several member churches or their agencies decided to make grants available to one or more movements."

PCR Educational and Programmatic Work

Although the Special Fund to Combat Racism has been the most controversial and newsworthy component of the WCC's Programme to Combat Racism, other aspects of the PCR have had a significant influence on Church and international

---

61. *Ibid.*

opinion regarding South Africa. The PCR, for instance, has a research and publications programme which has published, or assisted the publication of, a number of studies calling for international sanctions against South Africa.[62] This educational work has been influenced by the findings of several large international conferences held by the PCR/WCC. In this respect, it is noteworthy that ever since the 1969 Notting Hill Consultation, members of liberation movements (particularly the ANC) have always been present at these conferences and have played a leading part in their proceedings. Since the aim of the PCR has been to show 'solidarity' with the liberation movements, it has never been likely that such speakers would be criticised. Nor have they - as we have seen, their calls for action have invariably been ratified by the WCC with little or no dissent.

In the wake of the 1980 conference on racism, the PCR also developed what it calls 'programmatic work' which, it says, serves "as a channel of communication between the WCC member churches

---

62. For instance, the PCR published reports which led to the WCC Central Committee's decisions to call for a withdrawal of investments from Southern Africa (1972) and an end to bank loans to the South African Government and its agencies - *PCR Information*, 1980/No. 4, p. 35. It has also assisted the British organisation End Loans to South Africa (ELTSA) to publish its Barclay's Bank Shadow Reports, and also the publication of International Labour Reports on South Africa - *PCR Commission Minutes*, 1985.

and local groups struggling against racism...".[63] In order to gain financial support for this work, which is often carried out in conjunction with other WCC sub-units, a list of projects is presented to WCC member Churches and donor agencies each year. Unlike the Special Fund grants which have to gain the approval of the WCC Executive Committee, however, these grants are decided upon by the PCR staff and Commission alone, and are not made public.[64]

In terms of the long-term impact on the Church, perhaps the most significant of these projects has been 'Racism and Theology', since its objective has been to provide a theological justification for the PCR. As stated earlier, the activities of the PCR have been so at variance with the traditional work of the Church that, as the WCC has put it, the Church's traditional "theology and mission have to be reconsidered." **To put it starkly,**

---

63. *Programme to Combat Racism:* Information leaflet from the WCC. The June 1980 World Consultation on Racism identified the following thirteen 'programmatic categories': Racism and Theology; Southern Africa; Race and Minority Issues in Asia; Indian Movements in Latin America; Racism and Land Rights; Racism, Ethnic Minorities and Migration in Europe; Racism in Education and the Media; Racism and Doctrines of National Security; Racism in Church Structures; Research, Publications and Alternative Information; Economic Basis of Racism; Criminal Justice Systems and Legal Practices; Women under Racism.

64. Information is only available from WCC internal documents. For instance the minutes of the 1985 PCR Commission meeting show that the 'Southern Africa', project planned to give $20,000 to solidarity organisations and anti-apartheid groups; $10,000 to defendants in political trials in Namibia and South Africa, and $20,000 for the production of study, educational and action material on Southern Africa.

either traditional theology is correct and the PCR has been a mistaken activity which the Church should never have supported, or the PCR has been valid and it is theology itself which needs changing to bring it into line with the thrust of the PCR.

Not surprisingly, given its continued commitment to the PCR, the WCC has adopted this latter view. At its Central Committee meeting in Geneva in August 1980, it invited its member Churches to "challenge theology", asking "does it merely conform to or does it transcend and help to transform the society it comes out of?"[65] Traditional Christian theology has always maintained the need for a radical change in the lives of those who make up society, thus transcending and transforming it. What the WCC has in mind when speaking of theology transforming society is, however, something quite different. An indication of this is provided by the 1984 Unit ll Core Group meeting of the WCC,[66] which stated that the "PCR could help the churches to understand theologically that the commitment to peace and justice may well involve conflict and violence."[67]

In order to produce a theology which would help to "transform society", both the 1980 and the 1984 Central Committee meetings of the WCC called for more *contextualisation* of theology, and, to this end, the Racism in Theology project (which in 1985 had a budget of $130,000) has co-operated closely

---

65. Minutes, PCR Commission, 1985.
66. The PCR is a sub-unit of the WCC's Unit ll.
67. Minutes, PCR Commission, 1985.

with another WCC Programme, the Theological Education Fund. This was established in 1958, originally to raise the level of scholarship and academic excellence in theological training in the Third World. However, after the Uppsala Assembly its mandate was changed so that nearly all the projects assisted since then have in some way been concerned with developing what have become known as contextual theologies.[68] The Racism in Theology Project has also co-operated with the Ecumenical Association of Third World Theologians (EATWOT), an organisation set up in 1976 which has been described as "by far the most influential association of theologians in the world today."[69] It, too, has been active in spreading contextual theology to many parts of the Third World (see Appendix 4). As we shall see in the following chapters, the development of contextual theology has been an important aspect of the radicalisation of sections of the South African Church.

---

68. In the early 1970s the grants amounted to over $1 million a year. See Johnson, *op. cit.,* pp. 91-4.
69. Albert Nolan and Richard Broderick, *To Nourish our Faith: The Theology of Liberation in Southern Africa* (Order of Preachers, Hilton, South Africa, 1987), p. 18.

2. RADICAL THEOLOGY

It emerged in the previous chapter that one aspect of the work of the WCC's Programme to Combat Racism has been the efforts to develop a theological justification for the programme, including the controversial Special Fund grants to African liberation movements. This has involved the WCC in supporting and encouraging work on the *contextualisation* of theology. What does this mean, and how have such theological developments affected the Church both within South Africa and elsewhere?

Contextual Theologies

The *contextualisation* of theology is a term used to describe a general approach to theology which is fundamentally different from that of orthodox Christian theology. Traditionally, theology has as its starting point the Bible or, for those in the Catholic tradition, the Bible and the body of teaching of the Catholic Church. Based on these sources, orthodox theology seeks to discover and present truths about God and about God's dealing with the human race. These truths are eternal and universal. This means that what is known about God and the way He wants his people to behave is essentially unchanging both throughout history and throughout the world.

By contrast, contextual 'theology' is deeply relativistic; it is also essentially humanistic, focussing on man rather than God. Indeed one leading advocate of liberation theology, the best-known type of contextual theology, has described theology as "man's critical reflection on himself."[1] Contextual theology's starting point, both in terms of its chronological development and in terms of its general methodology, is not the Bible or the historic teaching of the Church but is, rather, an active commitment to 'liberation' from some oppression. Examples of this are the decision of some Latin American Catholic priests in the 1960s to side with (and in some cases join) guerilla movements fighting against authoritarian regimes, and the WCC's support for African 'liberation' movements. The 'first act' of theology is thus a historical *praxis* - that is, some experience of political oppression and a political action, often of a revolutionary nature, designed to liberate the oppressed.[2]

The 'second act', in the contextual approach to theology, is a *critical reflection* on this action in the light of the Bible or Catholic faith.[3] The result of this is a highly selective reading of the Bible, which makes use only of those passages (typically the Exodus of the Israelites from their slavery in Egypt, the Magnificat, and Luke 4: 18-19) which might be interpreted in such a way as to show God's support

---

1. Gustavo Gutiérrez, *A Theology of Liberation* (SCM Press, London, 1974), p. 11.
2. This is sometimes referred to as "doing theology".
3. Some contextual theologies also use non-Christian sources as the basis for their reflection. Indeed, the South African Institute for Contextual Theology (ICT) - see below - has stated that it needs to develop a 'prophetic theology' which "draws on other religions" - see *ICT Annual Report,* 1990.

for 'liberating' political action. Prominent South African contextual theologian, Fr. Albert Nolan, for instance, has described the Exodus as follows:[4]

> "God chose the Israelites not because of their virtues but because of their sufferings. He chose one small group of oppressed people, the Hebrew slaves in Egypt, for the sake of all oppressed peoples and in order to bring about the liberation and salvation of the whole human race."

Orthodox Christian theology would, of course, describe the Exodus quite differently. The fact that the Israelites were chosen by God was not because of their oppression and slavery but, rather, because God had previously formed a covenant relationship with the father of the nation, Abraham - He had promised that He would be their God, and they would be His people. Israel was delivered as a nation not in order to be some sort of model of political liberation for all oppressed people but, rather, in order to serve God and receive and obey His moral law.[5]

It might be thought that Nolan's reference to "liberation and salvation" refers to the coming of Jesus Christ to the nation of Israel. However, in contextual theology there is little reference to Christ's

---

4. Albert Nolan and Richard Broderick, *op. cit.*, p. 41.
5. Some of the contextual theologians also attack orthodox Christian morality. The South African Institute for Contextual Theology stated in 1984, for instance, that the aims of one of its projects was to "look into the problem of the church's conception of sin, and work to the dismantling of the mainline's conception." See *Minutes ICT AGM*, 1984.

work of salvation - the liberation from sin and alienation from God brought about through His death upon the Cross and freely offered to all who will believe in Him. When the Cross is referred to (which is not often), it too is interpreted politically. To quote Nolan again:[6]

> "Jesus suffered and died on a Roman cross because ...(he) was horrified by the sufferings of the people, shared in their sufferings and was determined to do something about their plight. Jesus was one of the oppressed struggling to free all who suffered under the yoke of repression. That is the meaning of the cross."

Since it is expected that the 'reflection' part of the process of contextual theology will lead to further action which will in turn lead to further reflection and so on, this approach is sometimes referred to as Action-Reflection-Action or the 'hermeneutical circle'. It is said to be *contextual* because the action and the reflection upon it - and hence the 'theology' - is entirely determined by the context. For this reason there could, in theory, be as many contextual theologies as there are contexts of oppression.

As has already been mentioned, the best known type of contextual theology is liberation theology. This was developed in Latin America (perceived as a situation of generalised oppression of the poor) from the mid to late 1960s onwards, mainly

---

6. Albert Nolan, *God in South Africa: The challenge of the gospel* (Catholic Institute for International Relations, 1988).

by Roman Catholic priests.[7] Leading liberation theologian, Gustavo Gutiérrez, has defined its purpose and method as follows:[8]

> "The theology of liberation attempts to reflect on the experience and meaning of the faith based on the commitment to abolish injustice and to build a new society; this theology must be verified by the practice of that commitment, by active, effective participation in the struggle which the exploited classes have undertaken against their oppressors."

In other words, the purpose of liberation theology is not to teach about the creation of a new man through Christ's work of salvation but, rather, to commit the Church to radical political action to create a new society. This is seen in class-struggle terms as the struggle of the poor and exploited against their

---

7. The first outline of liberation theology was presented by the Peruvian priest, Gustavo Gutiérrez, at a conference in Peru in July 1968. Many of his ideas were subsequently adopted by the Second General Council of Latin American Bishops meeting in Medellin, Colombia, a few weeks later. The first systematic work on liberation theology, Ruben Alves, *A Theology of Human Hope,* was published in 1969, but Gutiérrez's *A Theology of Liberation,* first published in Peru in 1971, is regarded as the 'basic text' of liberation theology. Similar work by Hugo Assman and Leonardo Boff followed rapidly. There is now a vast literature associated with liberation theology. A reasonably simple overview of its main concepts and historical development is provided by Phillip Berryman, *Liberation Theology* (I. B. Tauris, London, 1987). A critical analysis of the economic and political implications of liberation theology is to be found in Michael Novak, *Will it Liberate?* (Paulist Press, New York, 1986).

8. Gutiérrez, *op. cit.,* p. 307.

oppressors. In this analysis Gutiérrez and other Latin American liberation theologians have taken much of their inspiration from Marxism. As Gutiérrez has said, "it is to a large extent due to Marxism's influence that theological thought, searching for its own sources, has begun to reflect on the meaning of the transformation of this world and the action of man in history."[9]

Although it was liberation theology which first systematised the Action-Reflection approach, and hence opened up the way for the development of other forms of contextual theology (indeed, some liberation theologians refer to an aspect of their work as the "liberation of theology" because it presented such a change in theological method), at about the same time, and relatively independently, radical black theologians in North America were developing 'Black Theology'. In their situation it was specifically black people who were regarded as the oppressed in need of liberation - in this case from white racism.[10] Other parts of the world have seen the development of 'Asian theology' (dealing with the perceived need for

---

9. *Ibid.,* p. 9.
10. Although Latin American liberation theology and North American Black Theology appear to have been conceived independently of each other, they both drew on common roots in the German 'hope' and 'political' theologies of Jurgen Moltman and Johannes Metz. The first encounter between liberation theologians and Black Theologians was organised by the WCC at its headquarters in Geneva in May 1973 - papers from this conference were published in *Risk,* Vol. 9, No. 2. This was followed by a larger conference held in Detroit in August 1975, papers from which were published in Torres and Eagleson (eds.), *Theologies in the Americas* (Orbis Books, 1976).

the liberation of Asians from their oppression by Western culture and Western religion);[11] 'minjung theology', as a specifically Korean version of liberation theology;[12] 'urban theology' (where it is the inner-city poor who are regarded as in need of liberation);[13] and 'feminist theology' (dealing with the need to liberate women from male chauvinism). As can be seen, all the contextual theologies are in fact a type of liberation theology and indeed are sometimes referred to as the *theologies of liberation;* they are also sometimes referred to as *people's theology* because they are supposedly "of the people by the people for the people."[14]

It should be clear that, for those who take the contextual approach to theology, theology is no longer regarded as something universal and applicable in all circumstances. Indeed, contextual theologians maintain that "all theology is, and

---

11. See, for instance, Aloysius Pieris, *An Asian Theology of Liberation* (T. & T. Clark, 1988) and V. Fabella (ed.), *Asia's Struggle for Full Humanity; Towards a Relevant Theology* (Orbis Books, Maryknoll, 1980).
12. Minjung is a Korean word for 'the people' - see Jung Young Lee (ed.), *An Emerging Theology in World Perspective; Commentary on Korean Minjung Theology* (Twenty-Third Publications, Mystic, Connecticut, 1988).
13. Attempts to develop this have mainly been made in Britain. See, for instance, John Vincent, *Into the City* (Epworth Press, 1982); Colin Marchant, *Signs in the City* (Hodder and Stoughton, 1985); and *Faith in the City: The Report of the Archbishop of Canterbury's Commission on Urban Priority Areas* (Church House Publishing, 1985), pp. 64-5.
14. Publicity document, Institute for Contextual Theology, April 1990.

always has been, contextual" but "in the past mosttheologians were not aware of this."[15] They therefore argue that, since traditional Biblical theology was originally developed by Western scholars, it is, in fact, a contextual theology of the Western bourgeoisie and applicable (if at all) only in such a context and is quite irrelevant anywhere else. A booklet on contextual theology, first published in South Africa by the Institute for Contextual Theology (ICT) and reprinted in Britain by the Catholic Institute for International Relations, for instance, quotes with favour the 'discovery' by the German theologian, Johannes Metz, that all traditional European theologies are "bourgeois and that they serve the interests of the middle class in a capitalist society."[16] Similarly, an issue of the ICT magazine, *ICT News*, has declared that:[17]

> "the Western theology that was presented to us as a neutral and universal theology has since been exposed to be actually a theology of the liberal capitalist ideology. It is a theology of oppression, exploitation and domination."

It can be seen from this that contextual 'theology' amounts to a major assault on the historic teaching of the Christian Church, which it largely empties of its universal and spiritual content. As one traditionalist Catholic theologian, Father Rodgriguez

---

15. Nolan and Broderick, *op. cit.*, p. 13.
16. *What is Contextual Theology?* (Institute for Contextual Theology), reprinted as *Whose Theology?* (Catholic Institute for International Relations, 1985).
17. *ICT News,* March 1985.

Y Rodriguez has said of contextual theologians:[18]

> "Totally inverting the theological method, these authors do no proceed *thematically* from God to man, from the interior to the exterior, from the person to society, from individual sin to social or structural sin, but precisely the other way round."

In other words, contextual theology essentially reconstructs God in the image of man - He becomes merely what a certain group of people in specific situations do. For this reason, some commentators have argued that contextual 'theology' is not theology at all, but rather a form of anthropology, sociology, or political theory. Nevertheless, as we shall see, contextual theology is proving highly effective in bringing the teaching of the Church into line with the radical political activity already being undertaken by sections of the Church, whilst demanding that other sections of the Church should adopt such action too. Contextual theology thus has enormously significant spiritual and political consequences.

Black Theology

Within South Africa the adoption of the contextual theology approach started in the early 1970s, and was

---

18. Fr. Victorino Rogriguez Y Rodriguez, *Godless 'Theology' and Enslaving 'Liberation'* (TFP, 1988). The TFP (Tradition, Family, Property) is a Catholic organisation with many branches in Latin America opposing the spread of liberation theology. It has small branches in the UK (22 Milton Rd. East, Edinburgh, EH15 2NJ) and South Africa (PO Box 10906, Johannesburg, 2000) from which this publication may be obtained.

pioneered by a white Methodist Minister, Dr. Basil Moore, then director of theological concerns for the University Christian Movement (a multi-racial, theologically liberal, student Christian movement which existed only between 1968 and 1972). As Mokgethi Motlhabi has described:[19]

> "Black Theology was imported from the United States and placed under a separate project bearing that name, with its own director. Through this project Black Theology was propagated throughout South Africa by means of seminars and ministers' caucuses[20] which discussed the relevance of the church and its teaching in a situation of oppression such as South Africa."

American Black Theology

Of key importance in the teaching at these seminars was work by the black American theologian, James Cone, who, with his *Black Theology and Black*

---

19. Mokgethi Motlhabi, "The Historical Origins of Black Theology" in Itumeleng Mosala and Buti Tlhagale, *The Unquestionable Right to be Free: Essays in Black Theology* (Skotaville Publishers/ICT, 1986), p. 44.
20. Meetings were held in such places as the Wilgespruit Fellowship Centre near Johannesburg; the Edendale Ecumenical Centre near Pietermaritzburg, Natal; the Federal Theological Seminary at Alice, Cape Province; St Peter's Seminary, Hammanskraal, near Pretoria; and other centres in Zululand and the Transkei - see Basil Moore (ed.), *Black Theology: The South African Voice* (C. Hurst and Co., London, 1973). This book first appeared in South Africa as Mokgethi Motlhabi (ed.), *Essays on Black Theology* (University Christian Movement, Johannesburg, 1972).

Power, published in 1969, had produced the first systematic treatment of Black Theology in book form. He has himself described how he was asked to send a tape-recording of what subsequently became part of his next book, *A Black Theology of Liberation,*[21] for use in such seminars, and South African theologian, David Bosch, has explained that the "seminars held in 1971 were clearly profoundly influenced by Cone's thinking."[22] Examination of Cone's work shows, however, that his Black Theology redefines key Christian concepts in purely political - that is, Black Power - terms. As Cone has said, Black Theology:[23]

> "is the religious counterpart of the more secular term 'Black Power' ... Black Theology puts black identity in a theological context, showing that Black Power is not only *consistent* with the gospel of Jesus Christ, but that it *is* the gospel of Jesus Christ."

Because of its pivotal role in Black Theology, then, and also because of its influence upon the South African black consciousness movement, it is necessary to digress a little and say a few words about the American Black Power movement.

The American civil rights movement in the early 1960s had been a coalition of groups which,

---

21. Cone mentions this in Gayraud Wilmore and James Cone (eds.), *Black Theology: A Documentary History, 1966-79* (Orbis Books, New York, 1979), p. 223.
22. David Bosch, "Currents and Crosscurrents in South African Black Theology" in *ibid.,* p. 223.
23. James Cone, "Black Theology and Black Liberation" in Moore, *op. cit.,* p. 48.

under the overall leadership of Martin Luther King, adopted essentially non-violent means of attempting to bring about the full integration of black people into American society. From about 1963 onwards, however, the integrationist theme in the black community began to lose ground to the black nationalist philosophy of Malcolm X. Whilst serving a ten-year prison sentence for drug-related crime, Malcolm Little (as he then was) adopted the ideas of the 'Black Muslims' or 'Nation of Islam' whose leader, Georgia-born Elijah Muhammed, taught that Allah had revealed that all white people are cursed and that the total annihilation of the white man and his Christian religion was at hand, after which the Black Nation (or 'black, brown, yellow and red' races) would inherit the earth. According to Muhammed, the Nation of Islam (which he defined as the negro population of the United States) had been chosen by Allah as a special instrument for redemption of the entire black population. Muhammed set out to give his supporters, who were mainly unemployed or criminals from the Northern cities, an economic basis for a sense of self-pride and self-worth. He fostered black businesses and since, through this, supporters were provided with food and decent housing, more disaffected black people were drawn into the organisation. By the early 1960s it had an estimated quarter of a million members.

Malcolm X became a leading figure in the organisation and, as such, he asserted the right of blacks to self-determination, including the right of defence against the "white aggressor" with "all necessary means". He viewed Christianity simply as the white man's religion which had been used to subjugate blacks. Following trips to the Middle East, however, Malcolm X came to reject the religious aspect of the organisation and so established a rival, non-religious, highly militant body called the Organisation of Afro-American Unity which advocated a black, socialist revolution. To this end Malcolm X formed links with African liberation movements and also with Cuba and China. Although he was assassinated in February 1965,[24] his ideas lived on and, in 1966, a split occurred in the civil rights movement when his followers called for the rejection of Luther King's policies of non-violence and racial collaboration. After the split, sympathetic white liberals were largely excluded from the civil rights struggle and the emerging Black Power movement began to work not so much for black integration into white American society, as for the complete rejection of American institutions (which were regarded as deeply racist), an objective which Black Power leaders were prepared to bring about through the use of violence.[25]

Like Luther King, many of the civil-rights leaders were black churchmen and it was expected by most black and white Christians that they would denounce the Black Power movement for its hatred and violence. However, a group of black clergy quite

---

24. For more details of his life see *The Autobiography of Malcom X* (Grove Press, New York, 1965). Studies of the Black Muslims include E. U. Essien-Udom, *Black Nationalism: The Rise of the Black Muslims in the USA* (Pelican Books, 1966). For further general information on this period see The Times News Team, *The black man in search of power* (Times Newspapers, 1968).
25. See Stokely Carmichael and Charles Hamilton, *Black Power: The Politics of Liberation in America* (Jonathan Cape, London, 1968).

specifically refused to do this. In July 1966 a full-page advertisement supporting Black Power and signed by almost fifty black church leaders calling themselves the National Committee of Negro Churchmen (which later became the National Conference of Black Churchmen - NCBC) appeared in the *New York Times*.[26] The initiative for the action and the drafting of the statement came from Benjamin Payton, then executive director of the Commission on Religion and Race of the American National Council of Churches (an associated council of the WCC), who later became first president of the NCBC.[27] In October 1967 the NCBC was constituted as a permanent body which, as Cone later explained, would be:[28]

> "a permanent ecumenical organization that would be the vanguard in the struggle for black liberation in the church. Members of the NCBC were not only determined to make the black church more relevant to the black liberation struggle, but were equally determined to create a black theology that would be supportive of it."

---

26. Although the statement itself was couched in fairly moderate terms (see Wilmore and Cone, *op. cit.*, pp. 23-30), it was of crucial importance to the Black Power movement since it provided it with some moral respectability. Stokely Carmichael, the chief spokesman for Black Power, quoted from it freely in speeches across the country.

27. Apparently the connection with Payton was enormously important because it meant that the early activity of the NCBC could take place in the committee rooms and conference halls of the NCC. See Wilmore and Cone, *op. cit.*, p. 18.

28. Cone, *For My People: Black Theology and the Black Church* (Orbis Books, Maryknoll, New York, 1984), p. 17.

It was the NCBC which helped formulate the demands for white reparations to black people which, as we have seen, surfaced at the 1969 Notting Hill Consultation on Racism and ultimately resulted in the establishment of the WCC's Special Fund with its grants to liberation movements.[29]

It was out of this Black Power context, then, and with the rationale of supporting Black Power, that Cone's ideas on Black Theology were developed. Let us look at some of these ideas as they appeared in *A Black Theology of Liberation* in order to understand something of the influence of the Black Theology project in South Africa.

To begin with, and typical of other contextual theologies, Cone redefines theology so that it is no longer an objective knowledge of God and His relationship with Man derived from a study of the Bible. Theology is unreservedly partisan and 'arises' from the poor and oppressed who encounter God as they fight for their freedom. He states:[30]

"There is no 'abstract' revelation, independent of human experiences, to which theologians can

---

29. See "The Black Manifesto" and "The National Committee of Black Churchmen's Response to the Black Manifesto" in Wilmore and Cone, *op. cit.* These demands first surfaced at a National Black Economic Development Conference (BEDC) in Detroit in April 1969 and were presented in the form of a 'Black Manifesto' by James Foreman, the president of the BEDC and a committed Black Power activist.

30. Cone, *A Black Theology of Liberation,* (Orbis Books, Maryknoll, New York, 2nd Edition, 1986), p. xxi.

> appeal for evidence of what they say about the gospel. God meets us in the human situation, not as an idea or concept that is self-evidently true. God encounters us in the human condition of the liberator of the poor and the weak, empowering them to fight for freedom because they were made for it. Revelation as the word of God, witnessed in scripture and defined by the creeds and dogmas of Western Christianity, is too limiting to serve as an adequate way of doing theology today."

and he continues, [31]

> "..theology ceases to be a theology of the gospel when it fails to arise out of the community of the oppressed."

But who is this God who is encountered in the struggle for liberation? Cone makes it clear that he is not referring to a universal loving Father, but rather to some sort of black tribal deity. He states:[32]

> "The word 'God' is a symbol that opens up depths of reality in the world. If the symbol loses its power to point to the meaning of black liberation, then we must destroy it."

and continues:[33]

> "There is no place in black theology for a colourless God in a society where human beings

---

31. *Ibid.*, p.1.
32. *Ibid.*, p. 57.
33. *Ibid.*, p. 63.

suffer precisely because of their colour. The black theologian must reject any conception of God which stifles black-determination by picturing God as a God of all peoples."

And later, in a similar vein, he states:[34]

"If Jesus Christ is white and not black, he is an oppressor, and we must kill him. The appearance of black theology means that the black community is now ready to do something about the white Jesus, so that he cannot get in the way of our revolution."

Implicit in all that Cone says is the idea that blacks, simply because they are black, are in a sense God's elect. (At one point, he declares that whiteness is satanic, the symbol of the Antichrist).[35] 'Salvation', and therefore entry into the 'kingdom of God', is, however, reserved only for those blacks who join the revolutionary struggle. Thus he states:[36]

"The kingdom of God is a *black* happening. It is black persons saying no to whitey, forming caucuses and advancing into white confrontation ... The event of the kingdom today is the liberation struggle in the black community."

and:[37]

---

34. *Ibid.*, p.111.
35. *Ibid.*, p.8.
36. *Ibid.*, pp. 124, 125.
37. *Ibid.*, p. 128.

> "Salvation, then, primarily has to do with earthly reality and the injustice inflicted on those who are helpless and poor. To see the salvation of God is to see this people rise up against its oppressors, demanding that justice becomes a reality *now,* not tomorrow."

In traditional Christian theology it is sin, without God's saving grace through Jesus Christ, which prevents entry into the kingdom of God. In Cone's Black Theology sin may also prevent entry into 'the kingdom', but his view of sin is radically different from that of traditional theology. Thus, he says,[38]

> "Sin is not an abstract idea that defines ethical behaviour for all and sundry ... To be in sin has nothing to do with disobeying laws that are alien to the community's existence. Quite the contrary, failure to destroy the powers that seek to enforce alien laws on the community is to be in a state of sin."

> "According to black theology, the sin of the oppressed ... is that of trying to 'understand' enslavers, to 'love' them on their own terms. As the oppressed now recognize their situation in the light of God's revelation, they know that they should have killed their oppressors instead of trying to 'love' them."

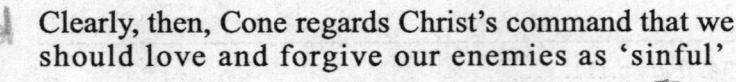

Clearly, then, Cone regards Christ's command that we should love and forgive our enemies as 'sinful'

---

38. *Ibid.,* pp. 104, 51.

because it may impede the black revolution. He declares:[39]

> "..with the assurance that God is on our side, we can begin to make ready for the inevitable - the decisive encounter between black and white existence. White appeals to 'wait and talk it over' are irrelevant ... We will not let whitey cool this one with his pious love ethic but will seek to enhance our hostility, bringing it to its full manifestation."

South African Black Theology

These, then, were the sort of ideas being studied in meetings and conferences of the UCM's Black Theology project in South Africa during the early 1970s. Some of the papers read there were later published in book form as *Essays on Black Theology*.[40] It was the first book on Black Theology to be published in South Africa, and, reflecting the situation of the time, was very much a mixed bag. Contributions from some of the black people who were trained theologians, for instance, adopted a fairly traditional approach to theology and were mainly concerned with criticising the way in which much Christianity in South Africa had been too associated with Western cultural values and forms of expression, which were not necessarily intrinsic to Christianity; for them 'Black Theology' mainly

---

39. *Ibid.*, p. 12.
40. See reference 20.

implied an emphasis on African cultural values.[41] Others, however, were clearly much more concerned with politics. For contributors such as Mokgethi Motlhabi, who took over as director of the Black Theology Project, as for two of the leaders of the South African Students' Organisation (SASO), Steve Biko and Nyameko (Barney) Pityana,[42] Black Theology was seen as being the theological extension of Black Consciousness. Pityana, for example, declared that "Black theology, then, is an extension of Black Consciousness",[43] and "the relationship between Black Theology and Black Consciousness is that one is a genus of the other."[44] Indeed,

---

41. The term 'Black Theology' has been used very inconsistently in South Africa. Some theologians have used it to describe a theology derived specifically from an African cultural context which might involve the fusion of Christianity and African forms of spirituality. This is not a 'theology of liberation' in the political sense, and is thus perhaps better described as 'African theology' rather than 'Black Theology'. Bonganjalo Goba has explained that although Black Theology and African Theology may have similar starting points - that is, an awareness of and positive approach to being a black African - the distinction between the two theologies "has to do with the kind of hermeneutic that one uses in his or her theological programme. Black Theology in its method of interpretation is intentionally political, on the other hand, African Theology tends to be more ethnographical particularly in its emphasis on African cultural values" - see Mosala and Tlhagale, *op. cit.*, p. 60.

42. Pityana was a co-founder of SASO with Biko but, according to reports, by late 1980 he had become a member of the ANC - see Tom Lodge, *Black Politics in South Africa since 1945* (Ravan Press, Johannesburg, 1983) and *Catholic Herald,* 20 November 1987. After being banned in South Africa in 1973, he came to England and eventually became an Anglican minister in Birmingham. In 1985 Pityana became a commissioner of the Programme to Combat Racism and its director in 1988, apparently on Archbishop Tutu's recommendation - see *Church Times,* 26 February 1988.

43. Moore, *op. cit.,* p. 62.

44. *Ibid.,* p. 63.

Bonganjalo Goba, another contributor to the volume, declared later that, "the relationship between Black Consciousness and Black Theology can be described as that of soul mates walking together in the ongoing struggle of black liberation."[45]

Apart from the fact that, at that time, it was somewhat ambiguous about the use of violence, Black Consciousness (which was largely developed by SASO - see Appendix 1) was very similar to the American Black Power movement, with its stress on black pride, black self-help, and opposition to working with white liberals or for integration into white society.[46] Thus, as American Black Theology was to be the theological arm of Black Power, so South African Black Theology was to be the theological arm of the country's emerging Black Consciousness movement. Ironically, however, in reading this volume, it becomes apparent that the only

---

45. Bonganjalo Goba, "The Black Consciousness Movement: Its Impact on Black Theology" in Mosala and Tlhagale, *op. cit.*

46. Allan Boesak, for instance, has described Black Consciousness and Black Power as follows: "Black Consciousness may be described as the awareness of black people that their humanity is constituted by their blackness. It means that black people are no longer ashamed that they are black, that they have a black history and a black culture distinct from the history and culture of white people. It means that blacks are determined to be judged no longer by, and to adhere no longer to white values. It is an attitude, a way of life. Viewed thus, Black Consciousness is an integral part of Black Power. But Black Power is also a clear critique of and a force for fundamental change in systems and patterns in society which oppress or which give rise to oppression of black people." See Allan Boesak, *Farewell to Innocence: A sociological study on Black Theology, Black Power* (Mowbrays, London & Oxford, 1978), p. 1.

person who really understood Cone's methodology, or began to actually *develop* a South African Black Theology at that time, was the white initiator of the project, Basil Moore. In other words, Black Theology was not a natural and spontaneous development amongst black South African Christians. Initially, it was a white-led theological import, which only began to take root amongst (some) black people in South Africa as its political potential began to be recognised and exploited.

This political potential was, in fact, enormous. Black theologians writing later have declared:[47]

> "...the appearance of that book heralded the dawn of a new kind of black militancy: The struggle for the liberation of the oppressed and exploited black people was to be waged at all levels of the social formation. Christianity and the Christian church had up till this time served as the ideological tool for the softening up of black people and as a means by which black culture had been undermined ... Black people were, as of this time, to draw the liberation struggle to the very centre of capitalist ideology, namely, the Christian theological realm."

The Black Theology project itself gradually fizzled out - partly because of the action taken by the South African authorities (who banned Basil Moore and the first director of the project, Sabelo Ntwasa, as well as *Essays on Black Theology*) and also, ironically, because the influence of the emerging

---

47. Mosala and Tlhagale, *op. cit.,* p.vii.

Black Consciousness ideas amongst black students was such as to lead to disenchantment with the multi-racialism and white liberal leadership of the University Christian Movement, and hence to its dissolution. This meant that the Black Theology project's support base had been destroyed and, although it then joined forces with SASO, funds were insufficient to keep it going.[48] Nevertheless, the project had succeeded in introducing Black Theology into South Africa and, from 1972 onwards, Black Theology began to appear in syllabuses of some theological training institutions.

Christian Institute

Black Theology also found support from the Christian Institute of Southern Africa. The Christian Institute had been founded in 1963 by a group of mainly Dutch Reformed Church ministers, led by Rev. Beyers Naudé, in the wake of the DRC's eventual rejection of the Cottesloe Statement. Modelling themselves to a large extent on the 'Confessing Church' movement which had sprung up in Germany in the 1930s to denounce Nazism, the Institute initially attempted to witness to the unity of the Church and to challenge apartheid by trying to change white attitudes through a mixture of education and moral appeal. As time went on, however, it became increasingly radical, a shift which was due largely to the effect Naudé's participation in the 1966 WCC Church and Society Conference had on his thinking.

---

48. However in 1975 a second conference on Black Theology was held in Lesotho, organised by Smangaliso Mkhatshwa.

Rather than attempting to bring about change by challenging white society, the Christian Institute shifted to strategies aimed at "empowering the powerless".[49] The Institute found it was able to attract funds from European (and later American) church groups and aid agencies to support a large staff and embark on programmes of more radical political action.[50] By the early 1970s, it had begun to play an important role in actively encouraging the development of the black consciousness movement and became a major source of support for black community leaders within the movement. The Christian Institute's magazine, *Pro Veritate,* also reflected this change in emphasis. As one (sympathetic) writer has put it, "by 1970 the editorials no longer bore a distinct Reformed, Confessing Church stamp, but were increasingly influenced by Latin American liberation theology, black theology, and the issues raised by the Programme to Combat Racism."[51]

From 1967 onwards the Christian Institute was a member of the South African Council of Churches. Partly through its influence, and also through the influence brought to bear by being an

---

49. Walshe, *op. cit.*
50. A former employee of the Christian Institute has described how he established contact with European (particularly Scandinavian) Church aid agencies in order to secure such funding. According to him, at this time the aid agencies were only too happy to provide money without strings if they believed it was going to help politically radical black groups. Private interview with the author, July 1991.
51. John de Gruchy, "A short history of the Christian Institute" in Charles Villa-Vicencio and John de Gruchy (eds.), *Resistance and Hope* (Eerdmans, Grand Rapids, USA, 1985).

associated council of the WCC,[52] the SACC gradually shifted its emphasis from traditional forms of Christian mission and evangelism to socio-political action. The protests it had made to the WCC about the Special Fund grants to liberation movements were not repeated after 1970, as the SACC "began to establish its reputation as a radical organisation ... a pioneer moving in new directions, urging churches to follow."[53] Some of its more evangelical members - like the Baptist Union and the Salvation Army - left the SACC in the process and, as with the Christian Institute and the WCC, this shift in its view of mission was supported by a corresponding shift in theology. In 1973, for instance, the SACC established a Division of Theological Training which made clear in its first report that it saw a need to 'contextualise' theology to meet the South African situation.

The Christian Institute was banned by the government in 1977 as part of its clampdown on the black consciousness movement and allied organisations at the time of the widespread disturbances in Soweto. Black Theology itself, however, was given a signficant boost that year with the publication of Rev. Allan Boesak's *Farewell to*

---

52. The SACC (or, to be precise, its forerunner, the Christian Council of Southern Africa) became an associate council of the WCC in 1962. Thereafter it reorganised its structure and, to a large extent, its thinking in line with that of the WCC.
53. David Thomas, *Councils in the Ecumenical Movement: South Africa 1904-1975* (SACC, Johannesburg, 1979), p. 54.

Innocence.[54] Boesak, then a young minister in the Dutch Reformed Mission Church (NGSK), had just completed six years doctoral study at the Theological Seminary of the Reformed Churches at Kampen, Holland, where he had specialised in Black Theology. *Farewell to Innocence,* which was his doctoral thesis, drew heavily on the work of Cone, which he propounded and applied to the South African situation with only a few reservations.

As with other contextual theologians, Boesak justified almost everything he had to say with reference to just two sections of the Bible - the Exodus, and Luke 4. 18-19, from which he concluded that, "Cone is right: The gospel of Jesus Christ *is* the gospel of liberation".[55] But this is a political liberation in which God "takes sides. He is neither indifferent nor aloof. He sides with the poor and the weak."[56] In South Africa this means that God sides with 'blacks' (by which is meant all non-whites) against whites and "blacks may participate in the struggle without any reservation knowing that they are doing the will of God."[57] This struggle is not for integration into, or reform of, white society but rather for 'radical change' of society, and the direction of the struggle is to be determined solely by black people. Since this struggle is determined by blacks, "blacks should have the right to determine whether

---

54. This was first published in Holland in 1976. It was published under this title in Johannesburg in 1977, and as *Black Theology, Black Power* (Mowbrays, London & Oxford, 1978). Quotes are taken from the British edition.
55. *Ibid.,* p. 17.
56. *Ibid.,* p. 43.
57. *Ibid.,* p. 76.

nonviolence is the only possible philosophy blacks should adhere to, or conversely that violence is the only possible expression left to blacks".[58] Boesak later states that "Cone argues - and we fully agree with him - white people with their sorry record of violence at every level are not morally equipped to preach the gospel of non-violence to black people."[59]

All this led Boesak into the redefinition of key Christian concepts. He maintains, for instance, that Black Theology "takes Christian love very seriously", but goes on to say that "any interpretation of Christian love that makes of it an ineffective sentimentality must be rejected." For, he says, "love is always love in righteousness" and "righteousness is that side of God's love which expresses itself through black liberation."[60] Similarly, although he refers several times to the need for reconciliation, he argues that the primary need is for black people to be reconciled with themselves and that any reconciliation with white people will only be possible when "righteousness and social justice" have been established.[61] Since he displays little faith in a process of reform, he therefore seems to agree with those American Black Theologians who state that "there is no other way for reconciliation to come but through revolution".[62]

Farewell to Innocence was the first book-length text on Black Theology to be produced by a

---

58. *Ibid.*, p. 66.
59. *Ibid.*, p. 126.
60. *Ibid.*, p. 146.
61. *Ibid.*, p. 93.
62. *Ibid.*, p. 128.

South African, and it soon became the basic text on the subject in theological faculties. Indeed, after his return from Holland, Allan Boesak emerged as one of the most influential Church leaders in South Africa, active in parish work, theological training, ecumenical affairs, and international Christian bodies at the highest level. In 1978 he became a member of the Examination Commission of the University of the Western Cape and, in 1982, joined the Governing Body of its Theological School. He was National Chairman of the Association of Christian Students of South Africa, Vice President of the South African Council of Churches, and theological adviser of the presidium of the All-Africa Conference of Churches. In 1982 he was elected President of the World Alliance of Reformed Churches, and in 1986 he became Moderator of the NGSK.[63] Boesak was also one of the driving forces behind the formation of the United Democratic Front (UDF) in 1983, and became one of its patrons.[64] All of these appointments presented Boesak with enormous opportunities for furthering his theological and political views both within South Africa and within the international Christian community.

Institute for Contextual Theology (ICT)

In spite of Boesak's influence, however, and the early interest of the South African Council of

---

63. Adelbert Scholtz, *The Story of Allan Boesak* (BusseSeewald, Herford, West Germany, 1989).
64. *Ibid,* pp. 78-79. After appearing close to the ANC for many years, Boesak joined the organisation in July 1991 and, with the support of Nelson Mandela, was elected chairman of the Western Cape region of the ANC in September 1991.

Churches, Black Theology only began to have a really substantial and sustained influence in South Africa after the establishment of the Institute for Contextual Theology (ICT). Although the ICT has always been a relatively small organisation,[65] it has been able to have an influence on the Church in South Africa wholly disproportionate to its size by acting, as research director Fr. Albert Nolan has put it, as a "hot-house" of ideas which have been fed into the mainline Churches and theological seminaries. In this the ICT has benefitted from the fact that, not being a Church, it has been able to do things without having to consider the possible opposition of its grassroots members, whilst at the same time it has enjoyed the support of both the SACC and the Southern African Catholic Bishops' Conference. The sympathy between the ICT, the SACC and the SACBC is indicated by the movement of senior personnel between the three organisations - the ICT's first General Secretary, Rev. Frank Chikane, (a former Black Consciousness activist, and a UDF leader), is presently the General Secretary of the SACC;[66]

---

65. At the end of 1991 it had a staff of just under twenty.

66. Chikane took over from Beyers Naudé as General Secretary of the SACC in 1987. He joined SASO in 1972 and was a founder member of AZAPO (see Appendix 1). He was ordained a pastor of the black Apostolic Faith Mission Church (AFM) in March 1980, but was suspended from the ministry by his Church district council in August 1991 because of his political activities. By 1982, when he joined the ICT (he became General Secretary in 1983), he had served four periods in detention because of such activities. In the early 1980s his politics shifted from Black Consciousness to an ANC 'Charterist' position and he became active in the UDF, acting as vice-president of the Transvaal region of the UDF between 1983 and 1985 and serving on the National Executive in 1984. In his autobiography, *No Life of My*

whilst the ICT's present General Secretary, Fr. Smangaliso Mkhatshwa, is a former Secretary General of the SACBC.

The ICT was set up in 1981 following discussions between a number of radical South African theologians, including Boesak and Beyers Naudé,[67] and members of the Ecumenical Association of Third World Theologians. Funded almost entirely by grants from overseas donors, which have included the British aid agencies CAFOD (Catholic Fund for Overseas Development), Christian Aid, and the Irish Catholic aid agency, Trocaire (see

---

Own (Catholic Institute for International Relations, 1988), he makes it clear that, in the third world, the "task of the theologian is to develop theological tools to help Christians participate in the struggle for justice..". Much of his activity at the ICT and subsequently at the SACC has been to that end. He was reinstated as a pastor of the AFM in 1990 but, as Smangaliso Mkhatshwa has said, "his reinstatement was not because of a change of heart by those who suspended him, but came about through pressure exerted by the people..." - see *New Nation* (SA), 27 April - 3 May 1990. Reports suggest that this 'pressure' was a threat by his sympathisers to burn down the building in which the Synod of the AFM was meeting if they did not agree to his reinstatement - see the Dutch paper, *Reformatorish Dagblad,* 17 May 1990.
67. Others included Prof. Charles Villa-Vicencio of the Department of Religious Studies, University of Cape Town; Rev. Francois Bill; and Rev. Cedric Mayson, former editor of the Christian Institute magazine, *Pro Veritate,* and one of the most active writers on religious issues within ANC circles.

Appendix 5),[68] the goal of the ICT has been "to contribute towards a theological base for the realisation of meaning, method and a theological source of a new society in Southern Africa."[69] Putting this more clearly, the overriding aim of the ICT has been to produce a specifically South African contextual theology justifying radical political change.

The political significance of such a programme should not be minimised. In secularised countries like Britain it is fairly easy for politicians to dismiss the political pronouncements of Church leaders because Christian allegiance is so low that, even if all active Christians took note of their leaders' calls and demands (which few do), it would not generally have much in the way of practical political impact. This is not so in South Africa, where an estimated 77% of the population adhere to Christianity,[70] where theology remains of great importance and interest, and where Church leaders still command enormous respect. Because of this, as Fr. Nolan has suggested, the theologies of liberation

---

68. In *Ten Years of Theology and Struggle* (ICT, 1991), published to celebrate the tenth anniversary of the ICT, Trocaire sent a message saluting "the Institute for Contextual Theology not alone for its obvious achievements in South Africa but also for its hidden achievements here in Ireland." A message of support was also sent by the Africa Secretary of the Council of Churches for Britain and Ireland.
69. *ICT Constitution*.
70. See J. Kritzinger, *A Statistical Description of the Religious Division of the People of South Africa* (Institute for Missiological Research, University of Pretoria, 1985). This study is in Afrikaans.

have been far more politically disturbing to South Africa than secular communism. If the same ideas had been promoted in a form other than theology they would have had little credibility, but presented in theological language they have been taken very seriously.[71]

Under Chikane's direction, the ICT set out to invigorate Black Theology. It immediately established a Black Theology Working Group, and a third national conference on Black Theology was held at the Wilgespruit Fellowship Centre in August 1983. This proved a very tense meeting.[72] As we have already seen, Black Theology was originally introduced and adopted by those involved in the Black Consciousness Movement and, for that reason, it was described as the theological expression of Black Consciousness. But although Black Consciousness was the sole internal uniting force in radical black politics in the early 1970s, this was certainly not true a decade later, particularly after the establishment in 1983 of the United Democratic Front which became essentially an internal arm of the exiled ANC (see Appendix 1). There were bitter ideological divisions between those in the Black Consciousness camp allied to the exiled black nationalist Pan Africanist Congress, and those in the ANC/UDF camp. The former took the view that racism was *the* cause of black oppression in South Africa and hence refused to join forces in 'the struggle' with sympathetic white people. The

---

71. Interview with author, June 1991.
72. See Mosala and Tlhagale, *op. cit.,* p. xviii. This book contains papers from both the 1983 and 1984 conferences.

ANC/UDF supporters, on the other hand, adopted a Marxist class-based analysis and, regarding capitalism as the ultimate cause of oppression in South Africa and racism as simply a particular aspect of capitalist oppression, were willing to join forces with progressive whites in the revolutionary struggle. Such ideological differences were reflected in the different views held by the radical theologians at the conference, with those who favoured the Black Consciousness wing of black politics drawing their theological inspiration from the race-based views of the American Black Theologians, whilst those who favoured the ANC/UDF wing drew their inspiration from the Marxist class-based analysis of the Latin American liberation theologians.

Partly because of the unresolved questions arising from the 1983 conference, the ICT organised another conference on Black Theology the following year in Cape Town. Here Black Theology was affirmed as "a weapon of the struggle for the liberation of the oppressed"[73] and agreement was reached that "what happens in the black struggle affects the process of theologising about this struggle and therefore Black Theology itself."[74] It was also agreed that it was not sufficient for Black Theologians simply to reflect on radical black political action from the haven of their theological faculties or seminaries, but that "a direct involvement in the struggle of the Black community is a

---

73. *ICT News,* December 1984.
74. See the preface to *Black Theology and Black Struggle*, the Report of the 1984 Conference on Black Theology (Institute for Contextual Theology).

prerequisite for Black Theological reflection"; Black Theologians "must die with the people and bear the pain with them in order to be able to write an authentic theology of liberation."[75] Since some argued that oppression in South Africa is based on both race *and* class, a new synthesis began to emerge whereby Black Theology would henceforth draw on both American Black Theology *and* Latin American liberation theology.[76] Furthermore, in order to ground it further in African culture, it would also occasionally call on distinctly African spiritual insights.

In this way, from a mixture of ideas derived from the American Black Theologians, the Latin American liberation theologians, and African 'cultural theology', a distinctive form of liberation theology has taken root in South Africa. The proportion of this mix has varied over time and from theologian to theologian in a somewhat confusing way. However, the important point to bear in mind all the time is not these differences, but rather the way in which this approach to theology, with its complete captivity to the vagaries of secular politics, and its

---

75. *Ibid.*
76. Boesak actually began this type of synthesis in *Farewell to Innocence*. Although, as we have seen, he drew very heavily on the work of Cone, nevertheless he stated that "racism is but one incidental dimension of oppression against which the total struggle should be waged.." and, for that reason, argued that the Latin American liberation theologians have important insights. He also criticised Cone for not not being sufficiently critical of American society as a whole, for he declared, "Black Theology ... must mean a search for a totally new social order." There are hints that what he has in mind for South Africa is some sort of African communitarian system.

readiness to justify violence, differs fundamentally from orthodox Biblical theology. This has significant implications for the way in which the Church views its mission to the world.

3. FROM RADICAL THEOLOGY TO ACTION

The previous chapter explained how a radical form of theology has grown up in South Africa, and discussed its links with similar theologies which have been developed in other parts of the world. For this to have much in the way of practical consequences, however, it is clear that these ideas needed to spread from the confines of the few people and organisations which initially developed them, to theological institutions and also directly to the people at the grassroots. Here, too, the Institute for Contextual Theology has played a key role.

Basic Christian Communities

In Latin America, where liberation theology has its origins, liberation theology is practised by what are known as 'Basic Christian Communities' (BCCs).[1] These are groups of generally poor people who meet regularly and are taught by a 'facilitator' how to apply the methodology of liberation theology in order to understand the social situations in which they find themselves. As liberation theologian, Leornardo Boff, has explained, "the Basic Christian Communities and Liberation Theology are but two distinct movements in the same process of mobilization of a people", the first representing "the practice of popular liberation"

---

1. These are also variously known as Base Ecclesial Communities (BECs) or CEBs.

and the second "the theory of this practice." BCC's are also sometimes known as the 'alternative Church' and their practice has been more fully described by radical South African theologian, Charles Villa-Vicencio, as follows:[2]

> "Worship, liturgy, the study of the Bible and other literature, sharing together, and corporate action in relation to particular events are important ingredients. Around these events social engagement becomes its distinguishing characteristic, with conscientizing of participants and the community being high on its agenda. The alternative church becomes a gathering point for the community in resistance and protest around specific issues."

Thousands of such groups now exist within the Latin American Catholic Church, particularly in Brazil and Nicaragua, where they have been a major factor in politicising and mobilising the people. In Nicaragua the work of the BCCs was a crucial element in the Marxist Sandinista take over of the country in 1979.[3]

When the ICT was first established it declared that one of its objectives was the establishment of BCCs,[4] and it has since worked to develop contextual theology programmes to be studied by such groups.

---

[2]. Charles Villa-Vicencio, "South Africa: a church within the church" in *Christianity and Crisis,* January 9, 1989.
[3]. For more information on BCCs, see *Transformation* (available from Paternoster Press, Exeter), July/September 1986. This contains several useful articles and a bibliography of the BCC movement.
[4]. *ICT Constitution,* para. 5.5.

Fr. Albert Nolan, who joined the staff of the ICT in 1984, has been the theologian most responsible for these programmes, and his book, *To Nourish our Faith: Theology of Liberation for Southern Africa,* as well as the ICT's *Contextual Theology for Groups,*[5] gives a good idea of the nature and structure of such courses. According to these publications, members of the groups are gradually introduced to the methodology of contextual theology; are taught to interpret the Bible for what it has to say about political oppression and liberation; are 'conscientised' through 'social analysis' (basically a Marxist approach to the social sciences) to see the world in simplistic, dualistic terms of oppressed and oppressor, and thus come to see the need for major structural changes in society.[6] They are then encouraged to further such ideas by studying and promoting some specific form of contextual theology such as feminist theology,[7] Black Theology, or liberation theology, and also to become practically involved in radical

---

5. This is a course consisting of four modules designed to be studied over two years. *Contextual Theology for Groups: 1st Module* makes it clear that "You cannot do this kind of theology alone or by reading books or by listening to lectures. It is essentially group theology..".
6. See Nolan and Broderick, *op. cit.,* pp. 52-55.
7. The ICT stated soon after its formation that it was keen to develop feminist theology - see *Minutes ICT AGM,* 1984 - and has had a department dedicated to this ever since. This is not, however, Western-style feminist theology where the main issue is one of gender and the struggle is just against male chauvinism. As the ICT has stated, "women do liberatory feminist theology through the eyes of the oppressed and exploited ... We believe in a prophetic theology, whereby our struggle is not simply against men but against all forms of oppression, exploitation and unbiblical domination." See *ICT News,* March/April 1989. South African feminist theology has thus been a way of specifically drawing women into the liberation struggle.

political action.

The ICT has also collaborated with the Lumko Institute, a Catholic organisation which has produced a great deal of detailed material about how to set up and run what it refers to as 'Small Christian Communities' (SCCs) - clearly only another name for BCCs. Like the ICT, the Lumko Institute is relatively small, but it has been making its influence felt on the wider Catholic Church in South Africa. In 1989, for instance, the Southern African Catholic Bishops' Conference (SACBC) produced a detailed Pastoral Plan, which it describes as being designed "for the transformation of the whole of life, for a change of heart and a change of society."[8] Drawing heavily on the work of the Lumko Institute, this Plan emphasises the need to transform the structure and the focus of the Catholic Church in Southern Africa by the establishment of SCCs which would adopt an approach referred to as the 'Pastoral Cycle'. This is described in the Plan as "a process with six steps or stages: 1. An event, experience or issue; 2. Social analysis; 3. Christian reflection and prayer; 4. Planning action; 5. Implementation; 6. Evaluation".[9] From this description it is clear that the 'Pastoral Cycle' uses the methodology of contextual theology, where Bible study and prayer are subservient to

---

8. *Community Serving Humanity: Pastoral Plan of the Catholic Church in Southern Africa* (Southern African Catholic Bishops' Conference, May 1989), p. 7. For a detailed and critical analysis of the Pastoral Plan, see *How Pastoral is the Catholic Bishops' Pastoral Plan? Religious and Political Implications of Small Christian Communities and Renew* (TFP, PO Box 10906, Johannesburg, 2000, 1991).
9. *Community Serving Humanity, op. cit.*, p. 42.

Marxist social analysis of issues.[10]

The radical *Belydende Kring* (i.e. confessing circle) movement within the family of Dutch Reformed Churches, has also been keen to develop Basic Christian Communities.[11] At a conference referred to as the 'National Assembly of Confessing Congregations' held in Johannesburg in 1987, the decision was taken to bring together "a national network of basic communities of people of Christian faith in the struggle to realize national liberation". A *Belydende Kring* Bulletin said of this later that: "A new christianity is emerging. Christians attending the assembly said they are ready to begin the transformation of their local churches and bring them in line with the struggle of the people of the land for liberation."[12]

The ICT also appears to have influenced yet another denomination - the Anglican Church of the

---

10. In Catholic circles, a similar approach to the 'pastoral cycle' is the 'See-Judge-Act' method. It has been used, for instance, in a cartoon-strip booklet, *Negotiating for a Just South Africa*, produced by the Justice and Peace Commission of the SACBC which is "designed to help groups in the Catholic Church to look at the issue of negotiations and see what is happening. After that the Bishops' Pastoral letter on Rerum Novarum and Negotiations can be read to judge what is happening. After that comes Action." It suggests that Catholic laity should persuade their parish priests to allow them to set up Church workshops to discuss the issue of negotiations for a new South African constitution, and to develop specific liturgies around the issue.
11. This has its origins in Beyers Naudé's call in the early 1960s to establish a 'Confessing Church'.
12. June 15, 1987. See also *The Road Ahead: Documentation on the Confessing Church debate* (The Belydende Kring, Cape Town, May 1987).

Province of South Africa (CPSA). In November 1987 it too committed itself to developing BCCs and the training of laity and clergy in 'social analysis'.[13]

Influencing the theological institutions

Given the complaints by some radicals that they have experienced some difficulty in mobilising Churches in the liberation struggle because the training provided by the seminaries has been "too academic and too theoretical",[14] it is easy to understand why the ICT has also been keen to encourage the development of contextual theology in South Africa's theological training institutions. In 1987, for example, it held a meeting which resolved that its theological education and training project (which has been responsible for developing the 'contextual theology for groups' programme) would cooperate with the South African Council for Theological Education, the Association of Southern African Theological Institutions, the South African Council of Churches and other theological institutions.[15] Two years later, in November 1989, it launched the Association of Committed Theologians (ACT) designed to bring together "those who teach

---

13. *Seek* (Journal of the CPSA), December 1987/January 1988. This decision was taken in the context of its acceptance of the Lusaka Statement (see below).
14. This complaint has been made, for instance, by Paddy Kearny, the director of Diakonia, a radical Durban-based organisation, in an interview in *New Nation* (SA), 7-13 July 1989. According to this report, he argued that theological training in South Africa should equip the clergy with the skills to set up a network of 'justice and peace' structures at all levels of the church, including the parishes.
15. *New Nation* (SA), 4-10 June, 1987.

launched the Association of Committed Theologians (ACT) designed to bring together "those who teach theology in seminaries or theological faculties and want to promote contextual theology in these places".[16] The main aim of ACT is to "organise theologians in support of the struggle for liberation...".[17]

In March 1991, the ICT was also able to announce the establishment of a cluster of theological institutions around Pietermaritzburg - the Federal Theological Seminary of Southern Africa (Anglican, Methodist, Congregational and Presbyterian), Saint Joseph's Theological Institute (seventeen orders and congregations of the Catholic Church), and the Department of Theological Studies of the University of Natal (ecumenical) - which were "committed to providing a contextual theological education in a changing South Africa."[18] As part of its task, the Pietermaritzburg Cluster of Theological Institutions recently launched a publishing house, Cluster Publications, specialising in works of contextual theology.[19] In these ways an increasing number of South Africa's theological training institutions have become, or are becoming, means of propagating a highly unorthodox and politicised approach to theology amongst those training to enter the Christian ministry.

---

16. *ICT Annual Report*, 1988.
17. ICT information document about ACT, 20 September 1989.
18. *ICT News*, March 1991.
19. Early titles include *We Shall Overcome: A Spirituality of Liberation; Biblical Hermeneutics of Liberation;* and *In Word and Deed: Towards a Practical Theology for Social Transformation.*

Attempting to influence the African Independent Churches

The work of the ICT amongst the African Independent Churches (AICs) has been to a similar purpose. The AICs are the largest group of Churches in South Africa and, with around eight million members, it has been estimated that they enjoy the support of between 35 and 40 percent of South Africa's black population.[20] The great majority of these Churches have either attempted to steer clear of politics altogether, or are moderate to conservative in their views. Most opposed the campaign for economic sanctions against South Africa and have refused to align themselves with the liberation movements. For this reason, with the exception of the Council of African Independent Churches (CAIC), a group of AICs with an estimated membership of about 50,000 who were initially brought together by the Christian Institute, the vast majority of the AICs have not joined the South African Council of Churches, as they have seen its activities as too political and too closely associated with the UDF/ANC. Indeed, a remarkable indication of the political conservatism of some of the AICs occurred in 1985 when the largest of these Churches, the Zion Christian Church, invited the then State President, P. W. Botha, to address their two million strong traditional Easter gathering at Mount Moria in the Transvaal.[21]

---

20. M. C. Kitshoff, "African Independent Churches: A Mighty Movement in a Changing South Africa" in *South Africa International*, January 1991. See also Lynette van Hoven, "Christian joy born from Africa" in *South Africa Panorama*, November/December 1990.
21. For details see *South African Digest*, 12 April 1985.

Given this background, it is highly significant that one of the first projects the ICT set itself in the early 1980s involved research into the existing theology of the AICs and the development of a "relevant contextualised course" of theology which could be used for AIC leadership training.[22] But although this programme may have gained some support from the CAIC,[23] it has had very little impact on the vast bulk of the AICs. Indeed, far more successful has been a quite different type of theological course - that run by the Timothy Training Institute to give AIC leaders (many of whom are very inadequately trained, and who have retained a belief in traditional African forms of spirituality like ancestor worship) an extremely thorough and completely orthodox grounding in the Bible. First established in 1985, this has been a great success and by mid-1991 the Institute was training over 2,600 AIC leaders in approximately 90 locations throughout South Africa.[24] The AICs also generally remain a great force for black political moderation.[25]

---

22. *ICT News,* No. 1, 1983.
23. In 1987 the CAIC held a conference which was addressed by ICT staff member, Alex Bhiman. Bhiman called on them to play an active role in the liberation struggle, suggesting that failure to do so would create doubts about their spirituality. The conference duly resolved that the churches should be more committed to the struggle. See *The New Nation* (SA), July 16-22, 1987.
24. Further information on the Timothy Training Institute may be obtained from PO Box 43, 2110 Mondeor, South Africa.
25. In 1991 there were rumours that one of the Zionist leaders might set up his own political party which would be prepared to enter into a 'Christian Democratic Alliance' with other moderate parties.

The Kairos Document

Without doubt, however, the most influential ICT initiative so far, and the most vivid demonstration of what contextual theology can mean when applied to practical political situations, has been *The Kairos Document*. This was published in September 1985 and presented to the world by the then General Secretary of the SACC, Dr. Beyers Naudé, at a press conference at the WCC's headquarters in Geneva.[26]

The Kairos Document, which was signed by just over 150 clergy and theologians from 22 Christian denominations in South Africa,[27] is frequently portrayed as a new and spontaneous response demanded by the developing political crisis of that time. In fact, however, many of the signatories had already worked together on the Black Theology projects or been involved in previous activities of the ICT. The Document grew out of the preparations for the ICT quarterly magazine, *ICT News,* and was written against the background of the events in South Africa in Summer 1985.[28] In order to understand the Kairos Document, or analyse it at all accurately, it is necessary to look at these events.

---

26. *The Kairos Document - Challenge to the Church: A Theological Comment on the Political Crisis in South Africa* (The Kairos Theologians, PO Box 32047, Braamfontein, 1985; Catholic Institute for International Relations/British Council of Churches, London 1985). References are to the British edition.
27. Prominent signatories included Beyers Naudé; Frank Chikane and Albert Nolan of the ICT; Smangaliso Mkhatshwa, General Secretary of the SACBC; and radical theologians from the University of Cape Town's Department of Religious Studies, John de Gruchy and Charles Villa-Vicencio.
28. *Crisis News* (South African Council of Churches), March 1986.

As Appendix 2 shows, a process of liberalisation of apartheid was already under way at that time. By 1985 virtually all white job reservations had been abolished, black trade unions had been legalised, black education had been improved, and many public amenities had been desegregated. In 1982 black local government was introduced and, in1983, a new constitution came into being establishing a tri-cameral parliamentary system which extended the franchise to Asians and coloureds, but not to blacks. Commentators differ on their interpretation of these events, and so it is difficult to be really objective, but probably the most credible view is that, although the Nationalist government had by this stage undergone little real change of heart about apartheid, nevertheless economic realities were producing change. Firstly, the demands of the labour market for skilled black workers brought about by white labour shortages had forced the abolition of white job reservations, and this had necessitated the provision of better black education and also led to increased black consumer power. This, in turn, had created economic pressures encouraging the desegregation of facilities like restaurants, hotels, theatres, etc. In other words, up to this period most aspects of the liberalisation process were very much 'market-led' and, given a vigorous economy, could be expected to continue.[29]

---

29. This sort of analysis has been put forward by John Kane-Berman in his testimony before various US Congress sub-committees in March 1988, reprinted as *The Erosion of Apartheid* (Times Media Ltd., Johannesburg), and also by Michael O'Dowd in "Understanding South Africa", *Journal of World Peace,* December 1988, reprinted by the British-South African Policy Studies Trust, as Policy Paper 1, 1991.

The 1983 constitutional changes, however, indicated both that the Nationalist government no longer had the confidence to maintain rigid 'white supremacy' but, at the same time, was not prepared to extend the franchise to black people. This, not unnaturally, infuriated many of them. Indeed, some regarded the extension of the franchise to Asians and coloureds as merely a cynical move by the white government to buy off other population groups and so reduce the pressure for a complete change in the system which (given the demographic make-up of the South African population) would result in black majority rule. Similarly, the introduction of black local government (that is, local government of the townships) was seen, not so much as a liberalisation measure, as a further entrenchment of the Group Areas Act which forced different population groups to live in strictly segregated areas. Thus by 1983 there was, on the one hand, a frustrated black population with rising expectations and growing confidence and organisational skills and, on the other hand, a government which, through its very preparedness to accept some reforms, was beginning to appear weak. Against this potentially explosive background, a plethora of black trade union and community groups (with some sympathetic coloured, Asian and white supporters) banded together in two broad coalitions. Their immediate goal was to fight the new constitutional proposals and make them unworkable, but they were also pressing for an end to all aspects of apartheid and, ultimately, for the adoption of socialism. In other words, neither of these two groups was working for continued liberalisation and reform but, rather, for an overthrow of the existing political and economic system.

Groups adopting black consciousness ideas banded together in the National Forum (the leading member of which was the Azanian Peoples' Organisation - AZAPO), whilst those inclined to ANC ideology formed the United Democratic Front. Both the National Forum and the UDF launched various campaigns to isolate the government from grassroots support, which meant that more moderate blacks, particularly those seen to be in some way associated with the white regime - for instance, policemen, or councillors in the newly-established black local authorities - were subject to gross intimidation. Political rivalries between the groups led to clashes between UDF and AZAPO supporters, and between the UDF and the mainly Zulu Inkatha movement. It was these developments, which, from September 1984 onwards, saw a rising tide of black-on-black violence in the townships and the first appearance of the horrific 'necklace' method of execution (mainly used as a summary method of execution of blacks accused of being 'sell-outs' to the white regime). It has been estimated that by May 1986, 3,477 private black homes, 1,220 black schools, as well as many churches and other community buildings had been badly damaged or destroyed, and 573 black people had been killed by other blacks, 295 of them by necklacing.[30] It was against this background, and in an attempt to control the violence

---

30. The 'necklace' is a tyre, filled with petrol and placed round the victim's neck. With his hands tied behind his back, or hacked off, there is nothing he can do to remove it when it is set alight. Death by burning and asphyxiation is slow and excruciatingly painful. It is estimated that 392 people died through necklacing between 1984 and 1987 - see *Business Day* (SA), 15 September 1988.

and unrest, that the South African government introduced a partial State of Emergency on 20th July 1985, extended to a total State of Emergency on 12th June 1986. This meant a media clampdown, restrictions on various political groups, and sweeping police powers of arrest and detention without trial.

The Kairos Document, then, was written against this background and was apparently designed to address the crisis. *Kairos* itself is a Greek word used in the Bible to mean God's appointed time relating to special occasions in His unfolding plan of salvation.[31] A German theologian, Professor Peter Beyerhaus, has pointed out that, in the Biblical sense, the *kairos* has three characteristics. First, "the chosen time comes through a free act of the sovereign God, an act in which man has no part and about which he can do nothing." Second, "God's *kairos* is centred in the sending of his Son Jesus Christ to implement his own plan of salvation to the world." Third, "the purpose of God's *kairos* is to enable man to receive at the appointed time within the limited interval of a given time period, salvation, the forgiveness of sins, and the grace to become God's son."[32] As we shall see, none of these aspects of God's *kairos* was actually contained in the Kairos Document.

Without offering any evidence that it had come about through God's special intervention, the

---

31. Galatians 4: 4-5 states, for instance, that "when the time (the *kairos*) had fully come, God sent forth his Son ... to redeem those who were under the law so that we might receive adoption as Sons."

32. Peter Beyerhaus, *The Kairos Document: Challenge or Danger to the Church?* (Gospel Defence League, Cape Town, 1987).

Kairos Document claimed that the man-made tensions and violence in 1985 meant that a *kairos* had arrived in South Africa. It was a "moment of truth" for apartheid - but it was a moment of truth which demanded political action. Using Marxist social analysis to present the situation in South Africa as a simple two-sided conflict between oppressor and oppressed where the cause of the oppressor was entirely unjust and that of the oppressed entirely just,[33] the Document ruled out the possibility of reforming the system with the sweeping and unproven assertion that "reforms that come from the top are never satisfactory. They seldom do more than make the oppression more effective and more acceptable." Then employing liberation theology's Exodus motif, the Document argued that "God does not bring his justice through reforms introduced by the Pharaoh's *(sic)* of this world". Rather, "true justice, God's justice, demands a radical change of structures. This can only come from below, from the oppressed themselves".[34] Thus it concluded that "the conflict and struggle will have to intensify in the months and years ahead because there is no other way to remove the injustice and oppression."[35]

In other words, instead of calling for peace and restraint during a time of enormous tension in the country (indeed it quite explicity stated that the "Church of Jesus Christ is not called to be a basion of caution and moderation" and that "the Church must avoid becoming a 'Third Force', a force between the

---

33. *The Kairos Document*, para. 4.1.
34. *Ibid.*, para. 3.2.
35. *Ibid.*, para. 4.4.

oppressor and the oppressed"),[36] this purportedly Christian document suggested that there was no alternative but to intensify the conflict. That this might involve the use of violence there could be no doubt. The Document appeared to excuse the killing of black moderates by terming them 'collaborators' and went out of its way to argue that the violence then being used by young people in the townships ought not to be called 'violence' at all but rather 'self-defence' since only oppressors can accurately be said to use violence. Thus it declared that "to call all physical force 'violence' is to try to be neutral and to refuse to make a judgement about who is right and who is wrong. The attempt to remain neutral in this kind of conflict is futile."[37]

The central message of the Kairos Document, however, was that this was also a *kairos* for the Church in South Africa. At present it was divided on both sides of the conflict, but God was issuing a challenge to decisive action.[38] On the one side there were those who supported the status quo; they were said to subscribe to heretical and blasphemous 'State Theology'.[39] The Document also attacked what it called the 'Church Theology' of many in the English-speaking Churches who were critical of apartheid, but rejected violence and continued to stress the need for reconciliation between all South Africans. Arguing that "it would be totally unChristian to plead for

---

36. *Ibid.*, paras. 5.6; 5.4.
37. *Ibid.*, para. 3.3.
38. *Ibid.*, Chapter 1.
39. It is interesting that the Document included in this category, not just those who supported the racism of apartheid, but also those who supported capitalism.

reconciliation and peace before the present injustices have been removed",[40] the Kairos Document declared that :[41]

> "There are conflicts that can only be described as the struggle between justice and injustice, good and evil, God and the devil. To speak of reconciling these two is not only a mistaken application of the Christian idea of reconciliation, it is a total betrayal of all that the Christian faith has ever meant."

Thus the Kairos Document stated that "Christians, if they are not doing so already, must quite simply participate in the struggle for liberation and justice."[42] This was 'Prophetic Theology'. It meant firstly that the Church should refuse to do anything which would seem to give moral legitimacy to the government. Secondly the Church "should not only pray for a change of government, it should also mobilise its members in every parish to think and work and plan for a change of government in South Africa." The Document then went on to declare that "the moral illegitimacy of the apartheid regime means that the

---

40. *Ibid.*, para. 3.1.
41. *Ibid.* This seems to have been rather a favourite theme of the ICT, or at least of general secretary, Frank Chikane. In *ICT News*, March 1985, he stated: "In the light of the new understanding of the incarnate life of our Lord we are called to abandon the old ideas of neutrality, unity and reconciliation ... We must begin to understand that there is no possibility of unity or reconciliation between the oppressed and the oppressor, the exploiter and the exploited, between good and evil, God and the Devil ... In the incarnation, we are called to abandon the old theology of reconciliation."
42. *Ibid.*, para. 5.2.

Church will have to be involved at times in *civil disobedience.*"[43]

Failings of the Kairos Document

It should be clear from all this, that the characteristics of the *kairos* of the Kairos Document bore little resemblance to those of the Biblical *kairos* referred to earlier. It had absolutely nothing to say about the way of salvation through Jesus Christ. Rather, it simply attempted to engage the Churches in the liberation struggle. In doing so it employed arguments which were grossly deficient both politically and theologically.

The Document was deficient politically in its simplistic portrayal of the South African situation as a civil war between oppressors and oppressed. It said nothing about the shades of opinion between white people, or of the fact that black people were engaged in conflict amongst themselves. So even if it really were right for the Church to side with the oppressed, as the Document demanded, then a legitimate question to ask was "Which oppressed?" Those in the UDF? Or the National Forum? Or Inkatha? And what about the many politically moderate blacks who, whilst hating apartheid, believed it was possible to achieve change through a liberalising process of reforms?

The Document was also deficient theologically, particularly in its rejection of reconciliation before the removal of all injustice.

---

43. *Ibid.,* para. 5.5.

During the Sermon on the Mount, Jesus told His disciples to "love your enemies and pray for those who persecute you".[44] In the Lord's prayer, too, we are instructed to "forgive those who trespass against us" - we are not told that we should only forgive those who ask for our forgiveness and who fully recompense us for any harm they have done. God's wisdom is greater than ours, and it may be the forgiveness and love we show to our enemies which brings them to repentance and makes possible reconciliation in the deepest sense. As the Bible says, "Do not be overcome by evil, but overcome evil with good".[45] To imagine that evil can or must be overcome by evil, as the Kairos Document implied, is quite contrary to authentic Christian doctrine.[46] By insisting that there were two sides to the conflict, between which no reconcilation was possible, and that the Church should become actively involved on one side, the Document was not only demanding that moral legitimacy be given to virtually everything done in the name of the struggle, it was also attempting to silence those forces in South African society most likely to be a restraining force on violence.

In this respect, it is important to look carefully at the Kairos Document's demand that the Church should be involved at times in civil disobedience.

---

44. Mathew 5: 44.
45. Romans 12: 21.
46. For a detailed theological critique of the Kairos Document from an evangelical perspective, see Rev. Dr. Philip Hughes, "Christianity and Revolution: The Kairos Document Considered" in *The Christian Challenge* (USA), December 1987 and January/February 1988.

Civil disobedience generally means a form of non-violent, but nevertheless effective, action against a State. By refusing to comply with its laws, an attempt is made to make the State ungovernable and hence, by extra-parliamentary means, to force some sort of political change. Although the form of civil disobedience may, in itself, be non-violent that does not mean that violence is necessarily avoided - civil disobedience may involve coercion of others to persuade them to join in the action and so make it effective, and it may also lead to violence either because the State uses force to keep civil order, or because order breaks down and civil disorder ensues. Civil disobedience is thus always a potentially dangerous option, and the decision by Christians to use civil disobedience must always involve a very careful assessment of ethical and practical considerations.

The Kairos Document was, in fact, not the first occasion that sections of the Church in South Africa had endorsed civil disobedience. The SACC had, in effect, supported the idea of civil disobedience ever since its 1979 National Conference passed an open-ended motion stating that "the South African Churches are under an obligation to withdraw, as far as that is possible, from cooperation with the State in all those areas in the ordering of our society where the law violates the justice of God" and had instructed its Justice and Reconciliation Division to "examine strategies of resistance." But the Kairos Document made this endorsement much clearer and, rather than calling for the Churches to carefully formulate its own strategy of civil disobedience, it argued that "the campaigns of the people, from consumer boycotts to stayaways, need to be supported and encouraged by the Church."[47]

Although 'consumer boycotts', 'utility strikes' and 'stayaways' may all superficially be regarded as non-violent forms of civil disobedience, some of the tactics used by young radicals in the 'peoples organisations' (i.e. the UDF and AZAPO) to force others to comply with them were, in fact, violent in the extreme. Much has been reported, for instance, about the fact that black people who refused to take part in utility strikes by, for example, continuing to pay their electricity bills when they had been ordered not to, were liable to have their houses burnt down, not infrequently when they were inside them. Similarly, those who broke consumer boycotts by continuing to patronise white-owned shops were frequently punished by the 'comrades' or 'young lions', as they came to be known, by being made to drink the cooking oil or eat the washing powder they had bought.[48] It could normally have been expected

---

47. *The Kairos Document, op. cit.,* para. 5.2.
48. In *Fast Facts,* June 1991, the South African Institute of Race Relations reports the following dreadful incidents of intimidation used during consumer boycotts and stayaways:
" * A Democratic Party-office bearer said that one of the party's black members in the Orange Free State was forced to drink a bottle of milk she had bought during a consumer boycott and then eat the plastic container. He also told of a man who was forced to swallow an entire bottle of tablets he had bought from a pharmacy during a consumer boycott and who died of the overdose.

* Four men between the ages of 34 and 63 were hauled in front of a people's court at 3 am in Soweto after ignoring a stayaway call which they had been told was optional. They were sentenced to 500 lashes each, stripped naked in front of ten-year-

that this sort of intimidation would have been condemned by the Churches, but the stance of the Kairos Document and the consistent support the South African Council of Churches has given to strategies of civil disobedience has meant that the mainline Churches have largely ignored such problems.[49]

Distribution of the Kairos Document

The Kairos Document was widely distributed within South Africa and also received significant worldwide support. According to the second edition, 35,000 copies of the first edition, and tens of thousands of summaries in English, Zulu, Xhosa, Sotho and Afrikaans were being distributed within a year. However, it was the international Christian community which appeared most excited by the Document. It was published in almost every

---

olds, spreadeagled over a drum and flogged.
* A woman was on her way home with groceries during a boycott. She was confronted by a group of youngsters, among them her son. He was told to take the groceries and destroy them, which he did. The mother was then allowed to pass and arrived home with no groceries, and therefore no supper for the family - much to the anger of her husband. When the son arrived home at 10 pm demanding his supper, his father lost control of himself and killed his son. He then turned himself over to the police."
49. Intimidation has continued to be a major fact of life in the black townships. In February and March 1991, the SAIRR conducted a survey of African adults in eleven major metropolitan areas and found that, in the previous year, a third had been forced to take part in consumer boycotts or stayaways, whilst one quarter had been dissuaded from paying their rents or service charges for electricity through various forms of threat.

European language and was distributed in Western Europe, East Germany, India, the Philippines, Australia, New Zealand, the USA and Latin America.[50] In Germany, the Evangelisches Missionwerk sent it to all delegates of the National Synod of the Evangelical Church in Germany (EKD). In Britain, it was published and distributed jointly by the British Council of Churches and the Catholic Institute of International Relations. According to a paper produced by the Kairos National Office, set up in South Africa in 1986 to co-ordinate activities and initiatives arising from the Document, many "Christians the world over have been challenged to reflect on their respective 'Kairoses' ... to critique the traditional, historical alignment of the Christian faith and the Church with the political status quo of the West, and are now developing prophetic theologies which will respond to the crises that they face in their particular contexts." Kairos groups have since been set up in a number of other countries - including Kairos USA, Kairos Canada, Kairos Europa, and Kairos Brazil.[51]

In other words, apart from its political impact within South Africa, one of the effects of the Kairos Document has been to further the spread of contextual theology to many parts of the world.

---

50. *The Kairos Document* (ICT/Skotaville Publishers, PO Box 32483, Braamfontein, 1986).
51. *ICT Annual Report,* 1990.

Implementing the Kairos Document: mobilising youth

Within South Africa itself, a Kairos national co-ordinating committee, national offices, and a regional structure were set up early in 1986 in order to co-ordinate the activities of individuals and groups committed to the thrust of the Kairos Document.[52] A high priority was give to work amongst youth groups. According to one report from this committee, since the youth in a church often have "periphery" status, and since the Kairos Document represents the sentiments of Christians "on the periphery", young people responded much more favourably to the Document than did Church leaders. A document produced by the Kairos National Office in May 1986 stated that Christian youth organisations, including SACC youth, the Student Union for Christian Action, Young Christian Students, the Catholic Students' Association, Anglican Youth, Catholic Youth, and InterChurch Youth had formed themselves into a committee to plan strategies that would "empower Christian youth for more effective action within the church and society within the framework of the Kairos Document."[53]

An ad-hoc Committee on "Kairos and Youth" drew up detailed three-phase plans for "translating the Kairos Document into Action" amongst young

---

52. For instance, the *Belydende Kring* 'confessing congregations' mainly date from this time, having been organised in response to the Kairos Document.
53. Document from the Kairos National Office, 10 May 1986.

people. These included:[54]

> Phase 1 - <u>Popularising the Kairos Document</u> by means of a concerted drive to distribute summaries of the document at universities, schools, church youth clubs etc. Also using drama, seminars and workshops to spread the message.
>
> Phase 2 - <u>Understanding the Kairos Document</u> by means of training events on the challenge and implications of the Kairos Document; campaigns to popularise the Bible as a theological basis for political activism along the lines of Latin American models; fortnightly house meetings for theological reflection and preparing for action.
>
> Phase 3 - <u>Kairos Action</u> - civil disobedience training; linking up with the 'broader struggle'; providing 'Kairos theology' input at funerals.[55]

This emphasis on young people is highly significant. During the late 1970s and in the 1980s, many black schoolchildren, responding to slogans like "liberation now, education later", abandoned their education and joined groups allied to the liberation movements. They were at the forefront of both the 1976 Soweto uprising and the political disturbances of 1984-6, and were responsible for some of the worst

---

54. "Kairos and Youth", Undated minutes from the Kairos National Office.
55. Funerals of those killed in political violence have often been used as opportunities for politically-charged sermons and further demonstrations, frequently erupting into more violence.

atrocities committed at these times and during the more recent outbreak of violence.[56] In South Africa in the 1990s many people now speak of a "lost generation" of children, uneducated, brutalised, and unemployable. It might have been hoped that Christian groups would have tried to restrain this culture of violence amongst the young, but the adoption of the Kairos Document by so many apparently Christian youth organisations, and these detailed plans to translate the recommendations of the Document into action, can only have added to the problem.

Implementing the Kairos Document: Kairos Worship

A further aspect of Phase 3 - translating the Kairos Document into action - was the preparation of monthly 'Kairos worship services'. The Kairos Document had stated that Church activities like Sunday services, communion services, baptisms, funerals, and so on, must be "reshaped" to "further the liberating mission of God and the Church in the world."[57] Taking up this idea, a Kairos Liturgy committee was formed in November 1985 in order to free the Church from "inhibitive, irrelevant forms of worship" and to "create new liturgical forms" which would "re-appropriate Church/Christian symbols to serve the needs of the poor".[58] The aim, then, was to

---

56. For some details see Keith Campbell, *Children of the Storm,* and Helene Roux, *How Revolutionaries Use Children,* both of which are available from Lone Tree Publications, Elim Building, 181 Proes Street, Pretoria, 0001. See also Ryan Malan, *My Traitor's Heart* (The Bodley Head, 1990).
57. *The Kairos Document,* para. 5.3.
58. Undated minutes from the Kairos Liturgy and Media Committee.

hold regular 'Kairos services' using liturgies which would quite explicitly use Christian symbols in a way which would further the liberation struggle. In March 1986, a book of Kairos liturgies for Good Friday and Easter Sunday was published. Service notes for Good Friday suggested, for instance, that sermons should stress that "Jesus was killed because in the name of God he sided with the poor and the oppressed and opposed their oppressors", whilst the aim of one Easter sermon was "to see the uprisings of the people ... as the resurrection of Christ in South Africa today". The conclusion of another suggested sermon was that "the struggle for liberation in South Africa today is a saving act of God. It is our passover from death to life. It is our Easter experience."[59] In other words, these most important of Christian festivals, celebrating the events which lie at the very core of Christianity - Christ's atoning death for our sins, and the offer of new and eternal life through Him - were to be reduced to mere political tools. In effect, the struggle itself had become the new God.

Concerned Evangelicals

Since it might be expected that Biblically-orthodox Christians, particularly evangelicals, would question the theology of the Kairos Document and the use of Kairos liturgies, it is noteworthy that the Kairos Liturgy and Media Committee decided to make "evangelical Churches a priority re integration of faith/worship and living in South African society" and also to challenge evangelists from overseas and

---

59. *Kairos Liturgies for Good Friday and Easter Sunday* (Southern Transvaal Kairos Liturgy Group, PO Box 32047, Braamfontein 2017), pp. 5, 16, 19.

those appearing on South African television about the 'other worldy' nature of their teaching.

More importantly, the ICT set up a project in September 1985 involving a group of 'concerned evangelicals' whose aim was to reflect on the *kairos* facing evangelical Christians in South Africa.[60] In 1988, under the leadership of the Rev. Caesar Molebatsi (one of the signatories of the Kairos Document), the group became a separate organisation working for an "evangelical mission that is contextual, transformative and empowering."[61] The most significant initiative of Concerned Evangelicals, however, was its publication in 1986 of a booklet called *Evangelical Witness in South Africa*.[62] This has been given a certain degree of credibility in Britain by being co-published by the largest umbrella organisation of evangelical groups in the country, the Evangelical Alliance, with a foreward by its general secretary.[63] Complaints by SACC-related organisations that they have experienced difficulty in spreading liberation theology at grassroots level because of the increase in evangelical and charismatic

---

60. ICT publicity leaflet, 1987.
61. Concerned Evangelicals has also stated that it intends to set up an Evangelical House of Studies, linked to the University of Natal, in order to proved a "contextual, progressive theological training for evangelicals." See Concerned Evangelicals publicity leaflet, undated.
62. Concerned Evangelicals, PO Box 200, Dobsonville 1865, South Africa.
63. *Evangelical Witness in South Africa: South African Evangelicals critique their own theology and practice* (The Evangelical Alliance & Regnum Books, 1986).

groups,[64] as well as the systematic campaign to discredit many evangelical organisations (which we shall consider in the next chapter), indicate, however, that the work of Concerned Evangelicals is unrepresentative of the vast majority of evangelical Christians in South Africa.[65]

Although *Evangelical Witness* was more subtle and sophisticated than the Kairos Document, its message was very similar. Written from the perspective of a group which would, in Kairos terms, normally adopt 'Church theology', it was a sort of public confession of failure for having assumed positions which "tend to maintain the status quo".[66] "The problem" stated the booklet "is that Jesus was radical, always geared to turning the world upside

---

64. In 1989, for instance, the Inter-Church Youth department of the Western Province Council of Churches (one of the SACC regional councils) complained about "the evangelical and charismatic movements which is *(sic)* growing rapidly and hindering our attempts to work towards the transformation of the Church." This is contained in a document entitled "Come With Me", SACC Youth Division, 1989.

65. The South African equivalent of the British Evangelical Alliance is the Evangelical Fellowship of South Africa (EFSA) which, in 1991, had 36 Churches or large evangelical organisations as members, including the Salvation Army, Apostolic Faith Mission, Assemblies of God, Youth for Christ, Youth with a Mission, etc. EFSA is a multiracial organisation, and by no means rules out Christian involvement in politics, but from an orthodox Biblical position, cautioning against the use of force and arguing that all Christians should actively seek for peaceful means by which just solutions to South Africa's problems may be found. See, for instance, *The Bible and Socio-Political Action* (EFSA, PO Mayors Walk, Pietermaritzburg 3208, 1989).

66. Evangelical witness in South Africa, *op. cit.*, p. 12.

down ... He was committed to a radical change and we are committed to moderation, to reformist liberal tendencies which leave the system intact."[67] Therefore, it said, "we believe that God, through Jesus Christ, is calling us to salvation, to a radical change of our lives and therefore to a radical change of structures of our society. We believe that we are called to effect these changes."[68] Arguing (like the Kairos Document) that "any reconciliation which happens without repentance cannot be reconciliation",[69] *Evangelical Witness* maintained that whites not only had to repent of sins relating to apartheid (which is reasonable enough) but also their 'sin' of wishing to work for power-sharing and of wishing to reform the system. Black South Africans, on the other hand, needed to confess their "complacence and permissiveness in the face of sin that reduced the image of God in them into nothingness" and their "sin of fear of harassment, detention, torture, etc."[70] In other words, blacks were guilty of not having been more fearlessly active in the liberation struggle. The overall, if implicit, message of *Evangelical Witness* was thus that, in obedience to Jesus Christ, all Christians should be involved in the liberation struggle and that true reconciliation would only be achieved when the struggle had been successful. Like the Kairos Document, *Evangelical Witness* chose to ignore the fact that the liberation struggle in South Africa at that time was manifesting itself largely through appalling black-on-black violence.

---

67. *Ibid.*, p. 15.
68. *Ibid.*, p. 22.
69. *Ibid.*, p. 19.
70. *Ibid.*, p. 19.

The Harare Declaration

It has already been mentioned that the Kairos Document was very widely distributed internationally and the support of the WCC was crucial in this. Its Programme to Combat Racism also promoted the document by devoting a special issue of its journal *PCR Information* in November 1985 to reproducing it in full, together with favourable detailed commentaries from various international theologians. Anwar Barkat, then director of the PCR, declared in his introduction that:

> "an appropriate response to the Document is to declare unequivocally on whose side the churches outside South Africa are and to indicate in clear terms what appropriate actions they are willing to take to enlarge the liberation stuggle internally and externally."

The WCC took this support further when, with the SACC, it organised an emergency consultation on South Africa in Harare, Zimbabwe, from 4-6th December 1985. This not only brought together a number of Church leaders from Western Europe, North America and Africa (including 37 from South Africa itself), but also included as observers senior members of the then-exiled liberation movements - five from the ANC and three from the Pan Africanist Congress (PAC).[71]

The conference set out its theological basis in a memorandum which stated:

---

71. The ANC members were Alfred Nzo, Thomas Nkobi, Jacob Zuma and Relly Mazinka; the PAC members were Ngila Muendane, Ibrahim Desai, and Vusi Ndlovu.

> "The struggle for liberation is a struggle grounded in faith. Christians cannot make a separation between prayer and political actions ... Their ministry today has to be one of involvement and participation in the struggle ... New ways of interpretation are needed with a view to undergirding the participation in the struggle, with fresh theological insights. In this connection we call attention to the issues and perspectives raised in the Kairos Document."

Against this understanding of Christian ministry, at least one of the South African Church leaders present made clear his support for violence in order to force the government to unban the liberation movements and release political prisoners. The Rev. B. Finca of the Reformed Presbyterian Church, in a statement which was subsequently widely distributed by the WCC,[72] declared that "what we need at this hour, at this time in South Africa is action calculated to intensify and escalate conflict." He continued:

> "the question that is facing the church catholic, and those of us who come from other countries, is whether it is prepared to move from the armchair resolution, conference kind of reflecting on the situation in South Africa to a campaign for costly intervention that will intensify the conflict and escalate the conflict, because that is the only way in which you can

---

72. It was sent, with some of the other statements from the Harare consultation, to all member Churches and associated councils of the WCC as part of the background literature accompanying the liturgy for a World Day of Prayer for South Africa - see below.

be of assistance to the oppressed of South Africa."

Using Kairos terminology, the Harare Declaration (see Appendix 6) stated that "we affirm that the moment of truth (Kairos) is now both for South Africa and the world community". Backing an initiative from the South African Council of Churches, the Declaration called on the Churches inside and outside South Africa to observe June 16th 1986 - the 10th Anniversary of the Soweto uprising - as a "World Day of Prayer to End Unjust Rule in South Africa", and subsequently distributed a Kairos-type liturgy to be used on the day.[73] It also called on

---

73. As the following prayer from the liturgy demonstrates, much of the liturgy (distributed by the WCC, the Lutheran World Federation and the World Alliance of Reformed Churches), was highly political and notably lacking in Christian forgiveness:
"Listen to our words, O Lord, and hear our sighs.
Listen to our protest.
For you are not a God who is friendly with oppressors,
neither do you support their devious ways,
nor are you influenced by their propaganda.
For you despise their arrogance,
you cannot stand the sight of these proud people,
and you hate their systematic repressions.
One cannot believe all they say.
Their official pronouncements are full of deadly deceit,
and they cannot be trusted.
They speak peace while increasing their production of arms,
they openly rumour of negotiation and reform,
whilst secretly planning ever more violent oppression..
Condemn and punish them, O God,
may their own plots cause their ruin,
drive them out of our presence
because of their many sins
and their rebellion against you.

the international community to prevent the extension, granting or rolling over of bank loans to South Africa and to apply immediate and comprehensive sanctions. Most controversially of all, however, and again in line with the Kairos Document and in keeping with the WCC's work through the Programme to Combat Racism, it called on the "Churches inside and outside South Africa to support South African movements working for the liberation of their country."

The Lusaka Statement

About eighteen months later, in May 1987, the Programme to Combat Racism organised a further international conference in order to review the implementation of the Harare Declaration, determine the role of the churches "in the search for justice and peace" in Southern Africa, and provide an opportunity for church leaders from the whole of Southern Africa "to meet with representatives of the liberation movements." It was held in Lusaka, Zambia, where the then-exiled ANC had its headquarters.

This was a larger conference with about 200 delegates, but it can hardly be said to have been a thoroughly balanced expression of international Christian opinion. Some of those listed as overseas delegates were, in fact, former South African political activists in exile,[74] and delegates from South Africa

---

74. For instance, Rev. Barney Pityana, who was a member of the committee and a UK delegate had, as we have already seen, been an early black consciousness activist and subsequent ANC member. The Rev. Brian Brown, also a UK delegate (he was head of the Africa desk of the British Council of Churches) had formerly been the administrative director of the radical Christian Institute in South Africa.

(thirty church leaders, together with a small number of representatives of trade unions, educational bodies, women's organisations, and youth organisations) were chosen by the South African Council of Churches which had long adopted a highly-politicised stance. Delegates from surrounding African countries largely came from their WCC-aligned Councils of Churches. This included twenty-eight delegates from the Council of Churches in Namibia (CCN) which, as has been well documented elsewhere, had extremely close links (including overlapping senior personnel) with the Namibian liberation movement, SWAPO.[75] Also, for the first time in a Church-organised conference of this kind, large contingents from the liberation movements were present as delegates, rather than as observers, and they played a major role in the proceedings.[76] SWAPO president, Sam Nujuma; ANC president, Oliver Tambo; and PAC chairman, Jonathan Mlambo, all addressed the conference.

In his address, Tambo argued that the source of violence in South Africa was apartheid, and that the ANC had no choice but to use violence to bring the apartheid system to an end and thus end the violence.[77] Mlambo, too, insisted that the PAC was convinced that "the most effective method of

---

75. See Alejandro Ezcurra Naon and Luis Daniel Merizalde, *SWA/Namibia: Dawn or Dusk?* (TFP, PO Box 10906, Johannesburg, 2000, 1989); *SWAPO, the Church and Human Rights* (International Society for Human Rights, British section, December 1986); and Elizabeth Endycott, "Swapo Shopped", in *The Spectator,* 16 September 1989.

76. There were seventeen from the ANC, seven from the PAC, and eighteen from SWAPO

77. For his full speech see the magazine of the ANC Department of Religious Affairs, Vol. 1, No. 1, 1987.

struggle, in the face of unabated reactionary violence, is the armed struggle."[78] Such arguments, which rely to a large extent on the Marxist concept of 'structural violence', ignore the possibility of abolishing apartheid by non-violent and reformist measures. Indeed, as Appendix 2 indicates, further reforms to the apartheid legislation had already been made by this time. The abolition of the pass laws, the partial restoration of South African citizenship to those in the homelands, and the granting of full property rights to black people, were all a tacit admission by the South African government of the fact that the grand apartheid scheme, with its establishment of tribal homelands (to which blacks had been forcibly removed) had been completely abandoned.

Some might argue that such reforms had come about as a result of the violence but, in fact, white South Africans were not suffering much as a consequence of revolutionary violence at that time. Rather, black people continued to suffer as a result of the rivalries between the internal organisations allied to the ANC and PAC with each other and with Inkatha, and also because of the failure of the liberation movements to command anything like total support from black people, and hence the use of intimidation to try and get that support. In this respect, Tambo's remarks about black-on-black violence are most revealing. He stated:[79]

> "the ANC has made strenuous efforts to mobilise all our people, both black and white, to join together in action against the Pretoria

78. *The Churches' Search for Justice and Peace in Southern Africa* (Programme to Combat Racism, WCC, 1987).
79. *Ibid.*

regime. At the same time, we have called repeatedly on those who serve within the machinery of apartheid to terminate such service and to join the struggle for their own liberation. It is clear that there are some who are refusing to listen ... I do not think that it is expected that we should excuse them simply because they are black. By their actions they have defined themselves as part of the enemy of all humanity."

Comments about black-on-black violence made elsewhere by other ANC leaders indicate that the ANC implicitly adopts a political definition of 'blackness'. In other words, moderate blacks who have been prepared to accept jobs or positions of authority within the existing structures in South Africa, are not 'black' at all. For instance, the ANC's radio station, Radio Freedom (beamed into South Africa from outside the country), commented on 3rd September 1986, that:[80]

"Our people are not attacking councillors because they are black, but because they are

---

80. Another broadcast on Radio Freedom (29 September 1986) can be regarded as incitement to violence against black moderates. It declared: "Those black people who serve this regime as soldiers, policemen and women, community councillors and bantustan leaders, civil servants, can no longer postpone the decision to come over to the side of the people ... You cannot survive if you continue to stand against the people. When your deeds catch up with you, as they surely will if you persist in serving the enemy, you will be buried as a traitor, despised by the people and spurned even by the enemy which finds your services so useful today. If you must die choose to be buried as a hero and not a traitor."

servants of the system which we want to destroy. There are no blacks killing black people, but our people are attacking agents of the system in the ongoing process of destroying the enemy organs of government."

As with earlier WCC conferences, the reports of the Lusaka conference and its final statement indicate that, in almost every way, it was the political liberation movements who set the agenda, which the other delegates, including Church leaders, endorsed.[81]

The Lusaka Statement (see Appendix 7) reaffirmed the Harare Declaration, but went much further. Whilst the Harare Declaration had stated that the South African government had "no credibility" and that it therefore supported those "calling for the resignation of the government", the Lusaka Statement declared the South African regime to be "illegitimate" and thus affirmed the "unquestionable right of the people of Namibia and South Africa to secure justice and peace through the liberation movements." Like the Kairos Document, it declared that this was a crucial time in the history of the country and argued that there was a "need for unity of purpose and action on the part of all those concerned with the process of

---

81. Although a discussion of the Namibian situation is outside the scope of this study, it is interesting to note that the Lusaka Statement endorsed SWAPO's claim to be the "sole and authentic representation of the people of Namibia". In fact, the 1989 Namibian elections (overseen by the UN, and judged by UN special representative, Mr Maarti Ahtisaari, to have been "free and fair") was contested by six other political parties or alliances other than SWAPO, and SWAPO only gained 57% of the vote.

liberation in the region, not least amongst the Churches themselves whose failings in this respect are a cause for repentance." In other words, the Churches should not act as a 'Third Force' for peace and reconciliation in the country but should, rather, be united behind the liberation movements. Most controversial of all, however, was the Statement's declaration that, whilst remaining committed to peaceful change, it recognised "that the nature of the South African regime *compels* (italics added) the movements to the use of force along with other means to end oppression".

The Lusaka Statement was later followed by a detailed Action Plan which essentially proposed using Churches inside and outside South Africa as campaigning organisations for the ANC and PAC. The Plan stated, for instance, that the WCC should encourage its member Churches to "recognise, support and relate to the liberation movements, actively endorsing the Lusaka Statement by working for its implementation"; that the WCC should campaign for "the recognition of the liberation movements of Namibia and South Africa as legitimate representatives of their countries"; that it should establish a "coordinating mechanism for implementation of the Lusaka and Harare declarations by churches"; and it should facilitate the "production of educational and informational resources on the liberation movements to be widely distributed to local congregations."

In July 1987 the AGM of the South African Council of Churches voted by a large majority to adopt the Lusaka Statement. Thereafter it set about getting its member Churches to endorse it too - the CPSA, for example, under the leadership of Archbishop Tutu, doing so at a meeting of its top executive body in November of that year.[82]

This adoption of the Lusaka Statement was of great significance. In the first place the SACC had, in effect, made a policy statement supporting the liberation movements' use of violence for the first time. This meant it had given up the right to stand above the political conflicts, judging the action of *all* groups by Christian moral standards. For how could it call a halt to the liberation movements' use of violence if it had said that they had no choice in the matter but were "compelled" to adopt violence?[83] Indeed, whilst the ICT, for instance, has been ready to blame the security forces and/or Inkatha for the spate of violence which has rocked South Africa since 1989/90,[84] both it and the SACC have done little if anything to condemn the violence perpetrated by the ANC and PAC and associated groups. When such

---

82. See *Seek*, December 1987/January 1988. Archbishop Tutu, however, has stated that "I support the ANC in its objectives to establish a non-racial, democratic South Africa; but I do not support its methods." Apparently in 1987 he attempted to persuade the ANC to suspend the armed struggle. See his letter to P. W. Botha, April 1988, available from the SACC.
83. At the SACC AGM, a motion was put forward by James Massey and the Rev. Peter Storey (chairman of the Methodist Church of Southern Africa, and a former pastor to both Nelson Mandela and the late Robert Sobukwe, founder of the PAC) which argued that nobody can be *compelled* to choose violence since it always involves choice. This was, however, heavily defeated. See reports in *The Star* (SA), 3 July 1987, and *Ecunews* (Journal of the SACC), August 1987.
84. See *Violence: The New Kairos* (ICT, September 1990).

violence has been mentioned, such Church bodies have continued to focus attention on the violence endemic in South Africa's social structures as the reason for countervailing political violence. For example, whilst in his address to the 1991 AGM of the SACC Frank Chikane stated that "Church leaders are seriously concerned about the culture of violence in the country" and, on 29th March the previous year, a number of Church leaders issued a statement expressing their concern that the unrest in the townships displayed an "apparent complete disregard for the value of human life", in both cases the blame for the violence was laid entirely at the feet of the apartheid system.[85]

The second important aspect of the SACC's endorsement of the Lusaka Statement was that it meant it now officially regarded the South African government as illegitimate. As General Secretary, Frank Chikane, pointed out in his speech to the SACC's AGM in 1988, "we are compelled to regard

---

85. One prominent Church leader and former general secretary of the SACC has, however, begun to question this interpretation of the situation. In a sermon delivered in Cape Town in March 1991, Archbishop Tutu stated that "a lot of the violence is due to political rivalry. Political groups in the black community are fighting for turf and they do not seem to know, or certainly some of their followers don't seem to know, that a cardinal tenet of democracy is that people must be free to choose whom they want to support. To coerce, to intimidate, is to admit that your policy can't persuade on its own merits. People must be free to choose whether they want to participate or not in boycotts, in mass action ... We black people must, of course, point to all the causes of violence ... but, ultimately, we must turn the spotlight on ourselves. We can't go on forever blaming apartheid." See *Saturday Star* (SA), 30 March 1991.

it (the government) as illegitimate and ... we are thus not obliged to obey its unjust laws."[86] This opened the way for the SACC to move from merely supporting the civil disobedience campaigns of organisations like AZAPO and the UDF, to the advocacy of civil disobedience by the Church itself. To quote Chikane again, the Church reached "a new praxis which has moved it from passive non-violence ... to active non-violent actions to change the system."[87]

The SACC and 'non-violent direct action'

In the second half of 1987, as part of this 'new praxis', the Justice and Reconciliation department of the SACC distributed to clergy of its member Churches over 3,000 copies of a book by American theologian, Walter Wink. Entitled *Violence and Nonviolence in South Africa,* this discussed the theology of, and strategies for, "militant nonviolent acts of civil disobedience and protest" seen as "Jesus' Third Way" between violence and non-violence.[88] Wink favoured 'nonviolent action' both on theological grounds and also because he considered it would be far more effective than violence in bringing

---

86. *Ecunews,* July 1988.
87. *Ibid*
88. Walter Wink, *Violence and Nonviolence in South Africa: Jesus' Third Way* (New Society Publishers, Philadelphia, 1987). The publication and distribution of the book was assisted by the international Fellowship of Reconciliation which also assisted a four-day workshop held by Wink in May 1988 at the Transformation Resource Centre in Roma, Lesotho. Approximately 40 participants from Botswana, Lesotho, Mozambique and South Africa met to discuss strategies of non-violent direct action to be used in their respective countries.

radical political change to South Africa, but he made it clear that he did not condemn violence. As he said,[89]

> "My gravest anxiety is that this book, rather than actually inciting people to engage in direct acts of nonviolent civil disobedience, will simply be used as an argument against violence. *This book is not an argument against violence* ... Rather than see concerned Christians limp between two opinions, I would urge them to commit themselves fully to militant nonviolence now, at last. Then, if nonviolence seems to have failed, I would urge them to take up arms and actually fight."

This initiative seems to have marked the end of any debate within SACC circles about the morality, or otherwise, of violence. In literature put out by the SACC in 1988, Frank Chikane stated that:[90]

> "the debate about violence and non-violence reaches a point at which it simply must end. There is a point beyond which such a debate is no longer possible ... In South Africa today there is no time or space left for discussion. At this critical point the debate ends and action begins."

But what was this action to be? For the liberation movements, if they judged it necessary, it obviously could be violence since the SACC had agreed that

---

89. *Ibid.*, pp. 104-5.
90. *Crisis News*, April/May 1988.

they were "compelled" to use it. More generally, however, the SACC favoured 'non-violent' civil disobedience campaigns both by the 'peoples' organisations', and by members of the Church. As far as the civil disobedience campaigns of the peoples' organisations were concerned, however, it appeared that no criticism would be made of what this might mean in terms of intimidation of black moderates.[91]

One well-publicised example of Church-organised civil disobedience occurred at the end of February 1988 when, in protest against severe restrictions placed by the government on the activities of seventeen organisations including the UDF and AZAPO, twenty-five Church leaders and other clergy marched from the Anglican Cathedral towards the parliament building in Cape Town. Under the emergency restrictions then in force the march was illegal; it was stopped by the police and the Church leaders concerned were detained for a few hours. Of potentially much greater long-term significance, however, was an Emergency Convocation of Churches held at the end of May that year which established the 'Standing for the Truth' (SFT) campaign to "discuss further the proposed programme of effective non-violent action and develop strategies of carrying out the campaign" and "mobilise and organise the churches and church groups to carry this

---

91. The 1987 AGM of the SACC adopted a resolution which declared that the rent boycotts persisting in different parts of South Africa were a "justified form of resistance" and made clear "its support for all those who are actively seeking the non-violent direct strategies to force change in South Africa towards a just society." It had nothing to say about the intimidation of black moderates involved in these 'strategies of resistance.'

out nationally."[92] A national committee (consisting of three representatives from each of the SACC and the SACBC, three representatives elected from the convocation, and three representatives of the Church leaders) was set up to co-ordinate the campaign and, in the second half of 1988 and throughout 1989, attempts were made to set up SFT groups all over the country. Working in conjunction with the Mass Democratic Movement (formed when the UDF joined forces with various unions), the SFT initiated marches and other forms of protest as part of the Mass Defiance Campaign against the government's emergency restrictions which were in place until 1990.[93] At the same time, SFT groups also set about educating and conscientising their membership through workshops in social analysis.

Although this high-profile confrontation with some Church leaders was a severe embarrassment to the South African government, according to the SFT's own literature, the campaign has so far not been as successful or effective as its organisers had originally hoped. Indeed, the degree to which radical Church leaders have been able to organise ordinary Christians to take part in such acts of civil disobedience should not be exaggerated. Nevertheless, by condoning the liberation movements' use of violence; by supporting

---

92. See *Standing for the Truth* (document obtainable from the ICT). For more information of the details surrounding these events see *Emergency Convocation of Churches in South Africa* (document obtainable from the SACC).
93. See *Negotiations, Defiance and the Church* (ICT on behalf of the Standing for the Truth Campaign, 1989). *Crisis News*, September 1989, gives a list of SFT defiance activities up to that date.

apparently non-violent forms of civil disobedience whose effectiveness in practice has often depended upon gross intimidation of black moderates; by constantly undermining the governments' reform process; by attempting to change the traditional Christian meaning of reconciliation, and arguing that the Churches should support the liberation movements rather than acting as a 'Third Force' in society - in all these ways, radical theologians and Church leaders have sent out signals into South African society which can only have contributed to the upsurge of violence and unrest seen from the mid-1980s onwards.[94]

---

94. It is interesting that, when they issued their statement about violence on 29th March 1990, the Church leaders involved called attention to the fact that "the unrest in the townships shows signs of a critical decline of Christian values." As this chapter has attempted to show, however, these Church leaders have preached a new form of 'Christianity' in South Africa, which has undermined traditional Christian values. For this reason, they themselves must be held at least partially responsible for this situation which they rightly find so deplorable.

4. THE CHURCH AS A 'SITE OF STRUGGLE'

The ANC and the Church

We have seen the way in which sections of the Church have come to support South Africa's liberation movements, the ANC and the PAC. The most significant of these, by far, is the ANC, and so it is also of interest to enquire how the ANC sees the Church.

In international Christian conferences, in order to gain support, spokesmen for the ANC frequently claim that the ANC has always been inspired by Christian ideals and will mention the fact that many of its early presidents - the Rev. John Dube, S. M. Magkatho, Z. R. Mahabane and Albert Lutuli - were all prominent churchmen.[1] Whilst this is true, it is

---

1. There has been a great deal of speculation as to whether Nelson Mandela is a committed Christian or not. He was baptised and brought up in the Methodist Church of South Africa and educated in Christian schools, and has stated that at an early age he developed a strong attachment to the Christian faith - see ANC Department of Religious Affairs magazine, Vol. 1, No. 2, 1987. In July 1989 the American evangelist, Billy Graham, stated in London that he had received a letter from Mandela saying that he had turned to Christianity - see *The Citizen* (SA), 10 July 1989. However, in an interview on South African television on 13 August 1990, when Mandela was asked if he was a religious man, he merely stressed the importance of the Christian Church as well as Hindus and Moslems in the anti-apartheid struggle.

also true that, as the ANC became more radical in the 1950s and 1960s, so its programme and methods appeared increasingly incompatible with orthodox Christianity. Some individual ANC members might be Christians but, as organisations, the ANC and the Church did not appear to have much in common. Indeed, because of the influence of its South African Communist Party (SACP) members, with their anti-religious Marxist-Leninist ideology, the ANC has frequently regarded the Church with hostility and suspicion. In spite of the support the ANC has received from sections of the Church in more recent years, this suspicion has not entirely vanished.

For instance, in 1990 an article in the SACP magazine, *Umsebenzi*, whilst stating that "a specific prohibition on believers joining the party" was not warranted, nevertheless went on to warn against "manifestations of idealism and unscientific analysis" in its ranks.[2] *Inqaba Ya Basebenzi*, the journal of the Marxist Workers' Tendency of the ANC, has also stated that:[3]

> "In the working class movement ... we ought to have no illusions about religion and its role ... Where the working class is downtrodden; remains in darkness and ignorance, religions strive to maintain it. Religion is used as a brake on the struggles of the workers."

In the main, however, the ANC and the SACP came to the view in the early to mid-1980s that, because so many people in South Africa are

---
2. *Umsebenzi*, Vol. 6, No 4, 1990.
3. *Inqaba Ya Basebenzi*, April 1988.

Christians, the liberation struggle could only be completely successful if they could gain Church support. Summarising such attitudes, the *African Communist* carried an article in 1986 which stated:[4]

> "in our country, the majority of those who will participate in the final overthrow of the apartheid colonial regime are church goers. Neglect of this factor .... may reduce the effectiveness of our vanguard role among the masses, and lose us sections of the potential fighting force ... Having realised that the majority of the working masses in our country are Christians, revolutionaries should then look for ways and means of involving the Church in the national liberation struggle in general and the working-class struggle in particular."

It continued:

> "Church ministers command a lot of reverence and respect. What they say and do goes a long way in shaping social attitudes. One important form of their involvement in the struggle is to lead their flock to the line of battle."

This article implicitly recognised, however, that although a section of Church opinion had developed a rationale for supporting the liberation movements, its active support from the grassroots membership of the Churches was still limited. As one of the most prominent ANC activists in Church

---

4. Thoko Mdlalose, *The African Communist*, No. 104, First Quarter, 1986.

affairs, Cedric Mayson,[5] stated in *The African Communist* in 1987, "The Church is not an army but a battlefield. It is one of the places where the struggle is being waged..".[6] In other words, until the whole Church supported the liberation struggle, it needed to

---

5. Cedric Mayson is a former Methodist minister who emigrated from England to South Africa in 1953 where he eventually became a South African citizen. From his autobiography, *A Certain Sound* (Epworth Press, 1984), it is clear that he either never attained an orthodox Christian faith or, if he did, he subsequently lost it. He maintains, for instance, that "the Bible has little to say about heaven or life after death" and argues that the concentration upon such subjects in hymn books and devotional material is "an aberration, an invention of religious practitioners for manipulating the credulous, not the content of the gospel" (pp.15, 16). He describes his own 'conversion' as the sudden realisation that "Jesus meant what he said about the kingdom of God on earth. The context of Christianity is not heaven but earth". He has stated that "the kingdom of God which Jesus proclaimed is not a religious kingdom. It is thoroughly political." According to him, this emerges "politically - in democracy, economically - in socialism, culturally - in community, ecologically - in wholeness, spiritually - in love." (pp. 15, 16, 18.) Mayson was one of the leading figures in the Christian Institute which he joined in 1973, becoming editor of its magazine *Pro Veritate*. As he describes in his autobiography, he changed from being a reformer who "hoped to push society into shape, into a revolutionary who sought to turn society upside down." (p. 79.) This led to a gradual involvement in the ANC, first supplying money, transport, and food, and then providing safe accomodation and medical supplies for people involved in the ANC's armed wing, the MK. He was detained by the South African authorities in 1981 and charged with high treason, but he jumped bail and came to England. However, he has continued to write on religious matters for ANC and SACP magazines, and has served on the ANC religious committee. He has also also spoken and written for sympathetic Christian groups in Britain.

6. *African Communist*, Third Quarter 1987.

be targeted to bring it on side. To quote Mayson again: "Some have the task of taking the struggle for liberation into the Church and establishing guerrilla bases in enemy occupied territory."[7]

Official ANC Policy

In line with this view, the ANC National Consultative Conference held at Kabwe, Zambia, in June 1985, saw the Church as one of the 'fronts' which needed to be mobilised for the struggle. As the report of the conference stated:[8]

> "The Movement (i.e. the ANC) recognises the fact that a large portion of our people are religious or come from particular religious backgrounds ... By raising the political consciousness of this community, influencing them to accept the politics of the Movement, especially the Freedom Charter, and a commitment to the creation of a non-racial, democratic South Africa, all should strive to convert them into centres of resistance and struggle."

To this end, the conference made the following recommendations:

> "1. We recommend that as a matter of urgency the comrade at Headquarters (i.e. dealing with religious matters) be reinforced with at least two comrades while more personnel are sought.

---

7. *Sechaba,* November 1983.
8. "Commission on Cadre Policy, Political and Ideological Work", ANC Internal Report on the Kabwe conference, p. 10.

2. The RPMC's[9] when creating their sub-structures, should also consider this front.

3. Seeing the importance of the Christian participation in the struggle, cadres going home should be given special briefing in this work.

4. We should aim to create ANC units both within the established churches and independent churches and other religious bodies.

5. We should work towards reaching churches in the rural areas, since in the majority of cases they are the main form of community activity. Even in resettlement areas churches become the first form of organisation that the people get involved in. We believe that our intensified work on church and religious organisations will ensure our organisation of the workers and peasants who are predominantly active in these organisations.

6. We recommend that the Movement should encourage trends within the churches and religious organisations that come closer to the struggling people. We should find ways of supporting the call by the churches to pray for the downfall of the fascist regime.

7. The Movement should give attention to the institutions like the Institute of Contextual Theology. We should aim at giving political content and direction to the work.

8. We should seek ways of intensifying church involvement in the End Conscription Campaign.

9. We should intensify our educational work amongst the church people. The distribution of

---

9. That is, the Regional Political Military Committees into which the ANC is organised.

propaganda especially directed to this constituency should be undertaken.

10. Churches could become important platforms to expose the regime's atrocities internally and externally."

In dealing with the other 'fronts' of the struggle, the conference made further recommendations of relevance to the Churches. For instance, on the youth front, the report stated that "we need to educate the youth in religious and cultural organisations to translate their religious beliefs towards the rejection of apartheid as a heresy and greater involvement in the struggle for liberation."[10] On the white community front the report recommended:[11]

> "the promotion of a white youth organisation to join the tide of resistance with youth congresses throughout the country. In this regard we should ensure that church youth together with the democratic left play a leading role in the creation of such an organisation."

Furthermore, under its consideration of the 'armed struggle', the report recommended that "we should organise for MK (i.e. *Umkhonto we Sizwe*, the armed wing of the ANC) even amongst the churches".[12]

This comprehensive list showed what an important aspect of the struggle the ANC now believed the Churches to be. One of the most

---

10. ANC Internal Report on the Kabwe Conference, p. 10.
11. *Ibid.*, p. 11.
12. *Ibid.*, p. 14.

interesting of the recommendations was that singling out the Institute for Contextual Theology, since the recommendation that the ANC should give political content and direction to its work, came at the time the ICT was beginning to work on the Kairos Document. Whether ANC members directly influenced the Kairos Document or not is unclear but, with its demands that the Church be involved in the liberation struggle at all levels, the Kairos Document was certainly useful to the ANC cause. Indeed, soon after it appeared, ANC President, Oliver Tambo, declared on Radio Freedom that:[13]

> "this document, fellow countrymen, could not have come at any better time than now ... Gone are the days when our people understood Christianity to mean neutrality and passivity in politics."

He continued,

> "however, this campaign of civil disobedience must never be mistaken for a substitution for our armed liberation struggle. Brothers, it must be seen as just another front of our broad liberation struggle. We shall still need to confront the enemy, a tooth for a tooth and an eye for an eye in the battlefield."

In other places, too, the ANC has repeatedly welcomed both the *Kairos Document* and

---

13. Radio Freedom, 3 October 1985.

Evangelical Witness in South Africa .[14]

ANC Department of Religious Affairs

To facilitate its objectives on the religious front, the ANC set up a Department of Religious Affairs,[15] based in Lusaka and headed by Father Fumanekile Gqiba, an Anglican (CPSA) priest and long-time political activist. The Department produced a magazine, which came to be called *Phakamani* (meaning "stand up"), as a vehicle for printing speeches by ANC leaders at Church conferences, as well as articles about the role the ANC envisaged for the Church. The first issue set the prevailing tone, with an article by Gqiba which stated:[16]

> "Revolutionary disciples are drawn together, united in, and by the holy spirit. God - the Alpha and the Omega - commands them to challenge the evils of this world and turn it upside down. He commands them to stand up now in his majesty and Glory and crush the wicked where they stand."

---

14. See, for instance, the editorial of the ANC Department of Religious Affairs magazine, Vol. 1, No. 1, 1987; also Cedric Mayson's article "The Comradeship of Marx and Jesus" in *The African Communist,* Third Quarter 1987.
15. An undated circular issued later from the ANC and addressed to "the religious community" stated that "..the ANC has upon the mandate of its 2nd National Consultative conference set up a Department of Religious Affairs, to lead and initiate an active and meaningful participation of the religious community in the struggle for a new democratic South Africa..".
16. ANC Department of Religious Affairs magazine, Vol. 1, No. 1, 1987.

In other words, the liberation struggle was viewed as a 'Holy War' and anything that stood in its way had to be destroyed. The Church, it seemed, had only one role - to strengthen the struggle. Thus, in 1988, *Phakamani* reprinted a leaflet produced by "ANC Christian Underground structures inside South Africa" which declared that:[17]

"The Church as an institution cannot be neutral nor can they present a 'Third Way' - there is no specifically Christian analysis, strategy and tactics. Both of these options hinder and obstruct our people's struggles, and thus postpone the day of liberation." Rather, "Let the churches be restructured so that the oppressed and exploited people can determine the choice of leaders, and the programmes and allocation of resources."

As mentioned earlier, one of the most regular writers on Church affairs for the ANC (and also for the South African Communist Party) has been Cedric Mayson, a former Methodist minister in South Africa, now resident in Britain. In his many articles, Mayson appears to see the relevance of the Church solely in terms of its contribution to the ANC's political agenda. He stated in *Phakamani* in 1989, for instance, that "the Church has no elevated role on a superior plane: its agenda for human society is the same as the Freedom Charter."[18] Elswhere he has declared that:[19]

---

17. *Phakamani,* Vol. 2, No. 1, 1988.
18. *Phakamani,* Vol. 3, No. 1, 1989.
19. *African Communist,* Third Quarter, 1987.

> "progressive Christians believe that Jesus is important for the revolution not by trying to make a god out of him (which he did not do for himself) but by putting his liberating message of the kingdom of God on Earth into action."

He, too, has been insistent that the role of the Church should not be to attempt to bring about reconciliation between different factions in the struggle, declaring, for instance, in *Phakamani* in 1989 that:[20]

> "The Church is a model of division and conflict, not reconciliation ... The church must avoid becoming a Third Force, a force between the oppressor and the oppressed. Christians, if they are not doing so already, must quite simply participate in the struggle for liberation and for the just society."

Such calls have also been made by the ANC's Radio Freedom. For instance, a broadcast on 1st March 1988, in the wake of the previous day's march by Church leaders in Cape Town, indicated that the ANC now saw the Church as perhaps its most useful ally in the liberation struggle. Stating that "what the church has done has been to bring millions of members into active struggle", the ANC made it clear

---

20. *Phakamani*, Vol. 3, No. 1, 1989. How far Mayson might be willing to take such participation in the struggle is indicated by a letter to the UK *Methodist Recorder* in 1986. In this he defended Winnie Mandela's remarks that "with our boxes of matches and our necklaces, we will liberate this country" by stating that " 'The Kingdom of God is amongst you' is not a religious expression. It means that the power of God is liberating his people ... and we have warrant for suspecting that when the time comes many will go in with matches in their pocket, dumping the bottles of petrol they no longer need."

that it intended to dictate how the Churches should now act. The broadcast stated that "the church must now be developed into a fierce battleground against the regime" and went on to demand that:

> "the democratic movement must be given a voice in all the churches - its directives must be relayed from inside the churches. From today, all the church services must be services that further the democratic call. The church must be for liberation. Its services must be for the struggle of the people against the apartheid regime."

The ANC has also recognised the importance and usefulness of the 'Standing for the Truth Campaign' which, as we have seen, was set up in May 1988 to encourage and co-ordinate 'non-violent direct action' by Church groups. In a document produced by its national executive committee in January 1990, the ANC reaffirmed its commitment to the four pillars of its revolutionary strategy - mass mobilisation, building up underground structures, international pressure, and armed struggle (see Appendix 1) - and declared:[21]

> "There is also a continuing responsibility on the part of the religious community of our country to deepen their engagement in the struggle to end apartheid. The 'Standing for the Truth Campaign' has played an important role in enabling parts of this community to contribute its share to the forward movement towards a

---

21. ANC document, 8 January 1990.

democratic South Africa. In the period ahead of us, greater rather than less involvement will be expected of the religious community."

In September 1989, the ANC's Department of Religious Affairs, held a conference in London which called upon all theologians to "identify completely with the national democratic struggle".[22] Following the conference, the Rev. John Lamola took over from Fr. Gqiba as the head of department.[23] Judging by his previous writings, however, Lamola's appointment did not signal any change of direction for the ANC. In 1988 Lamola had warned, for instance, that whilst the 'progressive' Church may be used in the struggle, the "bourgeois, sexist, authoritiarian Church" is still a target of the struggle,[24] and, in January 1989, he declared that:[25]

"it is not only a question of social responsibility for the church in South Africa to engage in the

---

22. *Phakamani*, Vol. 3, No. 2, 1989.
23. Lamola has had considerable experience in radical Church activity. Whilst a student, and as a black consciousness activist, he was a member of the ICT's Black Theology project. In 1984 he started working for the SACC's Department of Justice and Reconciliation as a fieldworker in Bophuthatswana. His work there brought him into conflict with the authorities and, in 1985, he was ordered out of the country. In 1987 he became a projects officer for the Institute for Contextual Theology; that year he was also a member of the SACC delegation at the Lusaka conference. He became secretary of the People's Progressive Party in Bophutatswana, but fled the country in 1988 because of his involvement in the abortive coup d'etat. He subsequently came to London where he became involved with the ANC - see *Vrye Weekblad* (SA), 8-14 November, 1991.
24. *Sechaba*, June 1988.
25. *Sechaba*, January 1989.

struggle for liberation, but that it is its central religious duty, an evangelical obligation to see to the overthrow of the apartheid regime."

To this end, Lamola had strenuously defended the right to use violence, stating that:[26]

"Abundant theoretical justification of the moral rightness of the attempts of the oppressed of South Africa to seek their freedom through armed struggle has already been done, convincingly and conclusively."

It might have been thought that the reforms announced by President De Klerk in February 1990, and particularly his unbanning of the liberation movements, would have produced some change in the ANC's attitude towards the role of the Church in South Africa - but not so. At a WCC Emergency Consultation on South Africa held in Harare later that month, for instance, Lamola stated that "our struggle has now entered a new terrain. That is the battle for the occupation of the moral high ground." He declared a little later that the role of the religious community in South Africa is "an affirmation of the morality of the liberation struggle, particularly as led by the ANC."[27] In April 1990, the radical weekly newspaper *New Nation* reported that the ANC had produced a draft memorandum on the role of its Religious Affairs Department as the movement attempted to re-establish itself inside South Africa.

---

26. *Ibid.*
27. *Sechaba*, April 1990.

This included:[28]

> "transforming as many communities of organised religion as possible into solid centres of resistance and struggle, and to lead these into participation in all aspects of the national liberation struggle as led by the African National Congress."

Bearing this in mind, it is interesting to speculate how the ANC sees Lamola's new role, announced in November 1991, as personal assistant to Frank Chikane, General Secretary of the South African Council of Churches.

'Progressive Christians' and the Church

It is not only the ANC which has seen the Church in South Africa as a 'site of struggle'. Perhaps not surprisingly, it is a view also held by those groups in the Church which have specifically sided with the liberation movements. As we have already seen, it was implicit in the 1985 Kairos Document, with its call for the Church to join the liberation struggle and its criticism of Christian groups who work for reconciliation in the traditional sense. More recently, such 'prophetic' or 'progressive' Christians (as they call themselves) have, like the ANC, openly declared

---

28. *New Nation,* April 5 - April 11, 1990. This same report speculated whether the role of the ICT and also of 'progressive' theological insitutions like the University of Cape Town and Pietermaritzburg would be affected by the establishment of the ANC's Department of Religious Affairs within South Africa, implying that there is considerable overlap of aims between these organisations.

that the Church is a site of struggle.

For instance, the ICT, the South African Council of Churches, and the Southern African Catholic Bishops' Conference jointly organised a conference in Harare in September 1989 which called on the Church to declare the South African regime illegitimate, on the international community to support the liberation movements, and on the people of South Africa to engage in all forms of civil disobedience. The organisations declared their work was "based on the understanding of the Church as a site of struggle" and that their coming together was "for the strategic concern of taking the struggle of workers into the churches."[29]

A document prepared earlier in 1989 for the AGM of the ICT had spelt out what this might mean in some detail. It stated that "the Church is like the factory, school, or community, in that it is also a site of struggle". Like the media and educational establishments, the Church "operates on the ideological level ... where the production of meaning takes place", but is especially important in that it "offers people a set of religious symbols that give meaning to the whole of one's life." The ICT concluded, therefore, that the struggle in the Church is essentially a competition for control of its "structures of power, practices, symbols, resources and services."[30] Dr. C. Wanamaker, an academic from the Department of Religious Studies at the University of Cape Town - perhaps the most

---

29. See *ICT News,* December 1989.
30. Document on the 'Standing for the Truth Campaign', ICT AGM 1989

progressive' theological department in South Africa - has also declared that the "stakes are high as two competing and antithetical interpretations of Christianity struggle against one another for control of that most important of all Christian symbols, the Bible."[31] **Hence, as the 1989 ICT document has itself accurately summed up, this struggle in the Church is essentially a battle "about the meaning of Christian faith."**

'Right wing Christian groups'

In this struggle, 'prophetic' Christians have shown that they are prepared to fight against all those in the Church who do not share their views. According to the ICT, in the first place this includes 'conservative' Christians - that is, both those prepared to actively oppose the liberation movements because of their economic and political programmes, and also those who argue that the Church should support the State because of the Biblical injunction "let every person be subject to the governing authorities" found in Romans 13. Secondly, it also includes Christians of the 'centre' who argue that the Church must develop its own specifically Christian solution to the political and social problems of South Africa, either by influencing society by means of personal conversions and spiritual renewal, or by acting as a reconciling 'third force' between the present government and those engaged in the liberation struggle.[32]

---

31. Charles Wanamaker, "Right Wing Christianity and the Bible in South Africa" in *Journal of Theology for Southern Africa*, December 1989.
32. ICT AGM 1989.

Frequently 'prophetic' Christians refer to these groups as "Right Wing Christian Groups" (RWCGs), although it should be clear from the above list that Christians do not need to hold views traditionally regarded as right-wing in the political sense in order to earn this label. Those who simply hold non-radical theological views may also be referred to as 'right-wing Christians'. As Smangaliso Mkhatshwa of the ICT has said, "Right-wing Christianity takes two forms. The first is the more subtle form that pretends to be apolitical and purely spiritual."[33] Thus literature produced by 'progressive' Christians (like the ICT, the SACC and SACC-affiliated Western Province Council of Churches, sections of the CPSA and the Catholic Church, theologians from the University of Cape Town, and others)[34] have variously described as 'right-wing' not only those small groups of Christians in South Africa who have strenuously opposed the spread of contextual theology,[35] but also large and generally apolitical charismatic and/or evangelistic groups like Ray McCauley's Rhema Bible Church, Youth With A Mission, Campus Crusade for Christ, and Christ for All Nations. Traditionalist Anglican groups within the CPSA, the evangelical Church of England in South Africa as a complete

---

33. Keynote address to the ICT AGM, 1989.
34. See also Paul Gifford, *The Religious Right in Southern Africa* (University of Zimbabwe and Baobab Books, 1988). This book is largely an attack on evangelical Christianity, including some of the best-known evangelical preachers like Billy Graham, Luis Palau, Benson Idahosa, etc.
35. These include, for instance, United Christian Action, *Signposts* magazine, and the Gospel Defence League.

denomination,[36] and groups of non-radical black independent Churches - like the Reformed Independent Churches Association (RICA) and the Western Cape Council of Churches - are also frequently labelled 'right-wing'. Such labelling, because of the associated, if often completely inaccurate,[37] negative political overtones of authoritarianism and fascism itself amounts to an aspect of the struggle within the Church, as the 'prophetic' Christians attempt to denigrate and discredit those who disagree with them.

Like so much other radical Christian activity in South Africa, this process has been spearheaded by

---

36. Very few people in Britain are aware of the fact that there are *two* Anglican denominations in South Africa - the CPSA, of which Archbishop Tutu is the head and which is affiliated to the South African Council of Churches, and the Church of England in South Africa (CESA). CESA does not belong to the SACC and is theologically far more evangelical than the CPSA, taking a position somewhat similar to the Church Society or the Proclamation Trust in Britain. Whilst CESA is the smaller Church, and is not invited to participate at Lambeth Conferences of the international Anglican Communion, it is growing rapidly, particularly in the Cape. This is partly because of the emphasis placed on active evangelism, and also because it has gained members from the CPSA.

37. The term 'right-wing' is often used loosely. On the one hand it may be used to describe those who advocate a relatively minimalist State and a generally free economy, whilst on the other it may be used to describe an almost diametrically opposed position - that is, those who support authoritarian regimes with a large and highly interventionist State sector, as is the case in Nazism or Fascism. However, because to varying degrees, Nazism, Fascism and ('left-wing') Marxism all increase the power of the State at the expense of the freedom of the individual, they have far more in common with each other than they do with 'right-wing' market liberalism or conservativism. This can lead to immense confusion in political debate.

the Institute for Contextual Theology which, in 1985, decided to study those groups which had criticised liberation theology and the Kairos Document.[38] This interest was stepped up in 1988 when the AGM of the ICT took as its theme a study of so-called 'right-wing religion' in South Africa, and, after numerous meetings that year, decided to collaborate with the Religious Studies Department of the University of Cape Town (UCT) in order to investigate the subject more thoroughly. UCT's involvement in turn led to a conference on 'right-wing religion' in Harare, Zimbabwe in August 1989, the papers from which were published as a complete issue of the *Journal of Theology for Southern Africa* in December of that year. Whilst it is not possible to study or critique any of these papers in the detail they deserve here, suffice it to say that their authors, without exception, adopt a position of great theological liberalism and appear as keen, if not keener, to attack the fundamental tenets of traditional Christianity as any political views which 'right-wing Christians' may hold. For instance, belief in the deity of Christ, His substitutionary atonement, His bodily resurrection, His virgin birth and second advent; giving the Bible a central role in every area of life; emphasising individual salvation; and acknowledging a cosmic battle between good and evil - all these aspects of 'right-wing' Christianity are, in various ways, discredited or at least slightly mocked.[39] The authors are also keen to attack any hint of order or hierarchy which might be derived from the Bible (presumably because this might impede the forces of revolution), suggesting that

---

38. ICT AGM 1985.
39. See, for instance, the paper by Wanamaker, *op. cit.*

Biblical passages which might point in this direction were merely culturally derived and should now be adapted to meet the specific demands of new situations. Thus editor Prof. Charles Villa-Vicencio declares that, in the Bible:[40]

> "The names and images imposed on the God of liberation were predominantly male, authoritarian and hierarchical. A careful investigation of the God-language of the Bible show that Yahweh contains not only many of the characteristics of other Middle Eastern deities but also of the dominant social structures of the time. God is called King, Lord, Master and Judge."

He concludes that "to cling rigidly to such names of God can be a form of idolatry - an attempt to create God in the image of the dominant society that does the naming."

'The Road to Damascus'

Although the papers in the *Journal of Theology for Southern Africa* amount to a sustained and comprehensive attack on many traditional

---

40. Charles Villa-Vicencio, "Right Wing Religion" in *Journal of Theology for Southern Africa*, December 1989. Prof. Villa-Vicencio's own political preferences may be indicated by his article "The Worker's Flag" in *New Nation*, 26 January 1990. In this he argues that the Church could stand accused of creating divisions amongst the oppressed if it distances itself from the South African Communist Party (SACP) and warns the Churches to safeguard against inheriting "the myths created around Communism in the western world".

Christian beliefs, the most significant attack on 'right wing' Christianity so far has come in *The Road to Damascus: Kairos and Conversion,* a 28-page pamphlet published in South Africa by the ICT in July 1989, and published in Britain jointly by the Catholic Institute for International Relations and Christian Aid. This contains much of the same form of analysis as the Kairos Document, but its main target of attack is not the State, but that part of the Church which has not yet joined the liberation struggle. It was signed by 539 of South Africa's leading radical theologians and Church activists,[41] together with others from six Third World countries - El Salvador, Guatemala, Korea, Namibia, Nicaragua, and the Philippines - where, because of the support of progressive Christians for popular or revolutionary movements, the Church was also seen as a site of struggle.

The *Road to Damascus* grew out of a meeting between the then ICT General Secretary, Frank Chikane, and members of the Ecumenical Association of Third World Theologians at their 1986 conference in Mexico. This led to talks between radical South African and Filipino Christians in January the following year and, with the subsequent support of the leadership of EATWOT, resulted in a two-year consultation process between "Third World Theologians in the Struggle for Liberation". The booklet describes the struggle in each of the seven

---

41. These included Desmond Tutu; Beyers Naudé; Allan Boesak; Frank Chikane; Smangaliso Mkhatshwa; Wolfram Kistner, formerly director of the SACC's Commission on Justice and Reconciliation; Caesar Molebatsi; and radical theologians John de Gruchy, Charles Villa-Vicencio, and Itumeleng Mosala.

countries as being between, on the one hand, the contextual theologies - "liberation theology, black theology, feminist theology, minjung theology, theology of struggle, the Church of the poor, the progressive church (and) basic Christian communities" and, on the other, "the religious right, right-wing Christianity, state theology, the theology of reconciliation, the neo-Christendom movements and anti-communist evangelicals."[42]

It is important to note that, according to this list, few Christian are excluded from the struggle and that even those working for reconciliation are regarded as part of the enemy camp. Indeed, the document later criticises those Christians who claim to be neutral as regards the political conflicts in these countries, stating that "neutrality plays into the hands of those in power because it enables them to continue and to discredit the Christians who oppose them."[43] It makes clear that its purpose is "not simply to deplore the divisions among Christians or to exhort both sides to seek unity".[44] Rather, it affirms that the only true Christians are those who have adopted a theology which "sides with the poor and oppressed" and that those who have not, are guilty, like Saul of Tarsus, of persecuting the Church. Having accused 'right-wing' Christians of apostasy, idolatry, heresy, hypocrisy, blasphemy, selfishness and even Satanism, they are called to a conversion like Saul experienced on the road to Damascus - in this case, however, a

---

42. *The Road to Damascus: Kairos and Conversion* (Catholic Institute for International Relations/Center of Concern/Christian Aid, July 1989), p. 1.
43. *Ibid.*, p. 8.
44. *Ibid.*, p. 1.

conversion to contextual theology which, in practical terms, would involve a decision to be part of the 'people's struggle'.

Like the Kairos Document, attempts were made to distribute *The Road to Damascus* widely. In Britain, for instance, it was sent to ministers on the Church of Scotland's regular mailing list and, in South Africa, it was translated into Afrikaans, Zulu and Sotho for widespread distribution amongst different population groups. Two comprehensive study guides were also compiled, one aiming at a general audience and the other aimed at students in post-ordination training amongst whom, according to the ICT, the document served "as a basis for skills development in analysis, contextual theology reflection and relevant sermon and liturgy construction."[45]

The Road to Damscus is so polemical, and so obviously lacking in the spirit of true Christian love, that it is highly unlikely that any 'right-wing' Christian reading it would feel the need to heed its call for conversion. Like the papers in the *Journal of Theology for Southern Africa,* however, it succeeds in displaying the preparedness of the 'prophetic' theologians to cruelly attack orthodox Christians both as a way of defending their own unorthodox views and, at the same time, taking forward the struggle in the Church.

---

45. ICT Annual Report, 1990.

Intimidation of Christians

It is all too easy for this struggle in the Church to sound merely like a rather bad-tempered academic debate. The implications of this debate on the ground, however, are grim. During a visit to South Africa in Autumn 1989 I visited a coloured pastor, a well-educated and deeply sincere Christian man, in his house in a township near Pretoria. He described to me how Kairos liturgies had been widely distributed in his area and the forms of pressure being brought to bear by young political radicals on orthodox Christian pastors and ministers to bring their teaching into line with the 'progressive' theology found in those liturgies. "At the moment", he said, "they use intimidation. But this may soon become persecution."

One organisation, 'Christians for Truth' (CFT) - closely associated with the KwaSizabantu mission station in Natal - has been working to expose various forms of intimidation of Christians. Through advertisements placed in national newspapers in September 1990, it appealed for information from Christians who had "suffered threats, intimidation or violence at the hands of the comrades". Since then CFT has published a regular newsletter which includes some of the information it has received. The following are two of the examples it has printed:[46]

---

46. Both of these examples are taken from the Christians for Truth newsletter, January/February 1991, available from Private Bag 250, Kranskop 3350. By November 1991 CFT had 16,000 members, most of whom are black Christians, many living in township areas.

- "Brethren from Soweto tell us that Christian children are forced to lead the comrades into battle. If a 'People's Court' is to be held in order to punish or kill an offender, it must be opened in prayer with a Bible reading by one of the Christians (who receives the nickname 'Mfundisi'/Preacher.)

Sometimes a whole school is called upon, during school hours, to launch an attack. The Christian children are forced to be in front and are carefully watched to see if they participate enthusiastically. If they show any hesitation they are immediately tagged as 'informers' or 'sell-outs'."

- "As a Christian, I believe in the fifth Commandment: 'Thou shalt not kill'.

The comrades knocked on my door at midnight forcing us to go to hostels and arm ourselves to kill hostel inmates. I then disagreed to that and I was stabbed in the shoulder and promised a necklace."

Is the Struggle Abating?

The acceleration in the reform process during 1990 and 1991, and the unbanning of the liberation movements, has made little difference to the attitude of the most committed of the 'prophetic Christians'. Although a handful of the Church leaders who took part in acts of defiance against the government are beginning to argue that the time has come for the "Church to be the Church" again, they have been condemned by their more radical colleagues.[47] For instance, in March 1991 the ICT announced it was now developing what it refers to as 'Post-Exilic Theology' specifically to address "the trends of 'neutrality' and 'reconciliation' that is creeping into the Church".[48] That same month, in a booklet with a foreward by SACC General Secretary, Frank Chikane, the 'Standing for the Truth Campaign' criticised those who argue that the liberation struggle can now be left to the ANC and PAC, and that the Churches should "retreat to the sanctuary" giving their main attention to purely spiritual matters. According to the SFT this is "liberal ideology" which sees "liberation (as) an optional extra, rather than the essence of being a christian." The booklet reaffirmed that the Church itself is a site of struggle and that Christians have to organise themselves into a progressive force in order to "pull other Christians in the church with them into the democratic movement" (i.e. the ANC). It particularly stressed that the "church is often the only place which offers resistance in rural areas" and that it is "crucial to link up the church prophetic movement in rural and urban areas." It advocated various means of revitalising the SFT, with a structure consisting of a national committee, regional committees, and area groups, trained by the ICT in the methods of contextual theology. Much of

---

47. This seems to be the position, for instance, of Dr. Stanley Mogoba, presiding bishop of the Methodist Church of Southern Africa. Dr. Mogoba has been a consistent and outspoken critic of apartheid, but he is now working to build bridges between the different ethnic and political groups in the country and so create a climate of genuine reconciliation - interview with author, June 1991.
48. *ICT News,* March 1991.

this was endorsed by an SFT consultation held in May 1991.

A few months before this, in November 1990, a National Conference of Churches, the largest gathering of Church leaders since the Cottesloe Conference had taken place in 1960, was held in Rustenburg. The conference was prompted by President De Klerk's 1989 Christmas message, when he called on the Churches to come together and formulate a joint position so they could speak to the Government with one voice. Jointly organised by Dennis House (Billy Graham's representative in South Africa) and Rev. Barney Pityana, head of the WCC's Programme to Combat Racism, the conference may be viewed as an attempt to bring together the two sides of the 'Church in struggle'. From what has been said so far, however, it should be clear that very little genuine reconciliation is possible between those subscribing to contextual theology and orthodox Christians without some dilution in their respective positions. For those who view the Church as a 'site of struggle' such a conference may be merely only another terrain of the struggle, where an attempt is made to persuade orthodox Christians to adopt some of the terminology and objectives of the contextual theologians. Indeed, partly because of their concern that this is exactly what did happen at the Rustenburg conference,[49] more than 700 representatives of 39 evangelical, pentecostal and reformed Churches met at the KwaSizabantu mission

---

49. See the *Rustenburg Declaration* (National Initiative for Reconciliation, PO Box 3053, Pretoria, 0001).

station in January 1991 to issue their own, thoroughly Bible-based, alternative declaration.[50]

Certainly the ICT has made its own view of the Rustenburg process clear. At its 1991 AGM, under the heading 'Standing for the Truth/Rustenburg', it passed a series of resolutions, urging all ICT members:[51]

- "to engage in the Rustenburg process";
- "to draw all those involved into existing structures of the prophetic movement in action";
- "to engage with the leaders of the mainline Churches in order for them to participate more regularly in the thrust of the prophetic movement";
- "to build SFT as a strong coordinating structure of the prophetic movement"
- "to be able to engage with these structures from a position of strength"

In other words, the ICT sees the Rustenburg process as a means by which other Christians may be drawn into the 'prophetic' Church. This initiative, together with the attempts mentioned earlier to develop a Base Community movement in South Africa, and the fact that the ICT has been showing an interest in learning from the Nicaraguan experience,[52] suggests that South Africa's radical Christians are

---

50. This is obtainable from Private Bag 250, Kranskop 3550.
51. *1991 Annual General Meeting Conference* (ICT, August 1991), p. 31.
52. In May 1990, the Christianity and Socialism project of the ICT sent a group of six people to Cuba and Nicaragua to study their experience of socialism - see *ICT News,* March 1991

working to create an 'alternative Church' network which is much more widely-based than it has been hitherto. In Nicaragua, the BCCs and the spread of liberation theology were not only crucial factors in the success of the 1979 Sandinista (FSLN) revolution, but were important in keeping the Sandinistas in power. As former Nicaraguan newspaper editor, Humberto Belli, has written:[53]

> "The revolutionary Christians in Nicaragua fit the ideology and purpose of the FSLN. They echoed in theological terms the Sandinista contention that true Christians in Nicaragua would unfailingly support the revolutionary process. They provided a theological way to revolutionize the main contents of the Christian faith. They worked hard to dispel the deep-seated fear of communism that so many Nicaraguans felt and to present Marxism as mainly a neutral social science. But their most important service to the Frente was to provide the government with a rationale for bringing the Nicaraguan Christian churches into submission to the state. The government could profile itself as favorable toward religion by maintaining cordial relations with the revolutionary Christians; it would seem to oppose not religion itself, but only religion which was an expression or tool of bourgeois and imperialistic interests. The revolutionary Christians themselves spearheaded the attack on the Christians who.

---

53. Humberto Belli, *Breaking Faith: The Sandinista Revolution and the Impact on Freedom and Christian Faith in Nicaragua* (The Puebla Institute, Michigan, 1985), p. 169.

did not unreservedly support the Sandinista revolution. The flip side of the revolutionary Christians' call to all Christians to throw their support entirely behind the FSLN was criticism of those unwilling to do so. Having defined the FSLN as the only vanguard of the oppressed ... failure to support it fully appeared as the most serious failure to put the gospel into practice."

In 1990, elections were held in Nicaragua, and the Sandinistas lost power. Against this background, remarks made by ICT General Secretary, Smangaliso Mkhatshwa, in his address to the 1990 AGM of the ICT, are particularly interesting. He stated:[54]

"When we visited Nicaragua recently, we discussed, inter alia, the relationship of the Church to the Sandinista led government. Progressive Christians admitted having made one major mistake since 1979. *And the mistake was that because they had such a friendly and progressive government they had stopped conscientising the people.* They felt that one of the reasons why the FSLN lost the elections in February was partly due to this neglect. In South Africa we are on the threshold of a new era. I am confident that it will be led by a people's government whose relations with the Church promises to be very friendly. But let us never forget that there are counterrevolutionary forces which will be waiting in the wings to reverse whatever gains the national struggle has made ... Hence the need for an ongoing

---

54. *1990 Annual General Meeting Conference* (ICT, 1990).

programme of conscientisation and theological reflection."

To put this in simple terms, the ICT has realised the necessity of sustaining theological support for liberation movements *after* they might take power in South Africa, by continuing to spread contextual theology and attempting to develop Basic Christian Communities. Because of this, some of South Africa's orthodox Christians fear that, in the same way that evangelical groups and the traditionalist Catholic Church suffered discrimination and persecution from the 'alternative Church'/Sandinista alliance once the Sandinistas took power in Nicaragua, so the same thing might happen in South Africa if the ANC takes total control. In other words, the political 'liberation' of South Africa might only herald a fiercer stage of the struggle in the Church. Certainly, there is as yet no sign that the 'prophetic Christians' or the ANC have ceased to see the Church 'as a site of struggle'.

5. WHO PAYS FOR THE STRUGGLE?

The Role of the South African Council of Churches

In this account we have seen the key role played by the South African Council of Churches in supporting the development of a South African liberation theology and the political liberation struggle of the ANC, PAC and allied groups. The SACC is an umbrella organisation for many of South Africa's mainline Church denominations and since, according to its constitution, its main aims are to "foster unity amongst the Churches, co-ordinate the work of Churches in South Africa, and undertake joint action on their behalf",[1] it has understandably been seen by the international community as the 'voice' of the Church in South Africa. For this reason, the attitudes of European Church leaders towards South Africa, and the sort of policies they have advocated that their governments should pursue, have invariably been largely determined by the SACC. Those South African Christians - of whatever colour - advocating less radical, more reformist, solutions to the country's problems, have had grave difficulties in getting their voices heard.

The degree to which the SACC is genuinely representative of the broad spectrum of Christian

---

1. SACC publicity leaflet, *What is the SACC?* (undated).

opinion in South Africa is, however, open to considerable doubt. This is for two reasons. In the first place, neither of the two largest denominations or Church groupings in the country are members. These are the (white) Dutch Reformed Church, and the vast majority of the African Independent Churches. Other significant denominations which do not belong to the SACC include the evangelical Church of England in South Africa (CESA), the Pentecostals, the Salvation Army, and the Baptist Union.

Secondly, and more significantly, it is doubtful how far the policies of the SACC are representative of the grassroots opinion of those Church denominations which do belong. The constitution of the SACC provides that its policies should be determined by an annual National Conference and an Executive Committee, both of which include representatives of member Churches. However, the Eloff Commission, which was set up in 1981 to inquire into the history and activities of the SACC, concluded in its detailed study published in 1983 that, with few exceptions, SACC policies were initiated by heads of department, not member Churches.[2] David

---

2. *Report of the Commission of Inquiry into South African Council of Churches* - hereafter referred to as the Eloff Report - (Government Printer, Pretoria,1983), pp. 135-140. This Commission was appointed by the State President, and comprised Justice Eloff (Judge of the Transvaal Division of the Supreme Court); Mr Blunden (Regional Court President); Professor Oosthuizen (Vice-Principal of the University of Pretoria); Mr F. Barrie (former Auditor-General); and Mr S. Patterson (chartered accountant). Because of South Africa's authoritarian political past, obvious caution is needed in referring to official documents of this nature. The sections of the Eloff Report referred to here are, however, thoroughly documented.

Thomas, in his history of the SACC (published by the SACC itself), also came to a similar conclusion. As he stated: "there can be no doubt that there is a gap between the administration and the constituency on occasion, and that even decisions taken by the National Conference of the SACC have been unacceptable to member churches".[3]

Source of SACC Funds

One telling indication of the member Churches' lack of support for, and also lack of influence over, the SACC is the extremely small proportion of the Council's budget which comes from its members' annual affiliation fees. The Eloff Commission found that, over the seven-year period 1975 to 1981, only a tiny 0.3% of the SACC's average yearly income of R2,565,435 came from its members; in three of the years, half of the SACC's members failed to pay any affiliation fees at all.[4] Within the SACC, and amongst donor organisations at that time, this was regarded as a very unsatisfactory state of affairs. Martin Conway of the British Council of Churches, for instance, concluded from his attendance of the SACC's 1981 National Conference that:[5]

> "Most worrying of all ... was the final page of the audited accounts showing that of the budget of more than R200,000 only R6,755 came from

---

3. David Thomas, *Councils in the Ecumenical Movement: South Africa, 1904-1975* (SACC, 1979), p. 62.
4. *Eloff Report*, p. 297.
5. Quoted in *ibid.*, p. 138.

the member churches' annual affiliation fees and comparatively few other sums from South African sources. This is not to say anything about the quality of the work that is done with the money, but it indicates a most unsatisfactory state of attitudes and relationships between the Council and its member churches."

Little seems to have changed in this respect more recently - indeed if anything the situation has got worse. As Appendix 8 indicates, in each of the years 1987 to 1990, members' affiliation fees were only 0.2% of total SACC income; in 1990, for example, twenty-one of the SACC's thirty-seven members had outstanding affiliation fees.

From where, then, did the SACC get its money? The answer is that virtually all of it came from overseas donations. Reference again to Appendix 8 shows that an average of 96.6% of the SACC's income during 1987 to 1990 came from grants and donations and, including 'interest earned' (much of which would obviously come from investments which had derived originally from grants and donations), this rose to around 99.6%. As Appendix 9 shows, however, over this period an average of only 0.6% of grant and donation income committed to projects came from South Africa itself. Allowing for the fact that some of the uncommitted funds may have come from South Africa (the source of uncommitted funds is not made clear in the SACC's annual accounts), it is still safe to conclude that, **from 1987 to 1990, an average of at least 98% of the SACC's income was derived from overseas.**

When the Eloff Commission reported it found a similar situation. It concluded that over the period 1975 to 1981 more than 97% of the SACC's funding had come from abroad - a significant increase on the 62.5% which had come from overseas in 1970, which itself had been a matter of some concern. This means that, since at least the early 1970s, the SACC has been able to pursue its activities virtually independently of its member Churches. This has been admitted by the Rev. Joe Wing, an honorary life President of the SACC, who stated to the National Conference in 1982:[6]

> "One of the main reasons why the SACC has had an independent existence in recent years is because 90% of its income has come from overseas, and Council officials, not member Churches, have raised the money. Any organisation which raises its own funds, with only a token contribution from its members, may claim a measure of freedom in expending those funds."

In other words, the SACC has not so much been the 'voice' of the South African Church, as that of SACC staff and its overseas donors.

As the SACC has involved itself in increasingly radical forms of socio-political action, so its overseas support has grown. Indeed, in his evidence before the Eloff Commission, Bishop Tutu, then General Secretary of the SACC, indicated that the more radical SACC projects appeared, the more

---

6. *Ibid.,* p. 138.

likely they were to attract overseas funding.[7] SACC grant and donation income, which had only been R646,457 in 1975, went up to R2,622,560 in 1980,[8] and then increased ten-fold over the next decade to R24,057,220 in 1990.[9] (At the 1990 rate of exchange, this was equal to about £6mn. - but in real purchasing power terms was probably more like £12mn.).

Virtually all this money came from European and North American church organisations. As Appendix 9 shows, during 1986 to 1990 the largest donor nations were Denmark (16.6% of total donations), Germany (14.0%), Norway (12.4%), the Netherlands (11.6%), Sweden (11.3%), and the UK (8.8%). In the UK, the largest donor by far has been Christian Aid, which gave R7,158,099 over the five-year period; other British donors have included Oxfam and the British Council of Churches. Similarly, in other large donor countries, most of the money has been given by Church-related aid agencies - Danchurchaid in Denmark; *Brot Fur Die Welt* (Bread for the World) in Germany; ICCO (Inter-Church Co-ordinating Commission for Development Projects) in the Netherlands; and the Church of Sweden Mission in Sweden. (Details of all donations above R5,000 are provided in Appendix 9).

---

7. *Ibid.*, p. 296.
8. *Ibid.*, p. 297.
9. See Appendix 8. In real terms donation income peaked in 1989 and has been falling since. Indeed, in both 1990 and 1991, the SACC was forced to slash its budget because income fell substantially below planned expenditure - its 1990 budget had originally been set at R34mn.; the 1991 budget, originally set at R26.9mn., had to be reduced to R20.5mn.

SACC Expenditure

As the budget of the SACC has increased, so has its ability to take practical action in line with its overall philosophy. Given the degree to which SACC statements no longer emphasise traditional Christian mission and evangelism, it is therefore perhaps not surprising that its Church and Mission Department - covering 'Mission and Evangelism', 'Youth Development', and 'Women's Ministries'[10] - should account for only 1.5% of its expenditure from 1987 to 1990. Even this, however, is deceptive.

One of the activities of the Mission and Evangelism division, for example, has been the translation of *The Kairos Document; The Road to Damascus;* and *Negotiations, Defiance and the Church* (a Standing for the Truth Campaign document advocating involvement in the MDM's mass defiance campaign) into Zulu and Sotho.[11] The emphasis of the SACC's Youth Development division and the Women's Ministries division has been similar. The Women's Ministries division, for instance, has worked with the ICT to develop a feminist liberation theology in South Africa. It has conducted a range of 'awareness-raising' programmes to encourage women to develop such an approach, organising workshops and seminars on the "feminist perspective of the Kairos Document" and on contextual theology in

---

10. The SACC underwent a reorganisation in 1991. This discussion of its departmental activities is in terms of its pre-1991 structure, as followed in its financial accounts over the years 1987-90.
11. *Annual Report of the Mission and Evangelism Department*, 1990 AGM of the SACC.

general.[12] An important aspect of the department's work, carried out in co-operation with the corresponding departments of the ICT and the Southern African Catholic Bishops' Conference, has been its participation in the WCC's Ecumenical Decade for Women. This was launched in 1988 with objectives which included "to develop in women a dynamic understanding of the link between Christianity and the struggle for liberation and the transformation of society."[13] A national conference of the Decade for Women held a year later put forward the recommendation that "the Church must transform the symbols and language of Church" and that "theological training must include liberation theology and feminist theology."[14]

Similarly, in 1987 and 1989 the Youth Development division organised a National Youth Theology workshop, the purpose of which was to explore the creation of a "liberating theological position of youth ministry in South Africa and further improve youth participation within Church structures and the political liberation process." Topics discussed included 'prophetic theology' and 'Church as a site of struggle."[15] A number of the SACC's regional councils have pursued this youth strategy at grassroots level. The Witwatersrand Regional Youth

---

12. See *Womenews* (Newsletter of the SACC Women's Ministries), March 1989.
13. *Ecumenical Decade for Churches in Solidarity with Women: A report of the pre-launch workshops,* May 1989, p. 15.
14. *Ecumenical Decade for Women National Conference 1989: Highlights and Recommendations,* para. 6.3.
15. *Annual Report of the Youth Department,* 1990 AGM of the SACC, p. 4.

Council, for example, has stated that its chief objective is to "educate the youth in the Church about contextual theology". And, understanding the importance of drama in reaching young people, the Western Province Regional Council of Churches has had a Christian Mobile Drama Group project with the aim of assisting "young Christians to develop a critical awareness about their lives and environment ... achieved by providing drama training which would include liberation theology presented contextually."[16]

These, then, have been some of the activities pursued by the SACC's Church and Mission department. As can be seen, one of the major concerns - even of the Mission and Evangelism division - has been the promotion of contextual theology which draws different sections of the population into the liberation struggle.

If the Church and Mission department has accounted for a mere 1.5% of total expenditure, on what else does the SACC spend its money? As Appendix 8 shows, the bulk of it goes on what it has termed 'Justice and Society' activities. Indeed, leaving aside spending on its twenty-two regional councils which carry out the range of SACC activities at a local level, the Justice and Society department accounted for an average of 83% of total SACC expenditure over the period 1987-90. Virtually all the rest went on General Secretariat activities like

---

16. *Come With Me,* SACC Youth Division, 1989. The Western Province Council of Churches has been acknowledged by the radical Cape-based newspaper, *South,* 7 to 13 March 1991, to have been "closely aligned with the ANC".

administration, communications and staff training.

It is these Justice and Society activities which form the practical outworkings of the SACC's commitment to 'political liberation' in South Africa. Some of the activities of this department are undoubtedly legitimate aspects of Christian social concern, particularly when they have attempted to rectify the serious discrimination and social disadvantage suffered by South Africa's black population. For instance, the African Bursary Fund, which was originally set up in 1969 to provide educational bursaries to enable children from rural areas to obtain crucial schooling (at a time when black children generally had to pay for their education) has continued to provide bursaries, mainly for high school and higher education, spending an average of approximately R3mn. per year during 1987-90. Few Christians would quibble with this work - although the fact that the Fund also runs an Outreach Programme to maintain contact with the bursars, bringing them together in seminars, and informing them about the SACC and its work, may also have meant that the Fund has been used to introduce at least some of them to the SACC's more radical political ideas. Similarly, the SACC's Ministry to Refugees, which averaged approximately R1.6 million per year from 1987-90, has undoubtedly performed essential relief work amongst refugees to South Africa from countries such as Mozambique, Angola and Lesotho. Papers produced by the division make it clear, however, that the SACC has also regarded as 'refugees' political activists who fled the country to escape arrest, or in order to join the ANC or PAC. This includes those who joined the guerilla wing of these movements.[17] It is not clear if this division was able to provide assistance to the exiles once they were out of the country, but it has certainly provided material assistance to their families remaining within South Africa.

The other programmes of the Justice and Society Department have had an even more obvious political impact. The Standing for the Truth Campaign, for instance, whose activities we have already looked at, had an income and expenditure at the height of its activities in 1989 of R286,000. Then there is the Justice and Reconciliation division, which had an average expenditure of approximately R250,000 per year over 1987-90. This was set up in 1972 in direct response to the establishment of the WCC's Programme to Combat Racism and, under the leadership of its (now retired) director, Dr. Wolfram Kistner, provided the main intellectual guidance for the work of the SACC, particularly considering the methods to be used to achieve social and political change.[18] As we have seen, it was this division which was responsible for distributing Walter Wink's book on 'non-violent direct action', and it was also mainly responsible for the promotion of the Kairos Document, both internationally and within South Africa itself. It has a network of fieldworkers, based with the regional councils, who are able to spread the ideas of the division both at a grassroots level and

---

17. See *Refugees and Exiles Challenge the Churches* (SACC Division of Refugees Ministries, 1987).
18. *Eloff Report*, pp. 52-54.

also overseas.[19]

With an average yearly expenditure during 1987-90 of over R5mn., the largest of the SACC's programmes is, however, its Dependants' Conference. This was initially established in 1963 by the International Defence and Aid Fund, and taken over by the SACC in 1965. Its policy has been to "minister to the needs of political prisoners, detainees, banned person and their dependants." The work of this division has been very extensive and has included the provision of legal aid for those accused of a range of offences, including terrorism; grants to the families of exiles; allowances to political prisoners and their families; additional allowances for those facing capital punishment, etc. In evidence given in a legal hearing in 1983, former SACC General Secretary, John Rees, testified that most of the beneficiaries of the Dependants' Conference in the early 1970s were members of the PAC and ANC.[20] From the general stance of SACC pronouncements, it is likely that the majority of people helped by the division during the 1980s were members of the UDF, or of linked organisations, which essentially developed into the internal arm of the ANC (see Appendix 1).

Closely associated with the Dependants' Conference, and the most politically contentious of all the SACC's programmes, is the Asingeni Relief Fund. It was set up in 1976 in the wake of the black-

---

19. *Report of the Director of the Division of Justice and Reconciliation,* SACC Justice and Reconciliation Committee, February 1987. In 1987 there were 15 such fieldworkers.
20. *Eloff Report,* p. 48.

consciousness inspired Soweto student uprising, when children protested about the introduction of Afrikaans as the teaching language in their schools, but continued rioting after this proposal had been dropped (see Appendix 1). On 16th June 1976 the staff of the SACC launched a fund to offer aid to those who had suffered bereavement and injury in the violence. In a press statement, it explained that *Asingeni* meant "we will not go in", chosen as an expression of solidarity with those students who refused to attend classes.[21] The initial object of the Fund was to help the black people of Soweto through such things as grants for funeral expenses; maintenance of families of persons who were killed or detained; medical and hospital fees; rent where the breadwinner was injured, killed, detained or lost his employment. According to the Eloff Report, the Fund also financed the legal defence of black people charged with various offences connected with the riots, including public violence, the possession of explosives, attempted arson, malicious injury to property, stone-throwing, etc.[22] This initiative captured the imagination of overseas donors who gave generously to the Fund, and it continued after the riots had subsided. Its power to attract overseas donations, however, subsequently began to wane and this was only reversed when Bishop Tutu announced in 1979 that the Fund was to have a more politically proactive thrust. As he stated:[23]

> "Originally the Asingeni Fund was set up to give rapid assistance and relief to those who had

---

21. *Ecunews,* No. 19, 1976.
22. *Eloff Report,* pp. 40-1, 92-3.
23. *Asingeni Report 19,* quoted in *ibid.,* p. 296.

been affected by the 1976 uprisings to give help with funeral expenses and then to provide legal expenses for those who were involved in political trials ... But our mandate tacitly involved assisting the victims of the apartheid system and to empower the powerless in their liberation struggle against the totally unjust and immoral system prevalent in our country. We are now making this tacit commitment more explicit in the assistance that we have been called upon more and more to provide."

Thereafter, as the Eloff Report summarised, the Asingeni Fund became the financial flagship through which the SACC and its General Secretary signalled their heightened commitment to, and support for, pressure groups they perceived as having the potential to bring about radical change. By the early 1980s such groups supported by the Fund included radical black consciousness groups like COSAS (Congress of South African Students) - which was in the forefront of the campaign to impose boycotts on school attendance in the townships - and AZASO (the Azanian Students' Organisation), as well as a number of black trade unions. The Asingeni Fund is a discretionary one, which means that (although in practice not all the Fund is used in this way),[24] the General Secretary can determine the purpose and the beneficiaries of the Fund at his discretion. There is also a great deal of secrecy surrounding the grants - although it was the second largest SACC programme

---

24. In 1991, for instance, R2.8mn.of the Fund was used for legal costs in conjunction with the work of the Dependants' Conference - see Report of the Dependants' Conference, 1991 AGM of the SACC.

over the period 1987-90, with an annual expenditure averaging just over R4 mn., no reports are made to the AGM of the SACC about its discretionary activities. The same is true of the National Emergency Fund.

From this fairly brief survey of SACC expenditure, it should be clear that very little of the income received from overseas Church organisations has been spent by the SACC on traditional Christian mission or evangelistic activities. Apart from compassionate social welfare programmes, much has gone on supporting those who have been involved in civil disobedience and violence. In this respect, it is important to remember that, given the pattern of violence which has prevailed in South Africa over the last few years, many of those provided with legal aid by the Dependants' Conference and Asingeni Fund may have been involved in intimidation of, or violence towards, other black people. It is therefore of particular concern to note that, of the R7,158,099 donated between 1986 and 1990 to the SACC by the British Church aid agency, Christian Aid, the greater part of it went to the SACC's two most obviously political programmes - R323,315 to the Dependants' Conference and R4,179,103 to the Asingeni Fund.[25]

---

25. For more information about Christian Aid see *Christian Aid - A Betrayal of Faith?* (International Freedom Foundation, UK, January 1992). See also Rachel Tingle, "A Political Charity" in *The Free Nation*, May 1983.

Assistance from the European Community

The SACC has also acted as a channel for considerable funding to groups in South Africa from the European Community. This programme, known as the Special Community Programme of Assistance for the Victims of Apartheid (VOA), emerged as a result of a meeting of EC Foreign Ministers in Luxembourg on 10th September 1985. In the wake of a European mission to South Africa at the beginning of that month, and subsequent talks by members of the EC Commission with representatives of the ANC, the Ministers resolved to adopt a series of 'restrictive' and 'positive' measures to encourage the abolition of apartheid. Amongst the positive measures announced in September 1985 were "programmes of assistance to non-violent anti-apartheid organisations, particularly the churches."[26]

The EC Commission has stated that, in formulating this programme, it worked closely with SACC and SACBC personnel, particularly Fr. Smangaliso Mkhatshwa.[27] They decided that EC aid should be channelled through the SACC and SACBC and, in addition, an "equivalent secular organisation should be established to allow wider access to the Community's assistance".[28] This secular organisation, the Kagiso Trust, was established early in 1986; its trustees were drawn from South Africa's circle of 'progressive' Church leaders - Dr. Beyers Naudé (chairman), Dr. Allan Boesak, the Rev. Frank

---

26. *EC Bulletin*, 9-1985, pp. 76-77.
27. Press Release, EC Commission, May 1986.
28. Background Briefing, EC Commission, 7 September 1990.

Chikane, Archbishop Desmond Tutu, Fr. Smangaliso Makhatshwa, and Archbishop Dennis Hurley (former president of the SACBC) - together with representatives of secular organisations, almost exclusively aligned with the UDF. It was also agreed that the trade unions should constitute a fourth distinct channel of EC funding.

When approval of the first grants was announced in July 1986, the EC Commission made it clear that the funds would be used to finance "welfare and humanitarian aid schemes, in particular educational and training programmes".[29] Another statement issued that month stated its assistance would also be extended to "those arrested in connection with the recent imposition of the State of Emergency" and, presumably because of this, the criteria were widened to include legal aid.[30] The EC has constantly reiterated that the main purpose of the Programme is for welfare and humanitarian purposes, stating that "no project which would support the activities of political organisations is eligible for Community financing under this programme. Only projects which are of a peaceful, non-violent nature may be supported."[31]

In its initial discussions, however, the EC had agreed that it would not seek to establish any mechanism of its own within South Africa to monitor

---

29. Press Release IP(86)374, EC Commission, 23 July 1986.
30. Answer QXW1793/87EN given by Mr Natali on behalf of the EC Commission, 29 March 1988.
31. Background Briefing, EC Commission, 7 September 1990.

spending,[32] and that it would be its South African partner organisations which would lay down the criteria by which funds would be allocated. At their insistence, then, the criteria ruled out assisting any government-related programmes or any programmes such as health care and social welfare which the 'apartheid regime' could legitimately be expected to finance within its government responsibilities. In spite of their obvious need for such aid, it also ruled out giving any assistance to projects initiated, organised or controlled by governments in the homelands or the semi-independent states of Transkei, Ciskei, Bophutatswana, or Venda - presumably as these were seen as structures which had been created under the grand apartheid design. Furthermore, development projects would only be supported if they contributed towards a "process of education for peaceful, but fundamental change". The result of these exclusions was to call into question the degree to which the objective of the programme was genuinely of a social-welfare nature, rather than essentially political. These fears were reinforced by the fact that, in spite of requests from members of the European Parliament, neither the EC Commission itself, nor its South African partners,

---

32. The procedure adopted in making grants has been as follows. Anyone seeking a grant applies to either the SACC, the SACBC, the Kagiso Trust, or Cosatu. Grants up to about R40,000 are administered directly by these organisations; larger grants are vetted by European non-governmental organisations with some expertise in the field and they make their recommendations to the EC. In the case of the SACC, for instance, grant applications are dealt with by a 'Victims of Apartheid Task Force' screening committee; large requests are passed on to its main European partners, Christian Aid, *Brot Fur die Welt*, Danchurchaid and ICCO, who advise the EC.

was prepared to release any details of the individual projects funded via the Programme. In his reply to a question in the European Parliament in September 1987, for instance, Mr Natali, on behalf of the Brussels Commission, stated that :[33]

> "The Commission has consistently declined to discuss the individual schemes supported by this programme, since this could directly or indirectly harm the interests of the beneficiaries concerned or suggest that confidentiality in regard to the programme was not being observed."

Many have found it difficult to understand why such a degree of confidentiality should be necessary if the grants really were of a social welfare and non-political nature.

Indeed, according to reports in *The Independent*, during 1987 officials of the British government (which provides about 20% of the funding for the VOA scheme) became increasingly concerned that the Kagiso Trust, in particular, was "too close to the UDF and the township radicals".[34]

---

33. Question 295/87(1), 16 September 1987. Mr Natali further stated in reply to question QXW1793/87EN, 29 March 1988, that the Commission: "provides the European Parliament with as much information as it considers compatible with the confidentiality necessary to safeguard the efficient implementation of the special programme ... (it) is not prepared to make public the details of individual projects since the intention of the Special Programme is primarily to assist individuals who are victims of the apartheid legislation while at the same time safeguarding their human dignity."
34. See reports by Richard Dowden in *The Independent*, 23 and 24 September 1987.

They especially objected to the funding of the radical South African Youth Congress (SAYCO) - the youth wing of the UDF which became notorious for supplying members of Winnie Mandela's bodyguard, the 'Mandela United Football Club'.[35] Instead, they wanted to see the money going to moderate organisations like the Urban Foundation, a business charity which funds improvements in the townships, and also to see money spent over a wider area, including the homelands. Because of mainly British concerns, in April 1987 the partner organisations in South Africa were asked by the Brussels committee controlling the scheme to submit information about the use made of the money. They refused. According to a report in the German newspaper, *Die Welt,* at the beginning of 1988 a representative of the EC was sent to South Africa to investigate the use of the money. Extracts of his confidential report published in the paper stated that:[36]

> "All talks in South Africa proved that the four organisations, especially the SACC and the SACBC are financing and organising actions which are nearly exclusively political. These include 'legal aid', education programmes

---

35. Sayco is now an affiliate of the ANC. At its 1990 congress it passed a resolution that "all youth in Sayco will be encouraged to join the ANC, rebuild it and popularise its perspective, aims and objectives. Sayco will begin a process, together with the ANC Youth Section, of formally establishing a mass based ANC Youth League in the country" - see *New Nation,* 20-24 April 1990. One of Sayco's affiliates, the Tembisa Youth Congress, in 1990 called for the reintroduction of 'people's courts', which have been associated with necklace killings - see *Daily News* (SA), 11 April 1990.
36. *Die Welt,* 19 March 1988.

> which are nearly exclusively political. These include 'legal aid', education programmes closely related to revolutionary aims and campaigns for white conscientous objectors or 'civil disobedience'."

The EC representative had interviewed Frank Chikane, General Secretary of the SACC, who, in answer to the question, "how were the EC funds used", stated that "the EC money was spend on existing projects. Last year 80 per cent of the money was invested in legal defence." According to the report, Chikane declared that "as far as the political work is concerned we are not able to make a distinction. There are no projects which are for the liberation struggle and must, at the same time, not be political".[37]

In other words, in spite of the assurances being given in the European parliament at the time that the VOA Special Programme was humanitarian and non-political, it is quite clear that members of the administering committee were well aware of the fact that they had no control over the use of funds and that the South African partner organisations were quite prepared to use the funds for essentially political purposes. Despite this, and the reservations of national governments like Britain (and, to a lesser extent, the Netherlands and Germany), the Programme has grown steadily - 10mn. ECU was made available in 1986; E20mn. in 1989; E25mn. in 1989; E30mn. in 1990; E60mn. in 1991; and E70mn. is budgeted for 1992. Up to June 1991, a total of

---

37. *Ibid.*

125mn ECU (ie. about £87.5mn. or about R420mn.) had actually been allocated to projects, all in South Africa apart from E4.7mn. in Namibia. Of the total, E43.3mn. had been channelled via the SACC and SACBC; E73.6mn via the Kagiso Trust; and E7.53mn. via the trade unions.[38]

This is, of course, a great deal of money. In a remarkably frank series of articles which appeared in the radical Cape-based newspaper, *South,* in March 1991, Rehana Rossouw calculated that a total of a least R500 mn. in foreign funding had been received by South Africa's anti-apartheid organisations the previous year, the largest conduit being the Kagiso Trust (which has received money from sources additional to the EC). One of the articles quoted Dr. Wolfram Kistner, formerly head of the department of Justice and Reconciliation at the SACC, as saying that "our activists today know all the psychological tricks to get money. They know exactly what words to put into their funding proposals." The result has been a huge industry - at that time, the Kagiso Trust alone was estimated to employ directly or indirectly almost 1,000 people - but, as leaders of some of the organisations receiving funds have admitted, this has bred a culture of "political corruption" and gross inefficiency. Moreover, they have said, "certain projects do little more than provide 'sheltered employment' for political activists."[39]

An additional concern amongst many South Africans is not simply that EC money has been used

---

38. Memo/91/34 produced by EC Commission, London, 10 June 1991.
39. See *South* (SA), March 7-13 1991; and March 14-20 1991.

for political purposes, but that it has been used in a one-sided way. John Kane-Berman, of the South African Institute of Race Relations, for instance, has claimed that the Kagiso Trust has denied EC money to "organisations that do not have the ANC's political seal of approval."[40] Certainly groups to the left and right of the ANC on the political spectrum feel they have had a bad deal from the VOA scheme. In a memorandum submitted to EC officials, the black consciousness group, AZAPO, complained that its applications for grants for educational community projects were refused by the Kagiso Trust,[41] and the PAC has made similar complaints.[42] It is the ANC's main opponent, Inkatha, however, which has been most concerned about the activities of the Kagiso Trust. This is both because Inkatha receives no funding from the Trust, and also because a disproportionate number of projects appear to have been funded in the Zulu heartland of Natal. This has been regarded by Inkatha as an attempt to strengthen the organisational capability of community groups linked to its political rivals.[43]

Other sources, apart from Inkatha, have confirmed this political bias. It is known, for instance, that the Kagiso Trust has funded the newspapers, *New African, Umafrika, Vrye Weekblad,*

---

40. *Sunday Telegraph*, 2 September 1990.
41. *Sunday Tribune* (SA), 29 April 1990.
42. *Sunday Telegraph*, 2 September 1990.
43. In June and July 1990 the Inkatha newspaper, *Ilanga*, published a series of five articles attacking the Kagiso Trust, giving details of the groups it has allegedly obtained from an ANC informer.

South, and *New Nation,* all of which are pro-ANC.[44] The *New Nation,* for instance, has been described by the (liberal) *Leadership* magazine as required reading on ANC thinking and its contents have been strongly criticised by the traditionalist Catholic organisation, TFP, for being highly politicised and contrary to traditional Catholic teaching.[45] The paper, which is now owned by the Catholic Bishops' Publishing Co., was launched in January 1986 by the SACBC with the support of Catholic development agencies in Europe, including CAFOD in Britain, SCIAF in Scotland, Tocaire in Ireland, Misereor in West Germany, and CCFD in France.[46] It is thought to have received EC funding via both the Kagiso Trust and the SACBC - in 1988, for instance, the SACBC applied for E1.25mn. for *New Nation.*

Privately, EC officials now admit that there was a "lack of transparency" about its VOA Programme.[47] Although the Budget allocation was doubled in 1991 and has been increased again for 1992, in the light of President De Klerk's reform measures, the EC has signalled that it wants to support many more initiatives which are genuinely developmental in their approach. It has already made clear that funding of radical newspapers like *New*

---

44. *Business Day* (SA), 20 June 1990.
45. See *The 'New Nation' and Liberation Theology* (TFP, PO Box 10906, Johannesburg, 2000, 1987). On the basis of an analysis of more recent issues of the paper, TFP repeated this criticism in advertisements placed in national newspapers in February and June 1990.
46. See document on the *New Nation* published by the UK Catholic Institute for International Relations (undated).
47. Telephone conversation with EC officials in Brussels, February 1992.

African should cease.[48] In February 1991 the EC opened a small office in Pretoria which will monitor the Programme on the ground - as the SACC has remarked, " the light and flexible procedures that governed the programme in the past seem to be over."[49] The EC's intention is that, although it will continue to channel funds via the SACC, SACBC, Kagiso Trust and the unions, these will no longer be the only avenues of support to South Africa and the office would itself identify additional projects for funding. Given the experience of the past five year, however, it would still seem highly desirable that the Programme become far more open and accountable to the European Parliament, with details of the projects funded available on request.

It is difficult to tell what were the real intentions of the EC's VOA scheme when it was first established. Was it intentionally political and merely hid behind the smokescreen of being of a welfare and humanitarian nature? Or did the EC genuinely intend the Programme to be as non-political as possible, but was naive in the advice it received and the organisations it chose to work through in South Africa? One thing that does emerge clearly is that, given the very significant change that has taken place in the way some of the Churches view their mision to the world, the decision to work via Church organisations is absolutely no guarantee against involvement in radical politics - nor is it any guarantee against contributing to the climate of violence. Unless the SACC, the SACBC and the

---

48. *Business Day* (SA), 26 October 1990.
49. *Report of the VOA Taskforce,* SACC AGM 1991.

Kagiso Trust change their stance rapidly and very significantly, to continue to channel any funds through these organisations is, in reality, to take sides in the power struggle between black groups taking place in South Africa today. This applies equally to funding from governmental organisations, and also to funding from Church groups and aid agencies.

SUMMARY AND CONCLUSION

Few could have guessed the practical implications of the change in Church thinking which began in ecumenical circles at the WCC Church and Society Conference in 1966. Largely as a result of this, the World Council of Churches established its Programme to Combat Racism which has now given almost $5mn. to liberation movements in Africa, virtually all of which have adopted the principles of Marxism-Leninism and have been prepared to use revolutionary violence in order to seize power. South Africa's two liberation movements, the ANC and the PAC, have respectively received a total of $1.3mn and $0.7mn from the PCR. The Programme has now continued for more than twenty years, with little protest from WCC member Churches. Neither the WCC itself, nor its member Churches, appears to have shown any concern about the dismal economic and human rights record of the liberation movements assisted by the PCR once they have taken power.

In order to justify the Programme, the WCC has encouraged the development of forms of theology which support radical political action. A whole family of 'contextual theologies' has now been developed in many parts of the world, the spread of which has been assisted both by the WCC itself and also by the Ecumenical Association of Third World Theologians. Within South Africa during the 1970s, North American Black Theology was adapted so as to provide theological support for the emerging black consciousness movement.

During the 1980s, such ideas were further developed and refined by the Institute for Contextual Theology. This has been responsible for formulating a specifically South African form of liberation theology, as found in the influential *Kairos Document* and *The Road to Damascus*. These widely-distributed booklets rejected a reformist solution to the country's political problems, and argued that Christians should not be working for peace and reconciliation but, rather, should participate in the "struggle for liberation and justice". Thus radical Church organisations came to condone the violence of South Africa's liberation movements. They also advocated the widespread use of civil disobedience by Church groups as a form of resistance against the government, apparently ignoring the degree to which civil disobedience frequently relies on intimidation of third-parties (particularly black moderates) in order to be effective. In these ways South Africa's radical Church organisations have contributed to the climate of violence which has rocked the country ever since Autumn 1984.

In the theology it adopts, and in its view of the role of the Church in the world, the Church in South Africa has become deeply divided. For some years now, apart from small break-away Afrikaner Churches in the Dutch Reformed tradition, all of the South African Churches have condemned apartheid. But those Christians and Church groups who adhere to orthodox theology, who emphasise the importance of preaching the spiritual gospel of salvation, and who would see their role in wider society as a 'Third Force' helping to bring about reconciliation between all racial and political groups, have been subjected to criticism, ridicule and other forms of attack by 'progressive Christians'. This has been compounded by the fact that, since at least 1985, the ANC has also developed a strategy to attempt to bring as many Church groups as possible into the national liberation struggle. Thus, whether the vast majority of ordinary Church-goers are aware of it or not, as the radical Christians have themselves made clear, a battle has been going on for control of Church practices, symbols, and resources. In other words, what is ultimately at stake is the meaning of the Christian faith.

Apart from the Institute for Contextual Theology, the main Church body which has been involved in this process is the South African Council of Churches. The SACC has enjoyed a yearly income between 1987 and 1990 averaging R23.28mn. (i.e. about £6mn.). Hardly any of this, however, has been spent on traditional Christian missionary or evangelistic activity. Indeed, even its 'Church and Mission' departments have been involved in promoting forms of radical, contextual theology. The SACC's 'Justice and Society' activities form the practical outworkings of its commitment to political liberation. Apart from social welfare programmes which would be acceptable to most Christians, much of the Justice and Society expenditure has gone on providing legal aid and other forms of support for those involved in civil disobedience and violence, including alleged terrorist offences. Only limited information is disclosed about the use of its semi-secret Asingeni Relief Fund (with an annual income averaging R3.9mn. between 1987 and 1990) but previous SACC General Secretary, Bishop Tutu, has stated that the purpose of the Fund is to "empower the powerless in their liberation struggle." Much of the SACC's activities have thus had very obvious political implications.

Although the ICT and the SACC have produced a range of influential publications and appear to the international community as the 'voice of the South African Church', the degree to which they, or other radical Christians, are genuinely representative of the great bulk of Christian opinion in South Africa is open to considerable doubt. It is noteworthy that, partly because of the obvious political nature of its work, the vast majority of the African Independent Churches (to which an estimated eight million black South Africans belong) have not joined the SACC. Moreover, both the ICT and the SACC derive only a fraction of their income from membership subscriptions - from 1988 to 1989, the ICT only received about 1% of its income from this source and, over the period 1987 to 1990, the SACC received a miniscule 0.2% from its member Churches and Church groups.

Because of this, neither the ICT nor the SACC would have been able to exist in anything like their present form if it were not for the support they have received from overseas, particularly from European Church aid agencies. Between 1987 and 1990, at least 98% of the SACC's income was derived from overseas, and in the years 1987 and 1988 the ICT's income from overseas averaged 96%. Two British aid agencies, the Catholic Fund for Overseas Development (CAFOD) and Christian Aid, have made grants to both the ICT and the SACC - more than half of the grant aid from Christian Aid to the SACC was to support two of its most obviously political programmes, the Dependants' Conference and the Asingeni Relief Fund. The British Council of Churches and Oxfam have also contributed to the SACC.

Between 1986 and the end of 1991, the European Community, allocated approximately 140mn. ECU (ie. about £98mn.) to Southern Africa under its Special Community Programme of Assistance to the Victims of Apartheid. A further E70mn. is budgeted for 1992. About one third of the money was channelled through the South African Council of Churches and the Southern African Catholic Bishops' Conference, and just under two-thirds via the Kagiso Trust, a secular trust set up jointly by the SACC and the SACBC. According to statements from the EC Commission, the grants were intended for welfare and humanitarian aid schemes, and were not supposed to support the activities of political organisations. However, the Commission has refused to give details to the European Parliament of projects financed, and there are many indications that not only has much of the money been used on programmes which are political in nature, but also that there is a strong bias in favour of ANC-aligned projects or groups. This reveals the fact that, given the very significant change in the way some of the Churches view their mission to the world, the decision to provide aid to a country like South Africa via Church organisations is no guarantee against becoming deeply involved in their political conflicts.

Thus, in enabling the ICT and the SACC to carry out their work, it can be argued that European Church aid agencies, including those in Britain, have also contributed towards the climate of violence in South Africa and the undermining of orthodox Christianity. This should be a matter of grave concern to many Christians in European countries who have donated to the agencies concerned.

British and other European Community taxpayers should be similarly concerned about the misuse of EC aid for political purposes in South Africa and the contribution that European governments may therefore have made towards exacerbating conflict in that country.

APPENDIX 1: Main Political Groups and Recent Political Events in South Africa

AFRICAN NATIONAL CONGRESS (ANC)
(See also South African Communist Party and United Democratic Front)
The ANC was originally founded in 1912 by a distinguished group of African leaders whose aim was forge some sort of unity out of the country's many black tribal and language groups and to persuade the white authorities to gradually abolish all forms of racial discrimination. At that time the organisation's ethos was Christian, nationalist, reformist, and rather elitist. It remained small for many years, almost sinking into extinction in the 1930s, but fortunes were revived in the 1940s under the presidency of Dr. Alfred Xuma who introduced a new constitution, streamlined the organisational structure and broadened the membership base. Increased membership resulted in the entry of younger, more radical members, including Oliver Tambo, Nelson Mandela, Walter Sisulu, and Govan Mbeki.

At the ANC annual conference in 1949, these younger member staged a coup which resulted in the ejection of Xuma from the presidency, and the election of Walter Sisulu as general secretary and of two communists to the National Executive Committee. This increased radicalism in the ANC leadership coincided with the beginnings of the new

Nationalist government's push to implement apartheid legislation. In reaction to this, in 1949, the ANC adopted a Programme of Action which called for non-cooperation with government institutions, boycotts and strikes. This was stepped up in 1952 to a Defiance Campaign in which activists invited arrest by defying the pass laws and refusing to comply with the separate amenities legislation.

ANC militancy also increased as a result of the 1950 Suppression of Communism Act which led to the dissolution of the Communist Party of South Africa and the movement of many of its black members into the ANC. Because of their influence, the ANC eventually abandoned its 'Africanist' or black nationalist ideology and instead adopted a class-based analysis of oppression. In 1959 this resulted in a split in the organisation and the creation of the rival Pan-Africanist Congress (PAC). During this period, the ANC also moved to increase its co-operation with non-black organisations including the South African Indian Congress and the all-white South African Congress of Deputies (both of which had also been strongly influenced by former members of the Communist Party). With the South African Coloured People's Congress and the South African Congress of Trade Unions (SACTU), these five organisations formed an alliance which, at the 1955 'Congress of the People', adopted the Freedom Charter as their manifesto for action. This moved well beyond obvious black aspirations for the complete abolition of apartheid; with its recommendations that the mines, the banks and other 'monopoly industries' should be nationalised and all other industry and trade controlled, it favoured a major restructuring of the economy on socialist lines.

The ANC call for a nation-wide strike in the wake of the tragedy of Sharpeville (when 67 black people were killed, and 187 were injured when the police opened fire on an apparently peaceful demonstration against the pass laws) led to its banning by the government in 1960, after which it operated underground or in exile. The following year, partly to compete with the radicalism of the PAC, an armed wing of the ANC known as *Umkhonto we Sizwe* (MK) or "Spear of the Nation" was formed with Nelson Mandela as first Commander. Its aim was to spark off a general uprising to force the government to negotiate. In 1963, however, after the MK had conducted a wave of bomb attacks against strategic installations, almost its entire leadership was captured at Rivonia, Johannesburg. Following a lengthy trial, Mandela, Sisulu, Govan Mbeki and others were found guilty of armed insurrection and sentenced to life imprisonment on Robben Island. The ANC underground network was thus virtually destroyed and Oliver Tambo, in exile, became the *de facto* leader of a decimated organisation.

Revitalization of the ANC only began with the 1969 Consultative Conference at Morogoro, Tanzania, which recommitted the ANC to the Freedom Charter and the transfer of power by revolutionary means.[1] It also opened ANC membership to all races, so allowing the influence of

---

1. *ANC Speaks! Documents and Statements of the African National Congress, 1955-1976* (African National Congress, 1977).

the white-dominated South African Communist Party (SACP) - an underground organisation formed when the Communist Party of South Africa was disbanded - to increase. With aid from the Eastern bloc, Libya, Sweden, the United Nations, and some Western Church agencies, the ANC set up headquarters in Lusaka, Zambia; bases in Angola, Botswana, Mozambique, Tanzania and Zimbabwe; offices in London, New Delhi, and Moscow; and a mission to the United Nations.[2] From such bases the ANC/SACP alliance was able to publish a steady stream of material,[3] and attempted to build up support amongst the international community as well as underground structures within South Africa.

Members of the MK were trained mainly in Angola by Cuban and Russian instructors; whilst potential leaders were trained in the Soviet Union itself.[4] MK members were infiltrated back into South Africa to carry out occasional terrorist bomb attacks. Until the early 1980s, the ANC's professed policy was to strike only at 'hard' targets such as police stations or vital national installations but, following its second consultative conference at Kabwe, Zambia in June 1985, it decided that there would be no attempt to distinguish between 'hard' and 'soft'

---

2. See Richard Neuhaus, *Dispensations: The Future of South Africa as South Africans See It* (William Eerdmans, Grand Rapids, 1986), pp. 270-1, and Michael Radu, "The African National Congress: Cadres and Credo" in *Problems of Communism*, July-August 1987.
3. Titles include *Sechaba, Dawn, The African Communist*, and *Umsebensi*.
4. See details provided by an ANC defector quoted in Keith Campbell, *ANC: A Soviet Task Force?* (Institute for the Study of Terrorism, London 1986), p. 49.

targets, and (black and white) civilians could expect to be caught in the crossfire. However, in spite of all its efforts and its international support, the ANC was unsuccessful in stimulating a revolutionary uprising in South Africa during the 1960s and 1970s. Partly because of this, in 1978 an ANC delegation led by Oliver Tambo visited Vietnam to study the methods of 'people's war' which had been developed by Mao Tse-tung. As a result, the ANC developed a three-year plan of operation aimed at politicising, mobilising and organising the people, followed in 1984 by the adoption of the 'four pillars of people's war' which comprised:[5]

- the activities of underground structures (cells, street and area committees, people's courts);
- united mass action;
- armed action by Umkhonto we Sizwe;
- the international isolation of South Africa.

After the creation of the United Democratic Front (UDF) in 1983 - see below - the ANC had, in effect, an internal arm which, from 1984 onwards, engaged particularly in the first two of these 'pillars of war'.[6]

From about 1986 onwards, Soviet support for the ANC began to dry up as the USSR entered into a new period of detente with the West and its own

---

5. See Dr. Anthea Jeffery, "Mass Mobilisation", *Spotlight* No. 1 (South African Institute of Race Relations, March 1991).
6. For more detailed information on the history of the ANC see Roland Stanbridge, "Contemporary African Political Organizations and Movements" in Robert Price and Carl Rosberg (eds.),*The Apartheid Regime;* Jordon Ngubane, *An African Explains Apartheid* (Praeger, New York) and Radu, *op. cit.*

economy started to disintegrate. The Soviets consequently appear to have put pressure on the ANC/SACP to negotiate with the South African government,[7] which the ANC/SACP at first resisted.[8] In August 1989, however, the ANC, in consultation with the Organisation of African Unity, set out in the *Harare Declaration* its preconditions for any negotiations with the government. This included the release of all political prisoners and detainees and the lifting of all bans and restrictions on proscribed and restricted organisations.

Under President De Klerk's process of reforms, moves were made towards meeting these demands: in October 1989 seven senior ANC officials, including Walter Sisulu, were released from prison; the ANC was unbanned the following February, and Nelson Mandela was released a few

---

7. The Soviet leadership at the 27th Party Congress in 1986 committed itself to the principle that all regional conflicts in the Third World should be solved by diplomatic-political means. A month later the Soviet leadership made it clear that this included the South African conflict - see text of a dinner speech by Gorbachev in honour of Samora Machel, published in the BBC Summary of World Broadcasts SU/8222, 2 April 1986. At the ANC's 1987 conference in Arusha a senior Soviet government official admonished the ANC for not doing enough to prepare the ground for negotiation and, in October 1989, the Soviet foreign minister for African Affairs, Anatoly Adamishin, suggested in an interview on Radio South Africa that the Soviet Union was prepared to help arrange negotiations beween the ANC and the government - see Gemma Porzgen, "Soviet Foreign Policy with Regard to South Africa" in *South Africa International* (SA), January 1991.

8. An article in the SACP magazine, *Umsebenzi* No. 2, 1988, made it clear that the SACP saw such Soviet suggestions as premature and harmful to the revolutionary cause.

days later. Immediately following his release, Mandela called for a continuation and intensification of the armed struggle,[9] but talks between the government and ANC representatives in May 1990 to discuss obstacles to negotiations produced an agreement (the 'Groote Schuur Minute') by which political prisoners should be released and exiles repatriated in return for the ANC's commitment to stability and a peaceful process of negotiation.[10] After a further meeting with the government in Pretoria in August 1990 (resulting in the 'Pretoria Minute'), the ANC announced that it was 'suspending' all armed actions with immediate effect. It should be noted, however, that the ANC has not agreed to *terminate* the armed struggle - at its July 1991 conference the ANC declared that "the armed

---

9. By this stage, however, the ANC was coming under some pressure from black African states to abandon the armed struggle. Under the terms of the Angola/South West Africa peace accord, the ANC was forced to move its military bases out of Angola. These were relocated in Tanzania and Uganda, but by Autumn 1989 the Tanzanian and Ugandan governments had taken steps to disarm ANC cadres. In March 1990, Dr Kaunda, president of Zambia, suggested that the ANC should suspend its armed operations inside South Africa. See *Race Relations Survey, 1989/90* (South African Institute of Race Relations, 1990).

10. There has been a debate within South Africa about how many genuine political prisoners remain in jail because, subsequent to the agreement, the ANC demanded that the government should extend the definition of political prisoners to include those involved in unrest-related actions such as arson and public violence. The government maintains that all genuine political prisoners had been released by the end of April 1991 - *The Times*, 2 July 1991.

struggle remains a pillar of our struggle",[11] and has made it clear that MK units are being developed and maintained in combat readiness.[12] Moreover, in spite of the fact that the ANC, in common with most of South Africa's political groups, signed a Peace Accord in September 1991 which bans private armies, the ANC has announced that it has no intention of dissolving the MK either now or in the future. Winnie Mandela and other ANC leaders have declared that the MK will be the "the future army of a democratic South Africa."[13]

In August 1990, the government agreed to terms relating to another ANC demand - the return of exiles to South Africa. Out of an estimated 40,000 South Africans then in exile, 20,000 were reckoned to be ANC members, 5,000 of whom were trained MK

---

11. ANC 48th National Conference, *Final Documents, Strategy and Tactics,* para. 3.1.
12. *Ibid.,* adopted Resolution on the MK. The Conference resolved that "the ANC shall maintain and develop MK"; that the "MK shall remain in constant combat readiness"; and that "the ANC shall establish structures of MK throughout the country at all levels." There have been reports that the ANC is continuing to stockpile weapons including AK-47 rifles, hand grenades and limpet mines - see *The Citizen* (SA), 19 October, 1991. In June 1991 Mr Mandela also admitted that the ANC leadership had ordered a back-up plan (Operation Vula) should negotiations between it and the government fail. The operation included the infiltration of ANC military commanders into South Africa and the establishment of arms caches with the aim of expanding a revolutionary army in South Africa - see *The Citizen* (SA), 24 June 1991.
13. For details see *Sunday Telegraph,* 15 September 1991.

guerillas in camps in Tanzania and Zambia.[14] The process of repatriation has been slower than originally planned, partly because of the problem facing the ANC and the repatriation organisations of finding jobs and housing for the returning exiles. In the case of MK members, however, some reports suggest that practically all of them were back in the country by the beginning of April 1991.[15]

The ANC has faced quite significant problems since its unbanning. It has been locked into a fierce political battle with the Inkatha Freedom Party (IFP), which has frequently spilled over into bloodshed. There have also been internal rivalries in the ANC between the 'old guard' returning from exile or recently released from prison, and the younger leaders from the associated internal organisations, the Congress of South African Trade Unions (COSATU) and the UDF, as well as tensions between members and non-members of the SACP (about half of the new ANC National Executive Committee are thought to be members of the SACP). More importantly, the ANC has been slow to transform itself into a genuinely mass-based movement. Hopes of recruiting a million members in 1990 were unfulfilled - by November 1990 its national membership had not reached 200,000,[16] and by June 1991 it was still only able to claim about 500,000 members.[17] One reason

---

14. For more details see Pippa Green, "Return of the Exiles" in *Leadership* (SA), October 1990.
15. *Sunday Telegraph*, 7 April 1991.
16. *Newsweek*, 15 October 1990.
17. Estimate made by Raymond Suttner of the ANC's Department of Political Education - see *The Citizen* (SA), 17 June 1991.

for this, admitted by the ANC secretary-general in his report to the July 1991 National Conference, is the alliance with the SACP which discourages whites, Indians, coloureds and moderate blacks from joining.[18]

Although there have been some signs of a softening of attitude, Nelson Mandela has continued to call for the maintenance of sanctions against South Africa - but to increasingly little effect. (Ironically it was former Soviet-bloc nations like Hungary and Czechoslovakia who were amongst the first to lift sanctions in 1990).[19] The ANC has lost some support from Western nations both because of the government's reform process and also because of Mandela's open support for PLO leader Yassir Arafat, Libya's Colonel Gaddafi and Cuba's Fidel Castro,[20] and emerging evidence of ANC atrocities against its own dissident members.[21] Nevertheless, during 1991

---

18. *Pretoria News* (SA), 12 July 1991.
19. The ANC has stated that it is determined to dictate the pace at which US regional sanctions and capital sanctions imposed by the World Bank and the International Monetary Fund are lifted - *The Times,* 12 July 1991.
20. This emerged during Mandela's 1990 tour of Western Europe and North America - see reports in the *Washington Inquirer,* 13 July 1990 and the *Sunday Telegraph,* 1 July 1990.
21. Mandela admitted on 13 April 1990 that the ANC had detained dissident members, saying that "it is true that some of these people who have complained were in fact tortured" - see *The Washington Post,* 15 April 1990. Most of these were MK members involved in a rebellion against their leaders in 1985; they were held without trial in prison camps in Angola. Some of these people are now back in South Africa and have formed the Returned Exiles Coordinating Committee (RECOC) in order to gather and publicise information on the whereabouts or fate of fellow prisoners.

the ANC received very considerable financial support from overseas and, according to reports, is now the richest political organisation in the country, with pledges during the year to September 1991 totalling at least R150mn.[22]

The degree to which the ANC is still committed to the nationalisation policies set out in the Freedom Charter is not clear. In June 1990, following a workshop in Harare attended by leaders of the ANC and COSATU, the ANC published a draft document on economic policy which demanded "increasing equality in the distribution of incomes, wealth and economic power" and stated that a future democratic state should retain ownership of existing state industries and, where necessary, new state corporations should be set up. Whilst the document avoided recommending which parts of the private sector should be nationalised, it said that the state should consider making strategic investments in the mines, as well as giving attention to "the extent of state ownership within the financial sector."[23] In June 1991, newspaper reports suggested that the ANC was now looking at only limited nationalisation and would rely mainly on a massive increase in personal and corporate taxes to close the wealth gap,[24] but the *Economic Manifesto* prepared for the ANC's July

---

22. These grants include: the Swedish International Development Agency - R54mn.; Swedish government - R40mn.; Australian government - R33mn. over three years; Germany - R30mn.; Switzerland - R30mn.; France - R25mn.; Nigeria - R5mn.; Algeria - R3mn.; Libya - R1mn.; Zimbabwe R1mn. See *The Citizen* (SA), 26 September 1991.
23. *Business Day* (SA), 5 June 1990.
24. *The Citizen* (SA), 5 June 1991.

1991 conference displayed a renewed commitment to nationalisation.[25]

As far as a strategy for gaining political power is concerned, the ANC has been pursuing a two-pronged approach - negotiating with the government on the one hand but, at the same time, continuing mass mobilisation, building up underground structures, preparing for armed struggle, and attempting to isolate South Africa internationally. Its July 1991 conference called repeatedly for an intensification of the struggle through these means and stressed that negotiation could only succeed in the context of intensified struggle on all fronts.[26] Civic associations allied to the ANC have been attempting to render the townships ungovernable by imposing rent and consumer boycotts, disrupting education, and isolating and intimidating black councillors so as to force their resignation and install ANC-controlled structures instead.[27] By the end of March 1991, almost half of the existing black local authorities had been destroyed in this way.[28] The violent clashes with Inkatha have also been used as an

---

25. Patrick Bond, "The ANC's Economic Manifesto: Can it satisfy the majority's basic needs?" in *Work in Progress,* June 1991.
26. ANC 48th National Conference, *Final Documents, Stategy and Tactics,* para. 5.
27. See Wayne Safro, *Special Report on Violence against Black Town Councillors and Policemen* (South African Institute of Race Relations, 1990), and reports in *Business Day* (SA), 8 November 1990, and *The Times,* 17 December 1990. For more details on mass mobilisation in general see Jeffery, *op. cit.*
28. See *The Star* (SA), 8 April 1991, and also Lawrence Schlemmer, "Power confrontation in the cities" in *South Africa Foundation Review,* February 1991.

argument for setting up 'self-defence' units in the townships under the control of returned MK guerillas. In proposals adopted at the ANC's December 1990 consultation and ratified at its July 1991 conference, the ANC made it clear that these units would operate right down to street level. They would receive regular military and political training (emphasising the importance of the liberation struggle) and be supplied with arms bought with the proceeds of a charge levied on the community.[29] Some commentators in South Africa are concerned that the effect of the September 1991 Peace Accord is to legitimise such units.

The main point of difference between the ANC and the government in the run-up to formal negotiations for a new constitution in South Africa stemmed from ANC demands that the constitution should be drawn up by a 'constituent assembly' elected immediately on the basis of one-person-one-vote, and that there should be an interim government to carry on the administration in the meantime. This policy, which was backed by Azapo and the PAC - see below - was endorsed at the ANC consultative conference in December 1990 and, at a rally in Soweto in June 1991, Nelson Mandela stated that there could be no compromise on this issue, "the ANC would take to the streets to press its demands."[30] This demand was resisted by the

---

29. This proposal first emerged during the ANC's 1985 Kabwe conference, but was developed further in a joint ANC-SACP-COSATU discussion document released in November 1990. See Mbulelo Sompetha, "Defending townships: Has the ANC done enough?" in *Work in Progress*, June 1991, and *Business Day* (SA), 16 April 1991.
30. *The Times*, 17 June 1991.

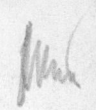

government because a constituent assembly elected in this way would almost certainly be dominated by the ANC which could then, in effect, dictate the new constitution. Instead, the government insisted that a new constitution should be negotiated by all political parties *before* new elections are held. The ANC has, however, been prepared to enter into formal negotiations with the National Party and other political parties through the Convention for a Democratic South Africa (CODESA) which first met in December 1991. Within the CODESA process (which has itself been emerging into a form of interim government and is expected to lead to the establishment of a multi-racial Interim Government Council by Summer 1992) the ANC appears to be dominating proceedings and has been successful in seeing many of its demands adopted.[31] This is in accord with ANC strategy which, as Mandela stated after the ANC national conference in July 1991, is based on "the premise that negotiation is a terrain of struggle leading to our central objective, the transfer

---

31. Referring to CODESA, Fr. Smangaliso Mkhatshwa has written in the February 1992 issue of the ICT's new magazine, *Challenge,* that "after a few setbacks, the ANC appears to be in the driver's seat again. It has wrested the initiative from the Nationalist Party and therefore the decisions taken by the ANC will have far-reaching consequences - for better or for worse."

of power to the people."[32]

AFRIKANER WEERSTANDSBEWEGING (AWB)
(Afrikaner Resistance Movement)

Originally an Afrikaner cultural organisation founded in 1973 by Mr Eugene Terre'Blanche, the AWB has in recent years assumed a high profile in far-right politics, organising rallies and making public statements with Fascist and Nazi overtones. Its political objectives are clear: it wants an Afrikaner nation state in the Transvaal, Orange Free State and parts of northern Natal, governed by a president free of the 'fetters' of parliamentary democracy. Although non-whites might be tolerated in this state, they would have no rights. The AWB has established paramilitary Brandwagte (outposts/guards) in every large town outside Cape Province whose main purpose is to crush a possible black uprising; they are encouraged to carry their own firearms. The AWB has been deeply critical of President De Klerk's reforms and in August 1991 staged a violent demonstration in Ventersdorp (where De Klerk was

---

32. *The Times,* 8 July 1991. The former head of the ANC's Religious Affairs Department, Rev. John Lamola, has also stated: "The issue of negotiations, as far as the ANC is concerned, is not to be isolated from the mainstream struggle to destroy apartheid. It is but another terrain of a number of interrelated terrains of our struggle, namely the activities of the ANC underground inside South Africa, mass protest action, mobilisation of the international community against the apartheid regime, and the armed struggle. Negotiations do not replace any of these, and must, until otherwise decided in the course of negotiations, go simultaneously with all of these other areas of struggle" - see the ANC magazine, *Sechaba,* April 1990.

speaking) in which three people were killed and 58 injured. Some right-wingers spoke of this event as the beginning of a "boer uprising". Following the 'yes' vote in the March 1992 white referendum over the reform process, Terre'Blanche said his private army was now preparing for a race war.[33] Membership of the AWB is variously estimated at 50-150,000, many of whom are also members of the Conservative Party.[34]

BLACK CONSCIOUSNESS MOVEMENT(BCM)

The Black Consciousness Movement in South Africa began with the formation of the **South African Students' Organisation (SASO)** in 1968 which established a number of self-help literacy and health care projects emphasising black solidarity and self-reliance. In doing this, SASO drew ideological inspiration from the African nationalist ideals of the then-banned Pan Africanist Congress (PAC) and, more importantly, the American black nationalist and Black Power movement which had emerged in the 1960s. Essentially black consciousness was concerned with fostering self-pride in black people and encouraging the rejection of all the notions of second-class status imposed upon them by whites. Blacks were defined as all non-white South Africans who were politically, economically or socially discriminated against - thus 'black' could include oppressed brown or coloured people, and not include relatively advantaged black people or those who

---

33. *The Times*, 21 March 1992.
34. For more information see Helen Zille, "The right wing in South African politics" in Peter Berger and Bobby Godsell (eds.), *A Future South Africa: Visions, Strategies and Realities* (Human and Rousseau/Tafelberg, 1988).

wished to adopt the white value system.[35] Black consciousness rejected integration and refused white participation in its organisations or programmes, and for that reason earned the charge of black racism.

In 1972, SASO joined forces with other black community and church groups to establish a **Black People's Convention (BPC)**. The BPC initially had a relatively low political profile, concentrating mainly on youth, church and educational programmes, leadership training courses and literacy classes. However, serious youth riots in Soweto and the Cape in 1976 were largely a direct result of BPC 'consciousness-raising' amongst young people.[36] The government responded to the township violence by banning seventeen BPC affiliated groups and imprisoning many of their leaders. Former SASO leader and BPC honorary president, Steve Biko, died in police custody in 1977. Many more national activists went underground and began to form civic organisations to address local issues such as rent, housing, and transport, and so build up a grassroots power base.

---

35. See Motlhabi, *Challenge to Apartheid: Toward a Moral National Resistance* (William Eerdmans, Grand Rapids, 1988).
36. The action was ostensibly sparked off in protest against the introduction of Afrikaans as the teaching language in the schools. The educational authorities responded by dropping the proposal and substituting English instead, but the riots continued. When Steve Biko was asked if he could point to any evidence of support for the BPC and black consciousness among the young generation in South Africa he is reported as replying: "In one word: Soweto! The boldness, dedication, sense of purpose and clarity of analysis of the situation - all these things are a direct result of Black Consciousness among the young in Soweto and elsewhere." See Biko, *Black Consciousness in South Africa* (Random House, 1978).

In 1978, Biko supporters launched the **Azanian People's Organisation (Azapo)**. It had roughly the same ideological approach as the BPC, but was more directly committed to political campaigning and organised itself as a political party with a national executive committee and a branch structure.[37] It led the demands for a cultural boycott of South Africa and in 1983 became the driving force in the **National Forum (NF)**, a coalition of political, community, labour, student and professional groups formed to present a common black front to fight the government's constitutional proposals to establish a tricameral parliamentary system with separate white, Indian and coloured (but not black) houses of parliament. Not all the NF groups adopted the black consciousness ideology, but (unlike the United Democratic Front which came into existence a couple of months later) the groups involved had to be predominantly black.

The key policy document of Azapo and the NF is the Azanian People's Manifesto, adopted in 1983. This sees the future of South Africa (Azania) as a one-party socialist state in which the means of production, including land and possibly housing, would be redistributed amongst the Azanian People. The struggle towards this end is to be in the hands of the black working class alone.[38] There are ideological and tactical differences between Azapo and the organisations adopting the ANC's Freedom Charter - for instance, Azapo questions the 'Charterists' degree

---

37. By the late 1980s, Azapo was claiming 86 branches and a paid up membership of 110,000. *Race Relations Survey,1987/88* (Institute of Race Relations, 1988).
38. *Ibid.* and Motlhabi, *op. cit.*, pp. 88-9.

of commitment to socialism and rejects their inclusion of white members. During 1984-86 these differences and the resulting power struggle between the ANC/UDF and Azapo led to numerous incidents of intimidation, terror and murder, committed particularly by young members of the two groups.[39] As part of its state of emergency, and apparently in an attempt to contain this unrest, government restrictions were placed upon Azapo and its youth wing in February 1988, which were subsequently lifted in February 1990. Sporadic incidents of violence between groups adopting the black consciousness approach and the Charterists continue, but at reduced intensity.

Azapo officials have on several occasions met Nelson Mandela in an attempt to work out some sort of consultative network of black political organisations. But differences with the ANC remain and, following his election as president of Azapo in March 1990, Dr Itumeleng Mosala (a Methodist minister and lecturer in black theology) rejected negotiations with the government and called for an intensification of the armed struggle.[40] Pandelani Nefolovhodwe, elected president the following year, declared 1991 a "year of struggle on all fronts including military" and Azapo's armed wing, the Azanian National Liberation Army (Azanla), has subsequently carried out a number of terrorist attacks within South Africa.[41]

---

39. See Keith Campbell, *op. cit.*, and Helene Roux, *op. cit.*
40. *Race Relations Survey, 1989/90.*
41. Mike Tissong, "AZAPO: fighting on two fronts" in *Work in Progress* (SA), March/April 1991.

In March 1991, Azapo called for a constituent assembly in which the test for membership would be whether organisations had been engaged in fighting to overthrow the regime and its apartheid policies.[42] Azapo refused to sign the September 1991 Peace Accord or to take part in the Convention for a Democratic South Africa (CODESA) to negotiate a new constitution.

CONSERVATIVE PARTY (CP)

The CP was established on 20 March 1982 after sixteen right-wing Nationalist MPs, under the leadership of Dr. Andries Treurnicht, broke away from the National Party because of the President's Council's recommendations for a new constitution. It has served as a rallying point for many smaller right-wing groups with widely divergent policies and strategies, who have come together in a tactical alliance in an attempt to defeat the National Party and its reform policy. Recognising that a return to old-style apartheid is no longer demographically or economically feasible, the CP now endorses simple partition of the country so that each 'nation' would have its own territory and a sovereign government of its own choice. In the 1987 general election the CP gained the support of 26% of the white electorate and 22 parliamentary seats, so replacing the Progressive Federal Party (19 seats) as the official opposition to the National Party. In the 1989 general election CP support increased to 31% of the vote and 39 seats, and by-election results since then have shown further large increases in support. The CP's success at the

---

42. Telephone interview quoted in *Countdown* (South African Institute of Race Relations, May 1991).

Potchefstroom by-election in February 1992 showed it had gained a majority of Afrikaner support. This prompted De Klerk to call a referendum of all white voters in March 1992 to establish he had a mandate to continue the process of reform - in the event De Klerk gained almost 70% of the vote thus delivering a crushing blow to the CP. The CP refused to sign the September 1991 Peace Accord, or to take part in CODESA.[43]

DEMOCRATIC PARTY (DP)

The DP was formed on 7th April 1989 by an amalgamation of the Progressive Federal Party (the official opposition to the National Party before it was displaced by the Conservative Party) and two smaller white liberal parties - the Independent Party and the National Democratic Movement, all of which had been firm opponents of apartheid. The DP, now led by prominent businessman and former PFP leader, Dr. Zach de Beer, has fully supported President De Klerk's reform measures and has participated in the formal talks for a new constitution. In the 1989 general election the Democratic Party gained 20.5% of the white vote, giving it 33 seats in parliament; it also contested the elections for the House of Delegates (the Indian House of Parliament) where it won 3 seats. More recently, by-election results show that the newly-liberal National Party has severely eroded the Democratic Party's traditional white liberal support base. The future of the DP now looks fairly bleak, although some think it could gain the support of politically moderate blacks.

---

43. For more information about the CP see Helen Zille, *op. cit.*

HERSTIGTE NASIONALE PARTY (HNP)
(Reconstituted National Party)

The HNP is the oldest and most extreme of all right-wing groups. It was formed in October 1969 by four members of parliament expelled from the National Party for opposing the then Vorster government's plans to allow 'mixed' national sporting teams to visit the country. It remains committed to the specifically Afrikaner interests and adheres to the original tenets of apartheid. It is opposed to any form of power-sharing and has rejected negotiations with the ANC. It won its first seat in a by-election in 1985, but lost it in the 1987 election when the party was crushed at the polls. HNP support fell even further in the 1989 elections when it stood on a platform favouring the reintroduction of old-style apartheid.[44]

INKATHA FREEDOM PARTY (IFP)

Inkatha was founded in 1975 by Mangosuthu Buthelezi, Chief Minister of the regional government of KwaZulu, with the encouragement of the then leadership of the ANC. They saw Inkatha as a means of bringing Zulus into the struggle against apartheid and as an organisation which would oppose homeland independence - Buthelezi claims that his resistance to the government's plans to grant full statehood to KwaZulu effectively killed off grand apartheid.[45] Buthelezi has not supported ANC policies on nationalisation, sanctions and, most particularly, the armed struggle, stating that he believes instead in dialogue and negotiation with the white regime.

---

44. *Ibid.*
45. Mangosutho Buthelezi, *South Africa: My Vision of the Future* (Weidenfeld and Nicolson, 1990).

Because of this, he refused to allow Inkatha to become effectively an internal arm of the ANC and, in 1979, these differences boiled over into a major row between the two organisations. Buthelezi continued, however, to attempt to negotiate the unbanning of the ANC and the release of Nelson Mandela and other political prisoners.[46]

By the 1980s Inkatha had developed a well-structured branch organisation overseen by a policy-making National Council meeting once or twice a year. Its headquarters are based in Ulundi (the adminstrative capital of KwaZulu), and it has several other offices in the country and abroad. Although Buthelezi has remained opposed to the armed struggle, since 1989 his followers have been involved in bitter fighting against the ANC as the two groups have fought for control of territory both in Natal/KwaZulu and townships in the Tranvaal. Peace talks between leaders of the two organisations and the Peace Accord signed in September 1991 have so far failed to bring this violence to a halt.

In March 1990 Buthelezi unveiled *The 1990 Inkatha Declaration* (seen as a rival to the ANC's *Harare Declaration)* which set out the Inkatha view of a future South Africa. In summary, it is a Western-style liberal democracy, with a universal adult

---

46. This was admitted by Nelson Mandela when, shortly after his release, he stated at a rally in Durban: "Although there are fundamental differences between us, we commend Inkatha for their demand over the years for the unbanning of the ANC and the release of political prisoners, as well as for their stand of refusing to participate in a negotiated settlement without the creation of the necessary climate." *Sowetan* (SA), 26 March 1989.

franchise, freedom of speech, an independent judiciary, the right to private property, freedom of religion, etc. In marked contrast to the ANC, Inkatha stresses that wealth redistribution should come about largely through the provision of equal opportunities, hence Buthelezi has argued for deregulation of the economy and the general provision of educational and training skills. In his address to the Inkatha Business Forum in July 1990, Buthelezi stated that Inkatha would not follow policies which had failed in the Soviet Union, but would proceed from the basic assumption of an 'enterprise-driven' economy.[47]

In July 1990, Inkatha relaunched and reorganised itself as a multi-racial political party, the Inkatha Freedom Party (IFP). At that time it stated it had a membership of 1.8 million members which, according to a party spokesman, rose to approximately 2.2 million members a year later - 42% of whom were claimed to be non-Zulu, including an estimated 100,000 whites.[48]

Initially Inkatha fully supported De Klerk's reform process, and stated in February 1990 that it was ready to start serious negotiations with the government immediately. The IFP has stated that constitutionally a one-man one-vote system of government in a unitary South Africa is ideal, but "for expediency is prepared to negotiate a federal, canton, or other system of government which expresses the basic principles of democracy."[49] It has been opposed

---

47. For further details see *Race Relations Survey, 1989/90*.
48. Interview with Suzanne Vos, July 1991.
49. *Echo* (SA), 16 November 1989.

to the ANC demand for a constituent assembly on the grounds that this would limit multiparty negotiations since "one party could dominate it numerically and write provisions into the consitution to benefit itself alone."[50]

The IFP suffered a severe political setback in Summer 1991 by the news that in 1989 and 1990 it had received a total of R250,000 (about £52,000) from secret government funds in order to enable it to stage political rallies and generally to strengthen it vis-a-vis the ANC. This has called its political independence into doubt. However, compared with the ANC, the IFP has received very little money from overseas. As far as increasing its black support is concerned, Inkatha is hampered by being seen as a predominantly Zulu organisation. Its support is heavily concentrated in the province of Natal - the Zulu heartland - and its best chance of significant power-sharing in the new South Africa would be via some sort of federal system. IFP leaders refused to sign the 'Statement of Intent' arising from the December 1991 CODESA meeting presumably because its commitment to "bring about an undivided South Africa" appeared to rule out such a federal system.

LABOUR PARTY (LP)

The Labour Party was established in 1965 by a group of coloured South Africans opposed to apartheid. In the 1989 tri-cameral elections it won 69 seats in the

---

50. Dr. Gavin Woods, executive director of the Inkatha Institute, quoted in *Business Day* (SA), 1 February 1991.

85-seat coloured chamber of parliament (House of Representatives) and so formed the ruling party under the leadership of the Rev. Allan Hendrickse. The LP has advocated a democratic, multi-racial society based on a mainly free-enterprise economic system. Within parliament, it has suffered a series of defections to the National Party and it is expected that this will continue, both in parliament and at grassroots level.

NATIONAL PARTY (NP)
The National Party has been the ruling political party in South Africa since 1948, and was responsible for introducing the apartheid system. In recent years, however, the party has embarked on a programme of political reform (see Appendix 2) and this has been greatly accelerated under F. W. De Klerk who took over the leadership of the party in 1989. In September 1989 the National Party produced a Plan of Action which declared that "discrimination between groups or against individuals based on race, colour, sex, religion or group affiliation is unacceptable. Where discrimination still exists it must be eliminated in an orderly fashion." Accordingly, the present National Party government has now abolished virtually all of South Africa's apartheid legislation. In so doing, it has been losing much of its traditional Afrikaner support to the Conservative Party, although it has gained white liberal support from the Democratic Party. In 1990 the NP voted to open its ranks to all races and, according to surveys during 1991, approximately one half of all coloureds would now support the National Party,[51] and even

---

51. *International Update* (SA), May 1991.

possibly 18% of urban blacks.[52]

In the past the NP has favoured a highly-regulated, semi-socialist approach to the economy (approximately 60% of industry and commerce was controlled by the State) but soon after taking office De Klerk took some steps to deregulate the economy and privatise a few State concerns. This was opposed by the ANC and the programme has been shelved.

The NP now accepts the idea of one nation in an undivided South Africa and is committed to the extension of the vote to all South Africans for a unitary parliament. Its preference would be for a constitution which would protect minority rights and include some sort of decentralisation of power, devolution of authority, constitutional checks and balances, and an independent judiciary.[53] In September 1991, the NP published detailed proposals for such a constitution which, if adopted, would result in a power-sharing agreement between political parties. These were immediately dismissed by the ANC, and many of these proposals were dropped in December 1991 at the start of the formal negotiations for a new constitution at the Convention for a Democratic South Africa (CODESA).

The NP opposed ANC/Azapo/PAC demands for a constituent assembly, arguing that a new constitution must be negotiated by the representatives of all parties committed to a peaceful and negotiated

---

52. Markinor survey reported in *Sunday Times* (SA), 16 June 1991.
53. F. W. De Klerk, parliamentary speech, 19 April 1990.

settlement.[54] It also opposed their initial demands for an interim government, saying that the present legally-constituted government cannot simply relinquish its powers.[55] The NP has, however, been trying to negotiate an acceptable new transitional constitution with those political parties and homeland leaders taking part in CODESA. Having gained overwhelming support for his reforms in a whites-only referendum held in March 1992, De Klerk now feels he has the mandate to move ahead to the etablishment of an all-party, multi-racial Interim Government Council (IGC) which will be representative of all organisations participating in CODESA and could be in place by Summer 1992. De Klerk, his Cabinet and the present three-chamber parliament would remain in place during this phase, but would legislate only in close consultation with CODESA-appointed comissions and committees that will have powers to draft legislation and veto Cabinet initiatives. In other words, CODESA is emerging as a *de facto* interim coalition government, dominated by the National Party and the ANC.

PAN AFRICAN CONGRESS (PAC)

The PAC was formed in 1959 by a group of ANC members, led by Robert Sobukwe, who left the movement because of the growing influence of the South African Communist Party and the resultant abandonment of black nationalism. The PAC's long-term political goal for South Africa is an African socialist state (Azania) in which all land would be

---

54. *Hansard* (SA), 1 col. 6, 1 February 1991.
55. *Hansard* (SA), 1 col. 7, 1 February 1991.

redistributed amongst the Africans and which would be part of a wider 'United States of Africa'.[56] Like the ANC, the PAC was banned in 1960 and went into exile, establishing bases in Tanzania and Zimbabwe. It was shunned by the Soviet Union, but survived largely thanks to Libyan and Chinese support. It is committed to the armed struggle and has a military wing, *Poqo* ("pure" - meaning a purely African character), which modelled itself on the Kenyan *Mau Mau* and under the slogan of "one settler one bullet" was responsible in the 1960s for a number of terrorist attacks on whites and moderate blacks, particularly in the Cape.

The PAC was unbanned in February 1990, following which it initially gained a surge of support at the expense of the ANC. The PAC attitude to the government remains inflexible: the 1991 Congress confirmed its rejection of the government's invitation to negotiations; called for a strengthening of sanctions; and stood by its demand that land and resources should be returned to the African people. The president, Clarence Makwetu, also affirmed that the PAC would maintain the armed struggle. The PAC has also kept up its contact with the People's Republic of China.[57]

There are marked ideological and tactical differences between the PAC and ANC, but in Summer 1991 efforts by the Patriotic Front of Zimbabwe brought the leaders of the two

---

56. See Mokgethi Motlhabi, *op. cit.*, pp. 45-46.
57. At the invitation of the central committee of the Chinese Communist Party, a PAC delegation visited China in November 1990. See *Race Relations Survey, 1989/90*.

organisations together in Harare to discuss the possible establishment of a 'broad-based national front'. A PAC/ANC liaison committee was set up and, in October 1991, 450 organisations largely aligned to the PAC or ANC came together at a 'Patriotic Front' Conference in Durban to work out a common strategy for talks with the government.[58] The PAC supported the ANC demand for a constituent assembly and has refused to sign the September 1991 Peace Accord, or to take part in the CODESA negotiations for a new constitution.

SOLIDARITY

Solidarity is the ruling party in the House of Delegates (the Indian chamber of Parliament). It favours a multi-party federal constitution in a single South African Parliament, with representation for minorities at all levels of government. Ultimately it favours a highly free-enterprise economy, but argues that South Africa will need a mixed economy for many years to come to redress racially-based economic imbalances.

SOUTH AFRICAN COMMUNIST PARTY (SACP)
(See also ANC)

The Communist Party of South Africa (CPSA), founded in 1921, was the first Communist Party in Africa. It was accepted for affiliation to the Third Communist International (Comintern) created by Lenin to unite and direct the communist movements

---

58. *The Times,* 16 April 1991 and *Pretoria News* (SA), 18 June 1991

of the world, and has been loyal to the Soviet Union ever since.[59] In 1927 it was directed by Moscow to form a 'black republic' in South Africa and, in pursuit of this objective, it set about trying to gain control of the ANC. Ironically, this process was accelerated by the 1950 Suppression of Communism Act, in anticipation of which the CPSA dissolved, black members joined the ANC, and Indians and whites joined the SA Indian Congress and SA Congress of Deputies respectively. In addition, an illegal underground South African Communist Party (SACP) was created. It is the SACP which is thought to have been behind the establishment of *Umkhonto we Sizwe*, the armed wing of the ANC, and responsible for the ANC's guiding policy document, the *Freedom Charter*.[60]

---

59. For instance, it supported the Soviet invasion of Hungary, Czechoslovakia and Afghanistan and backed the Polish government against Solidarity - see Professor Heribert Adam, "Eastern Europe and South African Socialism - Engaging Joe Slovo" in *South Africa International,* July 1990. ANC Executive member and Director of Information, Pallo Jordan, has denounced the SACP for "consistently praising every violation of freedom perpetrated by the Soviet leadership before and after Stalin's death." See *The Times,* 19 June 1990.

60. See Ngubane *op. cit.* Bartholemew Hlapane, a former member of the Central Committee of the South African Communist Party and of the National Executive of the ANC, testified before a United States' Senate Subcommittee (the Denton Committee) hearing in November 1982 that: "the Military Wing of the ANC, also known as Umkhonto we Sizwe, was the brainchild of the SACP, and, after the decision to create it had been taken, Joe Slovo and J. B. Marks were sent by the Central Commitee of the SACP to Moscow to organize arms and ammunition and to raise funds for Umkhonto we Sizwe."

Although relatively small, the SACP is highly significant in South African politics because it has continued to exercise considerable, if not controlling, influence over the ANC ever since the mid-1950s.[61] For instance, before the ANC's July 1991 Congress, various estimates put the proportion of ANC National Executive Committee members who were also members of the SACP at anything from one half to two thirds.[62] After that Congress, at least 45 members of the expanded 90-strong NEC were thought to be SACP members.[63]

At its Seventh Congress, held in Cuba in July 1989, the SACP adopted a new official programme, *The Path to Power*. This envisages a two-stage

---

61. Hlapane stated to the Denton committee that, during the years in which he served the ANC and SACP, "no major decision could be taken by the ANC without the concurrence and approval of the Central Committee of the South African Communist Party. Most major developments were in fact initiated by the Central Committee."

62. A report in the *Sunday Telegraph*, 1 July 1990, stated that "intelligence reports show that more than 400 of the top 500 people in the ANC are also members of the SACP, and that recent claims that 27 of the 35 members of the ANC's National Executive Committee are SACP members are 'substantially correct'." Further details were provided in an article by Warwick Davies-Webb in the *Sunday Times* (SA), 5 May 1991, who concluded that "SACP influence throughout ANC structures is all-encompassing." In a statement issued on the 79th anniversary of the ANC, Nelson Mandela declared that: "this unity also requires that we further reinforce our alliance with the South African Communist Party and COSATU and defeat the hostile efforts to drive wedges among the member organisations of this alliance." (ANC London office, 8 January 1991).

63. See *The Times*, 8 July 1991 and *The Citizen* (SA), 8 July 1991 and 10 July 1991.

revolution in South Africa - first a 'national democratic state' based on the principles of the Freedom Charter, with a mixed economy but expanding 'popular control' over vital sectors of the economy, would be established; later this would be followed by a second stage during which a fully socialist state would be set up. The programme also argues that the armed struggle needed to shift away from guerilla warfare to mass insurrection.[64]

The SACP was unbanned on 2nd February 1990 and held its first major 'above-ground' meeting on 29th July of that year. Soon after the unbanning, the then general secretary, Joe Slovo, declared that the "emphasis of the SACP will now be on building a mass, above-board party whose membership is not secret". Since then, membership of the SACP has risen from an estimated 2,000 to 25,000 in December 1991.[65]

The SACP has been in some ideological confusion since the collapse of communism in Eastern Europe and the former Soviet Union. Slovo, who stated that until 1989 he was an "unrepentant Stalinist", continued to stress the virtues of Marxism

---

64. *New Era,* August 1989. See also Sisa Majola, "The Two Stages of our Revolution" in *The African Communist,* March 1987.
65. *Sunday Telegraph,* 8 December 1991.

in his 1990 pamphlet, *Has Socialism Failed?*,[66] but more recently, to the chagrin of some of his more hard-line comrades, he began to espouse a social democratic future for the SACP. In December 1991, the SACP held its first legal Congress within South Africa for forty years, and Chris Hani (formerly head of the MK) was elected SACP general secretary in place of Slovo who was forced to resign because of failing health. This Congress reaffirmed its support for Marxism-Leninism - Hani has since stated that socialist governments collapsed in Eastern Europe and the Soviet Union only because they "practised a distorted form of socialism."[67] According to Hani, the Congress also decided that there should be "mass action by the people to push the process of liberation forward" and that "if negotiations fail, we'll have no choice but to fight."[68]

During 1990/91 some signs of strain in the ANC/SACP alliance began to emerge, particularly relating to the ANC decision to 'suspend' the armed struggle. For this reason the SACP has begun to develop independent grassroots support bases. These

---

66. He stated that: "We believe ... that the theory of Marxism, in all its essential respects, remains valid and provides an indispensable theoretical guide to achieve a society free of all forms of exploitation of person by person." He went on to state that "the major weaknesses which have emerged in the practice of socialism are the results of distortions and misapplications. They do not flow naturally from the basic concepts of Marxism whose core is essentially humane and democratic and which project a social order with an economic potential vastly superior to capitalism."
67. Interview with Hani in *Learn and Teach* (SA), February 1992.
68. *Ibid.*

are chiefly within COSATU, where many senior organisers have revealed themselves to be SACP members, and also within the newly-established civic associations which are members of the Civic Associations of Southern Transvaal (CAST).[69] Nevertheless, it is still its presence within the ANC which gives the SACP most power and influence. The ANC's December 1991 Congress strongly reaffirmed the ANC/SACP/COSATU alliance.

UNITED DEMOCRATIC FRONT (UDF)

The UDF was launched in August 1983 as an alliance of political, civic, youth, student and trade union organisations, with patrons including Nelson Mandela, and Church leaders like Beyers Naudé and Allan Boesak. At one time the UDF claimed to have between 700 and 800 affiliated groups and more than 2.5 million members.[70] Like the National Forum - see Black Consciousness Movement above - its immediate objective was to present a united front to oppose the government's plans to establish a tricameral parliamentary system, with Indian and coloured but not black houses of parliament. However, adopting a 'Charterist' rather than black consciousness ideology (the UDF formally adopted the ANC Freedom Charter in 1987), the UDF included groups of all races and all classes.

---

69. Warwick Davies-Webb, *Umkhonto we Sizwe and the South African Communist Party* (International Freedom Foundation, June 1991).
70. *Race Relations Survey, 1987/88*. However, since many of these groups were very small, with overlapping membership, it is possible that these claims were exaggerated - see Radu, *op. cit.*

The broader aim of the UDF was to destabilise the country as part of the wider 'liberation struggle' by first attempting to isolate the government from any sort of support at national or local level. This involved demands that the government should unban the ANC and release all political prisoners and that the international community should impose tough economic sanctions against South Africa. It also saw the beginnings of widespread mass action with worker stay-aways, disruption of black education, rent strikes, and the boycotting of shops belonging to whites. Starting in September 1984 there was an upsurge of violence in the townships as young radicals in the UDF and the National Forum vied with each other for support, clashed with followers of Inkatha, or forced more moderate blacks to support the strikes and boycots. Intimidation included the use of 'people's courts' and the horrendous 'necklace' method of execution for 'informers' and those like black councillors and police officers who were regarded as stooges of the white regime. It was this rising tide of violence in the townships which resulted in the government's declaration of a partial state of emergency in July 1985, lifted in February 1986, but imposed again as a national state of emergy in June 1986. On 24 February 1988, under the emergency regulations, the government placed severe restrictions on the activities of the UDF and sixteen other organisations, fourteen of which were associated with the UDF. This was a severe blow as it meant that the UDF was unable to accept overseas money, from which it derived more than half of its funds.[71] The organisation increased its support base by entering

---

71. Radu, *op. cit.*

into an alliance with Congress of South African Trade Unions and associated organisations to form the **Mass Democratic Movement (MDM)**.

The aims of the UDF have been closely linked to those of the ANC and, during the years when the ANC was banned and in exile, it was viewed by many as the ANC's 'internal wing'. With the unbanning of the ANC, the UDF decided to disband on 20 August 1991 and, prior to this, it issued a statement which "urged its affiliates to devote their energies to the building of the ANC, our ideological senior and mentor".[72] National secretary, Popo Molefe said that although not all UDF members were ANC members, the majority were, and he and many former UDF leaders have now assumed leadership positions within the ANC. At the July 1991 ANC National Congress, fourteen former UDF leaders were voted onto the new ANC National Executive Committee.

---

72. See Kaizer Nyatsumba, "The UDF and the future" in *South Africa Foundation Review*, March 1991.

APPENDIX 2: The Reform Process

From 1948 onwards, South Africa's ruling National Party extended apartheid restrictions into virtually every area of life so that where people lived, their right to own property, their standard of education, their type of work, whom they married, their access to public amenities and services, their right to vote, and their general social status, were all determined by their race classification. Starting in the 1970s, however, these restrictions and certain other security restrictions have been progressively relaxed as follows:

1973
• Restrictions on black people doing semi-skilled jobs relaxed.

1978-1985
• Most hotels, restaurants, cinemas, theatres, libraries, public transport and sports facilities (including the beaches) made multi-racial.

1979-1984
• Desegregation of trade unions and work places.

1981
- Black trade unions legalised.
- Job reservations for whites (except for some in the mining industry) eliminated.

1982
- Introduction of black local government.
- Black South Africans join government and parastatal boards.

1983
- New South African constitution extends national voting rights to Asians and coloureds.
- Black local government elections.
- Universities desegregated.

1984
- Uniform income tax laws for all population groups.

1985
- Abolition of the Prohibition of Mixed Marriages Act and the 1950 and 1957 Immorality Acts (which banned sexual intercourse across the colour bar).
- Granting of permanent residential rights to blacks who had been resident in a primarily white area since birth or for longer than ten years.
- Abolition of the Prohibition of Political Interference Act, so enabling the formation of racially mixed political parties.
- First cabinet to include non-whites.
- Urban business districts opened to businesses of all races.

- All racial clauses contained in immigration regulations removed.

1986
- Abolition of controls on the movement of blacks in South Africa.
- Issue of uniform identity documents to all South Africans without reference to race.
- South African citizenship restored to all, regardless of race or tribal 'homeland' (however, about 8-9 million citizens in the 'independent homelands' - Transkei, Bophuthatswana, Venda, and Ciskei - are unaffected by this legislation).
- Granting of property rights to blacks so enabling them to buy property in the townships.
- All-white Provincial councils abolished. Blacks, whites, coloureds and Asians appointed to executive committees to govern the provinces.
- Separate black courts abolished.
- Partial relaxation of the Group Areas Act, so making it easier for blacks to live in designated white areas.

1987
- Establishment of a joint executive authority between Natal and KwaZulu.

1988
- Provision for non-racial local government within free settlement areas.
- Desegregation of suburban train services.
- Removal of white job protection in the mining industry.

1990
- Lifting of the prohibition on the ANC, PAC, South African Communist Party and related organisations.
- Release of Nelson Mandela and other political prisoners.
- Lifting of emergency regulation restrictions on 33 organisations.
- Abolition of emergency regulations relating to education and the media.
- Partial scrapping of Group Areas Act, so opening industrial and business areas to all races.
- Lifting of State of Emergency in all areas excluding Natal and KwaZulu (8 June).
- Use of death penalty greatly restricted and automatic review procedures introduced.
- Reservation of Public Amenities Act scrapped so opening all public facilities to all races. (There is, however, no specific legislation outlawing the segregation of facilities and a number of Conservative Party controlled munipalities have continued to practice *de facto* segregation through very high fees.)
- Government announces desegregation of all health services and proposes single health policy (in practice, however, the administrators of a number of hospitals have still not desegregated them).
- Government announces that white state schools will be allowed to vote on whether to admit black pupils.
- Lifting of State of Emergency in Natal and KwaZulu.

1991
- 10% of white schools vote to open their doors to

black pupils.
• Additional funds allocated in the Budget for the upgrading of black housing, education and welfare. The gap between black and white old-aged pension reduced by 20%, although differentials remain.
• Internal Security and Intimidation Amendment Act reduces police powers of detention to ten days and makes the promotion of communism no longer an offence.
• Repeal of the Land Acts of 1913 and 1936, the Group Areas Act of 1966, and other legislation which had placed racially-based restrictions on where people could live and their tenure of land.
• Population Registration Act 1950 scrapped. Newborn babies freed from race classification (but existing race classifications in the population register to remain until the present constitution is abolished).
• 1982 Internal Security Act amended so as to impose strict limits on detention of terrorist suspects, curtail government powers to ban organisations, and abolish restrictions on publications and individuals.
• Multi-party negotiations start for a new constitution which would give all races the vote.

APPENDIX 3: WCC Grants to 'Organisations Combating Racism'
(thousands of US dollars)

	1970	1971	1973	1974	1975	1976	1979	1978	1979	1980	1981
ANGOLA											
UNITA	10	7.5	6	14	-	-	-	-	-	-	-
MPLA	20	25	10	23	-	-	-	-	-	-	-
GRAE	20	7.5	10	23	-	-	-	-	-	-	-
GUINEA-BISSAU											
PAIGC	20	25	25	100	-	-	-	-	-	-	-
MOZAMBIQUE											
FRELIMO	15	20	25	60	-	-	-	-	-	-	-
RHODESIA (ZIMBABWE)											
African National Council	-	-	-	-	83	-	-	-	-	-	-
Patriotic Front	20	10	-	30	-	85	85	-	35	-	-
SOUTH AFRICA											
ANC	10	5	2.5	15	45	50	25	25	-	150	65
PAC	-	-	2.5	15	45	50	25	25	-	-	45
SACTU	-	-	-	-	-	5	5	5	5	-	15
SOUTH WEST AFRICA (NAMIBIA)											
SWAPO	5	25	20	30	83.5	85	125	125	-	200	125
TANZANIA											
Sixth Pan African Congress	-	-	-	12.0	-	-	-	-	-	-	-
ZAMBIA											
Africa 2000 Congress	15.0	5.0	-	-	-	-	-	-	-	-	-
(WORLD TOTAL GRANTS)	200	200	200	450	479	560	530	434.5	349	775.5	587
GRANTS TO SOUTH AFRICA AS PERCENTAGE OF WORLD TOTAL GRANTS	5.0	2.5	2.5	6.7	18.8	18.7	10.4	12.6	1.4	19.3	21.3

Note: No grants were made in 1972.

	1982	1983	1984	1985	1986	1987	1988	1989	1990	1991	Total
ANGOLA											
UNITA	-	-	-	-	-	-	-	-	-	-	37.5
MPLA	-	-	-	-	-	-	-	-	-	-	78.0
GRAE	-	-	-	-	-	-	-	-	-	-	60.5
GUINEA-BISSAU											
PAIGC	-	-	-	-	-	-	-	-	-	-	170.0
MOZAMBIQUE											
FRELIMO	-	-	-	-	-	-	-	-	-	-	120.0
RHODESIA (ZIMBABWE)											
African National Council	-	-	-	-	-	-	-	-	-	-	83.5
Patriotic Front	-	-	-	-	-	-	-	-	-	-	265.5
SOUTH AFRICA											
ANC	65	70	70	77	80	110	105	100	141	141	1,351.5
PAC	45	50	30	33	26	35	45	67	94	94	726.5
SACTU	-	10	-	5	10	10	20	20	-	-	110.0
SOUTH WEST AFRICA (NAMIBIA)											
SWAPO	100	105	100	110	110	115	150	165	-	-	1,778.5
TANZANIA											
Sixth Pan African Congress	-	-	-	-	-	-	-	-	-	-	12.0
ZAMBIA											
Africa 2000 Congress	-	-	-	-	-	-	-	-	-	-	20.0
(WORLD TOTAL GRANTS)	489.5	446	400	396	400	529	635	635	549	505	9,749.5
GRANTS TO SOUTH AFRICA AS PERCENTAGE OF WORLD TOTAL GRANTS	22.5	29.1	25.0	29.0	29.0	29.3	26.7	29.4	42.8	46.5	

Sources: The figures for 1970-78 are taken from Appendix F in E. Lefever, *Amsterdam to Nairobi* (Ethics and Public Policy Center, 1979). The 1979-1991 figures have been compiled from annual press releases issued by the World Council of Churches.

Key to Abbreviations: UNITA - National Union for the Total Independence of Angola; MPLA - People's Movement for the Liberation of Angola; GRAE - Revolutionary Government of Angola in Exile; PAIGC - African Independence Party of Guinea and Cape Verde Islands; FRELIMO - Frente de Libertação de Angola; ANC - African National Congress; PAC - Pan Africanist Congress of Azania; SACTU - South African Congress of Trade Unions; SWAPO - South West African People's Organisation.

APPENDIX 4: Ecumenical Association of Third World Theologians

EATWOT grew out of two initiatives. In 1974 Fr. François Houtart of the European Centre for Latin American Studies at Louvain University, Belgium, started to examine the possibility of a conference amongst radical Catholic theologians in Africa, Asia and Latin America. Secondly, at a conference held in Detroit in 1975 (which brought together Latin American liberation theologians and American Black Theologians) the Latin Americans expressed an interest in meeting other radical theologians from Asia and Africa. They decided to join forces with those involved in the Louvain initiative and, following the 1975 General Assembly of the WCC in Nairobi at which contacts were made with like-minded Third World theologians, a steering committee was set up consisting of J. R. Chandran and D. S. Amalorpavadass (India), Ngindu Mushete (Zaire), Enrique Dussel (Mexico), José Míguez Bonino (Argentina) and Manas Buthelezi (South Africa). They contacted the WCC, the Theological Education Fund, the All Africa Conference of Churches, and the Christian Conference of Asia for support.

Their first conference, entitled an Ecumenical Dialogue of Third World Theologians, was held in Dar es Salaam, Tanzania, in August 1976. It was attended by twenty-two theologians from Africa, Asia and Latin America.

The conference adopted a highly pro-socialist and anti-Western political stance. According to the final statement, the main cause for underdevelopment in the Third World was "systematic exploitation of their peoples and countries by the European peoples" in the past, and exploitation by American, European and Japanese multinational companies in the present. The conference regarded with favour the economies of China, North Korea, North Vietnam, and Cuba as well as the newer socialist countries in Africa and elsewhere. It saw the Soviet Union and Eastern Europe as a "valuable counterbalance against imperialistic domination by the North Atlantic powers."[1]

Against this background, the conference considered the role of the Church and theology in the Third World. It concluded that there were now two major forms of theology - the theology of liberation, and the theologies from Europe and North America which were regarded as a form of "cultural domination". The final statement thus declared:[2]

> "we reject as irrelevant an academic type of theology that is divorced from action. We are prepared for a radical break in epistemology which makes commitment the first act of theology and engages in critical reflection on the praxis of the reality of the Third World."

---

1. S. Torres and V. Fabella (eds.), *The Emergent Gospel: Theology from the Underside of History* (Geoffrey Chapman, 1978), p. 263.
2. *Ibid.* p. 269.

It continued:[3]

> "We call for an active commitment to the promotion of justice and the prevention of exploitation, the accumulation of wealth in the hands of a few, racism, sexism, and all other forms of oppression, discrimination, and dehumanization ... this also means being committed to a lifestyle of solidarity with the poor and the oppressed and involvement in action with them ... Theology is not neutral ... In a sense all theology is committed, conditioned notably by the socio-cultural context in which it is developed."

Thus the statement put forward the following objectives:[4]

> "1. Sharing with one another the present trends of interpretation of the gospel in the different Third World countries, particularly bearing in mind the roles of theology in relation to other faiths and ideologies as well as the struggle for a just society;
> 2. promoting the exchange of theological views through writings in the books and periodicals of Third World countries;
> 3. promoting the mutual interaction between theological formulation and social analysis;
> 4. keeping close contacts as well as being involved with action-orientated movements for social change."

---
3. *Ibid.* p. 270.
4. *Ibid.* p. 273.

EATWOT was formed to further these objectives. It established research committees on Church History, Women, and Theological Studies, each of which holds periodical international gatherings. The Association held its second general conference in Accra in 1977 on the theme of African Theology, at which James Cone was a major contributor.[5] A third conference took place Sri Lanka in 1979;[6] and the fourth, in Säo Paulo in 1980, considered Basic Christian Communities.[7] Further international conferences have been held in New Dehli, in 1981,[8] and Geneva, in 1983.[9] In 1986 a second general assembly was held in Oaxtepec, Mexico.[10] The most recent international EATWOT meeting was its third general assembly, held in Nairobi in January 1992.

---

5. Kofi Appiah-Kubi and Sergio Torres (eds.), *African Theology en Route* (Orbis, 1979).
6. V. Fabella (ed.), *Asia's Struggle for Full Humanity* (Orbis, 1980).
7. S. Torres and J. Eagleson (eds.), *The Challenge of Basic Christian Communities* (Orbis, 1981).
8. V. Fabella and S. Torres (eds.), *Irruption of the Third World: Challenge to Theology* (Orbis, 1983).
9. V. Fabella and S. Torres (eds.), *Doing Theology in a Divided World* (Orbis, 1983).
10. K. C. Abraham (ed.), *Third World Theologies: commonalities and divergences* (Orbis, 1990).

APPENDIX 5: Grants Received by the Institute for Contextual Theology (Rand)

	1987	1988
Algemeen Gereformeerde	11,863	-
Christian Aid, UK	30,576	9,795
CAFOD, UK	18,984	-
Advieskommissie Missionaire Aktivititeiten (AMA), Netherlands	13,743	16,590
Commission on Inter Church Aid	8,040	35,674
CCODP	9,206	11,058
Church of Sweden	16,179	42,936
Diakonia, Sweden	38,250	16,893
Entraide et Fraternité	10,107	14,295
HEKS, Switzerland	30,202	38,671
Missionwerk - Protestant	24,559	-
Trocaire, Ireland	4,424	22,335
United Church of Canada	18,052	41,704
SA Catholic Bishops' Conference	4,662	-
Archbishop Hurley Trust	4,500	-
Comité Catholique Contre la Faim et pour le Développement (CCFD), France	-	19,230
Weltgebetstag der Frauen	-	3,500
Evangelisches Missionswerk,	-	27,321
Mission of Reformed Churches	-	11,970
Methodist Church in South Africa	-	3,315
Dreikoningstrat	-	33,778
Swiss Catholic Lenten Fund	-	14,865
(Less funds incorrectly allocated in previous years	-	(6,628)
TOTAL GRANTS RECEIVED	**243,347**	**357,303**
Membership Fees	3,039	3,422
Other income	2,853	17,709
TOTAL INCOME	**249,239**	**378,434**

Source: ICT Annual Financial Statements

APPENDIX 6: The Harare Declaration

We, leaders of churches from Western Europe, North America, Australia, South Africa and other parts of Africa, along with representatives of WCC (World Council of Churches), WARC (World Alliance of Reformed Churches), LWF (Lutheran World Federation) and AACC (All African Conference of Churches) met here in Harare, Zimbabwe, from the 4th to the 6th December 1985 on the invitation of the World Council of Churches.

We have come together to seek God's guidance at this time of profound crisis in South Africa, and have committed ourselves to a continuing theological reflection on the will of God for the church. We affirm that the moment of truth (KAIROS) is now, both for South Africa and the world community. We have heard the cries of anguish of the people of South Africa trapped in the oppressive structures of apartheid. In this moment, of immense potentiality, we agree that the apartheid structure is against God's will, and is morally indefensible. The government has no credibility. We call for an end to the State of Emergency, the release of Nelson Mandela and all political prisoners, the lifting of the state of emergency, the unbanning of all banned movements, and the return of exiles. The transferring of power to the majority of the people, based on universal suffrage, is the only lasting solution to the present crisis.

We understand and fully support those in South Africa who are calling for the resignation of the government. We regard this as the most appropriate and least costly process of change and as a contribution towards such change. As we await a new democratic and representative government in South Africa, then:
1. We call on the Church inside and outside South Africa to continue praying for the people of South Africa and to observe June 16th - the tenth anniversary of the Soweto uprising - as

World Day of Prayer and Fast to end unjust rule in South Africa.
2. We call on the international community to prevent the extension, rolling over, or renewal of bank loans to the South Africa government, banks, corporations and para-state institutions.
3. We call on the international community to apply immediate and comprehensive sanctions on South Africa.
4. We call on the Church inside and outside South Africa to support South African movements working for the liberation of their country.
5. We welcome and support the recent developments within the Trade Union movement for a united front against apartheid.
6. We demand the immediate implementation of the United Nations Resolution 435 on Namibia.

We, gathered here, commit ourselves to the implementation of the Harare Declaration as a matter of urgency. We are confident that the liberation of South Africa will be liberation for all the people in our country, black and white.

APPENDIX 7: The Lusaka Statement

We, representatives of churches, trade unions, Women's, Youth and anti-apartheid groups from South Africa, Namibia and other parts of the world, met in Lusaka, Zambia, May 4-8, 1987 at the invitation of the Programme to Combat Racism of the World Council Churches under the theme "The Churches' Search for Justice and Peace in Southern Africa."

THE THEOLOGY
It is our belief that civil authority is instituted of God to do good, and that under the biblical imperative all people are obliged to do justice and show special care for the oppressed and the poor. It is this understanding that leaves us with no alternative but to conclude that the South African regime and its colonial domination of Namibia is illegitimate.

We recognise that the people of South Africa and Namibia who are yearning for justice and peace, have identified the liberation movements of their countries to be authentic vehicles that express their aspirations for self-determination.

We as churches also recognise and repent of our failure to work as vigorously as possible for the implementation of the Harare Declaration as a basis for bringing the present regime in South Africa and Namibia to an end. We again commit ourselves to the Harare Declaration, and so to work for the removal of the present rulers who persistently usurp the stewardship of God's authority.

THE CHALLENGE
1. We call on the Churches and international community to recognise the overwhelming material sacrifice and suffering of the people of the Frontline States in combating apartheid and the destablilizing influence of the Pretoria regime in the region.

This necessitates an immediate and enhanced programme of aid and assistance to the Frontline States through the Southern Africa Development Co-ordination Council and other agencies in order to reduce their dependance upon South Africa and to enable them to continue to support both refugee victims of apartheid and those movements actively engaged in the struggle of liberation.

2. We affirm the unquestionable right of the people of Namibia and South Africa to secure justice and peace through the liberation movements. While remaining committed to peaceful change we recognize that the nature of the South African regime which wages war againgst its own inhabitants and neighbours compels the movements to the use of force along with other means to end oppression. We call upon the Churches and the international community to seek ways to give this affirmation practical effect in the struggle for liberation in the region and to strengthen their contacts with the liberation movements.

3. We affirm that the end to the conflict in Namibia and the attainment of self determination by the Namibian people lies in the implementation of UN Security Council Resolution 435 (1978). We therefore condemn the attempt by the United States, in collusion with other members of the Western Contact Group and with the minority government of South Africa, to bypass this resolution by linking the independence of Namibia to extraneous issues such as the withdrawal of Cuban troops from Angola. We recognise the willingness of SWAPO, the sole and authentic representative of the people of Namibia, to enter into an immediate ceasefire on the basis of UN Security Council Resolution 435. We call upon the churches to mark the 10th Anniversary year of the UN Security Council Resolution 435 with a programme of action to end the colonial domination of Namibia. We further call upon the church to observe May 4th as a World Day of Prayer for a free Namibia.

4. We urgently call upon the Churches in countries which, through economic and political co-operation with South Africa and Namibia, support the Apartheid regime, to exert increased pressure upon their governments to implement sanctions, and upon banks, corporations and trading institutions to withdraw

from doing business with South Africa and Namibia. We especially call upon the international community not to engage in newly devised deceptive forms of disinvestment which maintain the status quo, but instead to apply immediate and comprehensive sanctions to South Africa and Namibia.

5. We note with the gravest concern the growing number of those imprisoned, tortured, on trial, under sentence of death, and bereaved as a result of the actions of the apartheid regime. We call upon the Churches, especially those outside Namibia and South Africa to respond with prayer and increased efforts to publicise and meet with material assistance the needs and concerns of those who bear this particular burden of apartheid.

6. We condemn the censorship of the media and the concerted campaign of misinformation directed by the apartheid regime and its collaborators against the opponents and victims of apartheid. We call upon the Churches and the international community to take steps to secure the freedom of information about and within South Africa through their own, and if necessary, new mechanisms, thus insuring the fair and objective reporting of events in the region.

7. We recognise, at this crucial time (Kairos) in the history of Southern Africa, the need for unity of purpose and action of the part of all those concerned with the process of liberation in the region, not least amongst the Churches themselves whose failings in this respect are a cause for repentance. We see the suffering that results when unity is not present. We commit ourselves to further the cause of unity in our own churches, and in our ministry to the movements for liberation operating to bring an end to the illegitimate regime in South Africa and Namibia.

8. We call upon the WCC, in the light of the Harare Declaration and the previous resolutions, to establish, with urgency a mechanism whereby the progress of member Churches and others in implementing the Harare Declaration and these resolutions can be monitored, and through appropriate advice and encouragement, made more effective. Special attention should be given to the implementation of economic sanctions.

This monitoring process should occur at national, regional and international levels. We recommend that further meetings of churches, liberation movements and others be held within eighteen months to review the results of the monitoring process.

In the past we have often failed to move from resolution to practice. We recognise that it is God's imperative that we be God's obedient instrument in the struggle for justice and peace in Southern Africa. We pray for God's grace and covenant together to accompany our brothers and sisters in Namibia and South Africa on their journey to liberation.

THE LUSAKA ACTION PLAN
The WCC should send a delegation of Eminent Church Persons on a mission to the United States, United Kingdom, Federal Republic of Germany, Japan, the European Community Secretariat in Brussels, permanent member states of the Security Council of the United Nations and the Contact Group nations on Namibia. This group should:

1.1. call for the immediate and unconditional implementation of UN Security Council Resolution 435 (1978) and underline the critical urgency for the churches and the people of Namibia of an end to the prevailing impasse which generates increased pain and suffering;

1.2. call for the immediate implementation of comprehensive economic sanctions against South Africa. Churches should specifically press for
a. EEC countries to include coal in their sanctions package;
b. an end to the trade in oil, a crucial import for South Africa, by endorsing and supporting the international Shell oil boycott;
c. ways to boycott South African Airways and end its landing rights at international airports;
d. pressure on banks to stop the granting of credit to the government of South Africa, its institutions, private banks and the rest of the private sector in South Africa, as well to the public and private sectors in Namibia; banks should also refrain from rescheduling South African loans and make such rescheduling dependent on the resignation of the Botha government;

e. withdrawal of multinational corporations based in the countries visited who maintain trade and investment with South Africa and Namibia. Particular emphasis should be put on refraining from the exploitation of the resources of Namibia in accordance with the UN Decree 1;

f. increased and effective measures to comply with the UN Security Council Arms Embargo against South Africa (1977) and the prosecution of those who break it.

1.3. Urge the diplomatic isolation of the Afrikaner Nationalist regime and its expulsion from all United Nations agencies;

1.4. Urge Western governments to sign and ratify the International Convention on the Elimination and Repression of the Crime of Apartheid adopted by Resolution on the UN General Assembly in 1973 and ratified by some 8 member states;

1.5. Promote a climate of solidarity with the struggling peoples of Namibia and South Africa in the countries visited by meeting with South African liberation movement representatives in these countries.

2. NAMIBIA

2.1. PCR should embark upon a programme of Information on Resolution 435, its provisions and its implications for the future of Namibia. An information packet should be disseminated to all member churches for wide distribution and discussion at all levels.

2.2. The 4th May 1988 should be observed as a World Day of Prayer for a free Namibia; and the Anniversary of the Kassinga Massacre on 4th May should be marked by a special focus on continuing brutality and atrocities being committed in Namibia.

3. SOUTH AFRICA

The WCC should embark upon and intensify the campaign to expose the moral and theological illegitimacy of the South African regime by

3.1. encouraging member churches to recognise, support and

relate to the liberation movements actively endorsing the Lusaka Statement by working for its implementation as well as the Lusaka Action Plan;

3.2. campaigning for the recognition of the liberation movements of Namibia and South Africa as legitimate representatives of their countries;

3.3. encouraging Trade Unions to boycott the transport of goods to South Africa and Namibia seeking ways of working closer with unions campaigns and boycotts;

3.4. facilitating the production of educational and informational resources on the liberation movements to be widely distributed to local congregations;

3.5. establishing a coordinating mechanism for implementation of the Lusaka and Harare declarations by churches and anti-apartheid groups, especially all actions on sanctions mentioned under Point 1 of this document.

4. THE FRONTLINE STATES

4.1. This consultation commends the work of Frontline States in their care for refugees, notes especially the commitment of the Zambian Government and the Zambian Christian Council, our hosts in Lusaka, as well as other church agencies working among refugees.

4.2. Member churches should promote awareness of the pernicious consequences of apartheid policies on the economy and well-being of the Frontline States especially insofar as it means that scarce resources have to be diverted towards the defence of the countries.

4.3. The churches are encouraged to continue to campaign for a radical reform of the world economic order and give as much political and economic support as possible to the newly established African Fund of the Non-Aligned Movement.

4.4. The All Africa Conference of Churches should encourage its member churches to monitor the use being made by the South

African regime of agents in African states to violate sanctions especially with regard to oil shipments and the arms embargo, and to become more actively involved in anti-apartheid activities such as the Shell oil boycott.

4.5. Churches should oppose all support for UNITA in Angola and RENAMO in Mozambique, which are South African funded groups, and work to end US support for UNITA.

4.6. Churches should elicit moral and material support for the Frontline States, in particular by increasing aid to SADCC in its efforts to lessen dependency on South Africa.

4.7. Churches should support the call for sanctions/withdrawal/disinvestment from South Africa and Namibia and instead support investment in the SADCC countries.

4.8. The WCC should support and call on churches to
a. make financial contributions to the Documentation and Information Centre in Harare and
b. participate fully in the radio transmission venture by preparing religious programmes with a Kingdom-orientated approach on all aspects of liberation theology in order to counter right wing religious propaganda.

5. SOUTHERN AFRICA
5.1. Churches should provide mechanisms for Southern African students to study abroad.

5.2. Churches should increasingly work to encourage international youth groups to incorporate the issues of South Africa and Namibia in their ongoing activities.

5.3. Churches should raise the visibility of the plight of women in Southern Africa by convening seminars and workshops.

APPENDIX 8: South African Council of Churches: Income and Expenditure

(R'000s)

	1987 Income	1987 Exp.	1988 Income	1988 Exp.	1989 Income	1989 Exp.	1990 Income	1990 Exp.
General Secretariat								
Administration	1,658	1,666	1,639	1,478	1,502	2,044	2,061	1,686
General Secretary, Discretionary	27	27	27	27	54	54	49	49
Communications	405	236	5	316	438	570	366	366
Regional Councils	1,025	1,507	3,590	3,591	5,529	5,588	6,320	6,320
Staff development & training					216	216	175	175
Total	3,123	3,409	5,100	5,436	8,281	8,489	8,596	8,568
% of income/exp.	14.6%	16.6%	22.7%	24.1%	33.0%	29.2%	36.4%	33.2%
Justice and Society								
African Bursary Fund	2,023	1,745	1,429	2,257	1,177	3,725	3,140	4,281
Asingeni Relief Fund	4,493	4,027	6,241	4,795	2,211	3,428	2,531	3,853
Dependants' Conference	4,820	4,867	3,904	3,895	6,281	6,290	5,421	5,421
Justice and Reconciliation	371	186	185	235	(64)	321	274	257
Ministry to Refugees	878	983	1,142	1,279	2,531	2,394	1,733	1,733
National Emergency Fund	4,027	3,804	3,619	3,576	3,104	2,337	426	657
Standing for the Truth					286	286	11	11
Leadership Development					268	78	78	31
Total	16,612	15,612	16,520	16,037	15,794	18,859	13,615	16,245
% of income/exp.	77.6%	76.0%	73.5%	71.1%	62.9%	64.9%	57.7%	63.0%
Church and Mission								
Mission and Evangelism	110	82	89	69	55	125	122	122

Youth Development	72	93	77	109	173	248	137
Women's Ministries	115	74	91	120	194	378	180
Total	**297**	**249**	**257**	**298**	**492**	**748**	**439**
% of income/exp.	1.4%	1.2%	1.1%	1.3%	1.7%	3.2%	1.7%
Development and Service							
Hunger and Relief	1,049	966	325	470	788	254	180
Home and Family Life	142	94	117	165	236	229	188
Inter Church Aid - General	148	146	131	134	204	154	140
Inter Church Aid - Relief	22	57	11	26	6	11	17
Total	**1,361**	**1,263**	**584**	**795**	**1,234**	**648**	**525**
% of income/exp.	6.4%	6.1%	2.6%	3.5%	4.2%	2.7%	2.0%
Increase (Decrease) in Uncommitted Funds for the year	(375)	5	432	(714)		1,232	
Other items							
Total Income/exp	**21,020**	**20,538**	**22,885**	**22,566**	**24,380**	**29,073**	**24,839**	**25,777**
(Source of Income)							
Grants & Donations received	20,294	21,837	23,835	24,057			
Affiliation fees receivable	35	45	54	49			
Interest earned	662	985	476	637			
Other income	29	18	15	96			
Grants as % of total income	96.5%	95.4%	97.8%	96.8%			

Note: The Divisional incomes are expressed as a percentage of total committed income - that is, total income net of the increase/decrease in uncommitted funds for the year - see the notes to Appendix 8.

Source: Compiled from SACC Annual Financial Statements.

APPENDIX 9: South African Council of Churches: Grants and Donations
(Rand)

	1986	1987	1988	1989	1990
AUSTRALIA					
Australian Council of Churches	25,962	56,548	-	-	-
Australian Embassy	-	13,962	-	-	-
Community Aid Abroad	44,345	7,319	164,001	-	-
Uniting Church in Australia	-	-	-	-	6,000
Total	70,307	77,829	164,001	-	6,000
% of committed grants	0.4%	0.4%	0.8%	-	-
CANADA					
Anglican Church in Canada	-	330,688	353,613	200,927	609,162
Canadian Aid for SA Refugees	79,258	223,808	222,191	-	244,415
Canadian Council of Churches	1,273	-	-	-	-
Presbyterian Church	7,871	13,730	9,232	62,994	10,915
United Church of Canada	465,080	642,154	796,518	666,578	210,760
Total	553,482	1,210,380	1,381,554	930,499	1,075,252
% of committed grants	3.3%	5.8%	6.4%	3.8	4.7%
CARIBBEAN					
Caribbean Conference of Churches	2,997	-	-	-	
DENMARK					
Danida/Danchurchaid	3,224,801	3,127,757	4,504,693	3,687,835	2,991,179
Faeroe Students	100,424	-	-	-	-

	Total			
	3,325,225	3,127,757	4,504,693	3,687,835	2,991,179
	18.8%	15.1%	21.0%	15.0%	13.1%
FRANCE					
Defap	691	28,643	-	-	-
Department Evangelique Francois	3,054	-	-	-	-
Total	3,745	28,643	-	-	-
% of committed grants	-	0.1%	-	-	-
GERMANY					
BFDW (Brot Fur Die Welt)	1,070,290	1,862,932	2,761,114	2,524,858	2,079,948
Chrsanowsky, G.	120,000	-	12,822	-	-
ESP	-	-	239,913	120,000	120,000
Evan. FeR Kirche	-	-	-	10,463	-
Evan. Kirche in Deutschland (EKD)	318,653	355,846	181,702	127,697	-
Evan. Kirche in Westfalen	-	-	24,204	-	-
Evan. Kirchenkries Voel Kungen	175,942	4,246	20,402	-	-
Evan. Kirchentag	-	-	-	15,734	-
Evan. Kreditgenossenschaft	249,628	389,133	338,480	84,323	801,717
Evan. Missionwerk (EMW)	-	6,450	-	-	-
Evan. Propstei	38,172	8,895	-	-	-
Evan. Ref. Kirche in N.W. Germany	-	5,013	-	-	-
Evan. Reformed Landeskirchen	102,043	722,077	-	1,361,726	2,262,903
EZE	-	-	29,302	-	-
German Consulate	-	-	46,859	-	-
Kiechenkreisamt Hamburg	-	35,551	-	-	-
Kirchenkreisamt Hildsheim	-	-	-	-	-
Kirchenreisant Aurich	5,923	7,829	-	-	-
Lutheran World Federation	6,568	11,547	-	-	-
Maydell, I. von	-	-	-	-	-
Nordelbisches Kirchenkasse	87,324	74,260	26,830	-	-

Northelbian Centre for World Mission	43,639	52,731	53,733	88,256	142,905
Nordeleische Kirchenkasse	-	-	-	38,685	-
Protestant Church in Hessen	-	128,348	-	-	-
Trautwein, Dr. T.	6,237	-	-	-	-
United Evangelical Mission	12,069	12,069	-	-	-
Van der Linden	-	-	-	30,045	-
VELKD	-	223,924	137,851	139,480	163,788
Vereinigte Evan. Lutheran Kerk	-	-	56,004	4,696	-
OTHER	12,639	32,861	6,207	4,075	-
Total	2,249,127	3,933,712	3,935,423	4,550,866	5,571,261
% of committed grants	13.3%	19.0%	18.4%	18.5	24.4%
IRELAND					
Irish Council of Churches	8,693	5,798	-	-	-
ITALY					
Costa Lunga, Rev.	-	67,462	-	-	-
United Churches Merryland Playcentre	1,674	-	-	12,091	-
OTHER	-	8250	-	-	-
Total	1,674	75,712	-	12,091	-
% of committed grants		0.4%			
LESOTHO					
Mennonite Central Committee	115,490	95,700	35,429	49,018	50,924
% of committed grants	0.7%	0.4%	0.2%	0.2%	0.2%
NETHERLANDS					
Algemeen Diakonaal Bureau	198,891	251,000	290,766	226,000	220,446
Bisschoppelijke Vastenaktie	25,206	-	-	-	-
Commission of Interchurch Aid of the Netherlands Reformed Churches	211,900	163,573	92,828	99,682	149,052
Inter-Church Co-ordinating Commission for					

Development Projects (ICCO)	1,071,788	1,938,206	1,523,502	3,912,662	1,810,586
Kairos Christians	5,000	-	-	-	-
St Oecumenische Hulp aan Kerken	29,825	21,557	-	-	-
Stichting Wilde Ganzen	268,414	20,964	-	-	-
VD Gereformeerde Kerk	-	19,503	-	-	-
Zending Mission of the Reformed Churches	-	-	-	-	-
Total	**1,811,024**	**2,414,803**	**1,907,096**	**4,238,344**	**2,180,084**
% of committed grants	**10.7%**	**11.7%**	**8.9%**	**17.3%**	**9.5%**
NORWAY					
Church of Norway	1,356,572	1,944,534	2,050,000	3,661,417	3,388,533
Norwegian Church Aid	143,475	177,192	251,860	-	544,636
Total	**1,500,047**	**2,121,726**	**2,301,860**	**3,661,417**	**3,933,169**
% of committed grants	**8.9%**	**10.3%**	**10.7%**	**14.9%**	**17.2%**
SOUTH AFRICA					
Anglo-Vaal Limited	9,000	4,000	8,000	5,000	-
Catholic Bishops' Conference of SA	-	-	-	6,000	-
Church of the Province of SA	3,525	7,695	-	-	-
Community of the Resurrection, St. Peters	-	-	10,000	-	-
Congregation of Oakford	-	-	-	10,000	10,000
Control Data	-	25,000	50,000	-	-
Dominican Sisters of Kingwilliamstown	-	-	-	10,000	10,000
ICA Durban and District	5,000	5,500	7,000	7,000	7,500
Johannesburg Diocese	12,324	-	-	-	-
Joseph Helen	-	8,000	-	-	-
Methodist Church of SA	-	5,000	-	-	-
Tutu, Bishop (Refugees Fund)	5,903	12,656	-	-	-
3-M SA	-	-	20,000	32,500	52,000
Ex SA Church Hunger Fund	-	-	47,282	-	-
OTHER	20,228	63,473	28,570	23,193	19,625

Total	55,980	138,383	173,743	98,988	102,595
% of committed grants	0.3%	0.7%	0.8%	0.4%	0.4%

SWEDEN

Church of Sweden Aid	895,194	1,043,769	1,476,604	806,000	421,319
Church of Sweden Mission	210,434	779,034	53,966	1,062,157	1,334,009
Diakonia	649,062	159,307	891,254	1,102,427	1,221,440
Mission Covenant of Youth, Uppsala	1,396	-	-	-	-
Swedish National Christian Conference	-	-	-	34,425	-
Total	1,756,086	1,982,110	2,421,824	3,005,019	2,976,768
% of committed grants	10.4%	9.6%	11.3%	12.2%	13.0%

SWITZERLAND

Hilfswerk der Evangelischen Kirchen der Schweiz (HEKS)	24,412	275,423	15,714	175,967	152,075
Interchurch Support Group	92,057	161,530	103,887	158,966	121,189
Schweiz, Evan	-	-	-	83,139	-
Sutter, Dr. Erika	2,600	-	-	-	-
Total	119,069	436,953	119,601	418,072	273,264
% of committed grants	0.7%	2.1%	0.5%	1.7%	1.2%

UK

British Council of Churches	31,175	61,698	-	-	-
Cafod	-	-	-	24,938	-
Christian Aid	1,543,075	2,816,827	2,255,453	1,118,814	423,930
Greenbelt Festivals	-	-	6,817	-	-
Oxfam	509,731	166,502	-	-	-
St. Albans Diocesan Education	7,048	-	-	-	-
OTHER	7,120	7,983	1,060	-	-
Total	2,098,149	3,053,010	2,263,330	1,143,752	423,930
% of committed grants	12.4%	14.8%	10.6%	4.6%	1.8%

USA					
Adelphia Foundation	38,463				
Africa Fund	98,546	20,242	104,233	92,175	17,833
All Angels Episcopal Church	5,866	4,624	-	-	-
Church of the Brethren	-	10,288	34,692	-	-
Ford Foundation	143,946	-	101,375	-	-
Lutheran Church of the USA	32,352	-	-	76,989	88,025
LWF	-	-	-	-	-
Massachussetts Episcopal Diocese	40,054	10,084	4,170	-	-
Nat. Council of Churches of Christ	1,462,629	101,799	265,727	53,710	1,160,430
Nat. Council of Churches of the Orient	-	17,521	-	-	-
Plowshares Institute Inc.	2,658	8,829	3,527	9,736	-
Plymouth Congregational Church	-	4,819	3,113	-	5,492
Presbyterian Church,USA	7,808	63,392	4,111	24,329	115,835
A. Philip Randolph Education Fund Inc.	-	25,743	-	-	-
Reformed Churches in America	-	12,097	-	-	-
Religious Society of Friends	-	17,647	-	18,708	-
St. James' United Church	5,019	40,914	-	-	-
St. Mary's Presbyterian Church	-	-	-	-	-
St. Martin's Evan. Lutheran Church	7,086	-	-	-	-
Trinity Church	41,378	22,380	12,810	159,457	-
United Church Board for World Ministries	96,900	26,462	67,484	48,941	53,518
United Church of Christ	3,750	5,293	4,339	-	-
United Church on the Green	5,128	-	-	-	-
United Presbyterian Church	26,823	-	25,147	-	-
United Presbyterian Women	9,298	-	-	-	-
OTHER	28,290	16,062	4,747	-	5,030
Total	2,026,571	408,196	635,475	484,045	1,446,163
% of committed grants	12.0	2.0%	3.0%	2.0%	6.3%

263

WORLD COUNCIL OF CHURCHES	893,871	1,497,301	1,493,754	1,968,643	1,650,505
% of committed grants	5.3%	7.2%	7.0%	8.0%	7.2%
Sundry Overseas	23,531	60,483	58,558	284,117	74,537
Country of origin unclear	276,690	-	9,237	16,339	69,809
TOTAL GRANTS & DONATIONS COMMITTED TO PROJECTS	16,921,221	20,668,496	21,405,578	24,549,045	22,825,440
Increase/(Decrease) in Uncommitted Funds for the Year	99,771	(374,789)	431,682	(714,400)	1,231,780
TOTAL GRANTS & DONATIONS RECEIVED	17,020,992	20,293,707	21,837,260	23,834,64	524,057,220

Notes:
1. Donors normally commit grants to specific projects of the various departments of the SACC. These are all listed in the SACC Annual Financial Statements. The total donations committed to projects made by each donor has been calculated by summing all these individual project donations together.
2. Some grants are made without being committed to any projects - these are listed under uncommitted funds.
3. Unless a donor has contributed more than R5,000 in other years, individual grants under R5,000 are generally listed under "other".

Source: Compiled from SACC Annual Financial Statements.

INDEX

Abraham, K. C. 245
Adam, Heribert, 228n
Adler, Elisabeth 17n
Africa 2000 Congress 36, 240
African Communist 136, 137, 142n, 143n
African Independent Churches 95-96, 167, 195
African National Congress (ANC) 4, 5, 21, 29, 34, 36, 49, 80, 81, 82n, 84, 85, 95, 100, 118, 121, 122, 123, 127, 160, 165, 166, 175, 177, 181, 185n, 188, 192, 219, 222, 226, 238; armed struggle and 204-5; atrocities 207; bases 201, 204n; Christianity and 134-148; constituent assembly and 210-11; Department of Religious Affairs 142-43, 146, 147; financial support for 208, 240-41; four pillars of people's war 202, 209; history of 198-201; Kabwe conference 138-40, 210n; membership 206; nationalisation and 208-9; SACP and 228-229, 231; self-defence units and 210; UDF and 232, 234
African National Congress Youth League 6, 185n
African theology 72n, 86

Afrikaner Resistance Movement (AWB) 212-13
All Africa Conference of Churches 80, 242
Alves, Ruben 57n
Amalorpavadass, D. S. 242
Angola 44-45, 201, 207
apartheid - Conservative Party and 217; Dutch Reformed Churches and 7n, 12n; reform of 98-99, 123, 235-239
Appiah-Kubi, Kofi 245n
Apostolic Faith Mission Church 81n
Asian theology 58n
Assman, Hugo 57n
Association of Committed Theologians (ACT), 93-94
Azanian National Liberation Army (Azanla) 216
Azanian People's Manifesto 215
Azanian People's Organisation (AZAPO), 81n, 100, 108, 131, 188, 210, 215-17

Baptist Union (South Africa) 77, 167
Barclay, Oliver 43n
Barclay's Bank Shadow Reports 49n

Barkat, Anwar 118
Basic Christian Communities (BCCs) 88-89, 91-93, 156, 162-63, 165, 245
Bauer, P. T. 21n
Belhar Confession 7n
Belli, Humberto 163
Belydende Kring 92, 111
Berryman, Phillip 57n
Beyerhaus, Peter 101
Bhiman, Alex 96
Biko, Steve 72, 214
Bill, Francois 82n
Black Consciousness 63, 72-3, 76, 77, 81, 84, 100, 178, 179, 213-17, 232
Black Economic Development Conference (BEDC) 67
Black People's Convention (BPC) 214
Black Power 21, 24, 63
Black Theology 58, 76, 90, 145n, 156, 192; in America 62-71; in South Africa 61-62, 71-75, 77-79, 84-86; reconciliation and 79; violence and 69-80, 78-79; view of God 68-69, 78
Blake, Eugene Carson 41
Boesak, Allan 73, 77-80, 82, 86, 155n, 181, 232
Boff, Leonardo 57n, 88
Bond, Patrick 209
Bonino, José Míguez 242
Bosch 63n
Botha, P. W. 95, 127n
Broderick, Richard 52n, 55n, 60n, 90n
Brot Fur die Welt (Bread for the World) 171, 183n

Brown, Brian 121n
British Council of Churches 37n, 46, 97n, 110, 121n, 168, 171, 196
Buthelezi, Manas 242
Buthelezi, Mangosuthu 219-221
Burnett, Bill 26

Campbell, Keith 113n, 201n, 216n
Campus Crusade for Christ 151
Carmichael, Stokely 65n, 66n
Catholic Bishops' Publishing Co. 189
Catholic Fund for Overseas Development (CAFOD) 82, 189, 196, 246
Catholic Institute for International Relations 60, 97n, 110, 155, 189n
Catholic Pastoral Plan 91
CCFD 189, 246
Chandran, J. R. 242
Chikane, Frank 4, 5, 84, 97n, 104n, 128-9, 148, 155n, 160, 182, 186; biographical details 81n-82n
China 65, 226
Christ for All Nations 151
Christian Aid 82, 155, 180, 183n, 196, 246
Christian Conference of Asia, 242
Christian Institute 75-77, 95, 121n, 137n
Christians for Truth 158
Church of England in South Africa (CESA)

151, 152n, 167
Church of Sweden
 Mission 171
Church of the Province of
 South Africa (CPSA)
 11n, 93, 127, 151
Church Theology 103, 116
civic associations 209, 232
civil disobedience 106-9,
 129-133, 141, 149, 193,
 233
civil rights movement 63-65
Cluster Publications 94
Communist Party of
 South Africa 199, 227
Concerned Evangelicals
 114-18
Cone, James 62-63, 87, 245
Congress of South
 African Students
 (COSAS) 179
Congress of South
 African Trade Unions
 (COSATU) 183n, 206,
 229n, 232, 234
Conservative Party (CP)
 217-18, 223
contextual theology 51, 52,
 53-61, 77, 78, 83, 89, 94,
 110, 115, 151, 160, 161,
 172, 174, 192; theological
 training and 93-94
Convention for a
 Democratic South Africa
 (CODESA) 211, 217,
 218, 222, 224, 225, 227
Conway, Martin 168
Cottesloe Consultation 12,
 13n, 75
Council of African
 Independent Churches
 (CAIC) 95-96
Council of Churches for
 Britain and Ireland 83n
Council of Churches in
 Namibia 122
Cuba 45, 65, 162, 243, 201,
 207, 229

Danchurchaid 171, 183n
Davies-Webb, Warwick
 229n, 232n
de Beer, Zach 218
de Gruchy John, 10n, 12n,
 13n, 26n, 76, 97n, 155n
De Klerk, F. W. 3, 147,
 161, 218, 223, 224n, 225
Democratic Party 218, 223
Denton Committee 228n-
 229n
Diakonia 93n
Die Welt 185
Dowden, Richard 184n
Dube, John 134
Dussel, Enrique 242
Dutch Reformed Church
 (DRC) 7n, 12n, 11, 12,
 13, 167
Dutch Reformed Church in
 Africa (NGK in Afrika)
 12
Dutch Reformed Mission
 Church (NGSK) 7n, 12,
 78, 79

Eagleson, 58n, 245n
Ecumenical Association of
 Third World Theologians,
 (EATWOT) 52, 82, 155,
 192, 242-45
El Salvador 155
Ellul, Jacques 16
Eloff Commission 167, 168,
 170
Emergency Convocation of
 Churches 131, 132n

End Loans to South Africa (ELTSA) 49n
Endycott, Elizabeth 122n
Essien-Udom, E. U. 65n
European Community Special Programme of Assistance to the Victims of Apartheid 181-91, 196-97
European theology 243
Evangelical Alliance (UK) 115
Evangelical Fellowship of South Africa 116
Evangelical Witness in South Africa 115-17, 142
exiles 205-6

Fabella, V. 59n, 243n, 245n
feminist theology 59, 90, 156, 172, 173
Finca, Rev. B. 119
Foreman, James 67
Freedom Charter 199-200, 215, 228, 230, 232
Freedom House 44, 45n
FRELIMO 24n, 29, 36, 37, 44, 48, 240-41

Gifford, Paul 151n
Goba, Bonganjalo 72n, 73
Goodall, Norman 20n
Gospel Defence League 151n
Gqiba, Fumanekile 142, 145
GRAE 29, 240-41
Graham, Billy 134n, 151n
Green, Pippa 206
Griffiths, Brian 21n
Groote Schuur Minute 204
Guatemala 155
Guevara, Che 24n

Guttiérrez, Gustavo 54n, 57n, 58

Hamilton, Charles 65n
Hani, Chris 231
Harare Declaration 118-21, 247-48
Hein, Rodney and Ellie 45n
Hendrickse, Allan 223
Herstigte Nasionale Party (HNP) 219
Hlapane, Bartholemew 228n, 229n
Hoile, David 45n
hope theology 58n
Hudson, Darril 10n, 13n
Hughes, Philip 106n
Hurley, Dennis 182

ICCO 171, 183n
Ige, Bola 17
Inkatha/Inkatha Freedom Party (IFP) 4, 100, 123, 127, 188, 206, 219-222, 233
Inqaba Ya Basebenzi 135
Institute for Contextual Theology (ICT) 54n, 55n, 59n, 88, 115n, 127, 146n, 148n, 149, 151, 153, 160, 162, 173, 192, 194, 197; African Independent Churches and 95-96; ANC and 141; establishment of 81-82; income 246-47; influence on theological training 92-94; Kairos Document and 97; sees Church as 'site of struggle' 149-50;
institutional violence 18, 23

International Defence and
   Aid Fund 177
International Fellowship of
   Reconciliation 129n
International Labour Reports
   49n

Jeffery, Anthea 202, 209n
Jordan, Pallo 228n
*Journal of Theology for
   Southern Africa* 153-54,
   157

Kagiso Trust 181-191, 196
Kairos Document 97, 101-
   113, 119, 125, 141, 153,
   155, 172, 176, 192; civil
   disobedience and 106-9,
   112; deficiencies of 105-
   6; distribution of 109-10;
   rejects reconciliation 103-
   4; rejects reforms 102;
   violence and 103; youth
   and 111-13
Kairos liturgies 113-14, 120
Kane-Berman John 4, 5,
   98n, 188
Kearny, Paddy 93n
Kistner, Wolfram 155n,
   176, 187
Kitshoff, M. C. 95n
Korea, 155
Kritzinger, J. 83n
KwaSizabantu 158, 161

Labour Party 222-23
Lamola, John 145, 147,
   148, 212n
Lefever, Ernest 14n
liberation theology 54, 56-
   59, 76, 85, 86, 88, 90,
   102, 115, 153, 156, 163,
   173, 174, 192, 243

Libya 201, 207, 226
Lodge Tom 72n
Lumko Institute 91
Lusaka Statement 93n, 121-
   129, 249-255
Luther King, Martin 23, 64
Lutuli, Albert 134

Magkatho, S. M. 134
Mahabane, Z. R. 134
Majola, Sisa 230
Makwetu, Clarence 226
Malan, Ryan 113n
Malcolm X 24n, 64-65
Mandela, Nelson 80n, 134n,
   198, 200, 203, 205n, 207,
   210, 210, 220, 229n, 232
Mandela, Winnie 185, 205
Marchant, Colin 59n
Marcuse, Herbert 18
Marks, J. B. 228n
Marxism 14-15, 58, 85, 90,
   92, 123, 135, 163, 227,
   231
Mass Democratic Movement
   132, 234
Massey, James 127
Matthews, Joseph 21
Mayson, Cedric 82n, 137-
   38, 142n, 143
Mbeki, Govan 198, 200
Mdlalose, Thoko 136
Merizalde, Luis Daniel
   122n
Methodist Church of
   Southern Africa 11n,
   127n, 160n
Metz, Johannes 58n, 60
minjung theology 59, 156
Misereor 189
Mkhatshwa, Smangaliso
   75n, 82, 97n, 151, 155n,
   164, 181, 182, 211n

Mlambo, Jonathan 122
Mogoba, Stanley 160n
Molebatsi, Ceasar 115, 155n
Molefe, Popo 234
Moltman, Jurgen 58n
Moore, Dr Basil 62, 72n
Mosala, Itumeleng 62n, 72n, 73n, 74n, 84n, 155n, 216
Motlhabi, Mokgethi 62, 72, 214n, 226n
Mozambique, 44-45
MPLA 29, 36, 44, 48
Muhammed, Elijah 64
Mushete, Ngindu 242

O'Dowd, Michael 98n
Oxfam 171, 196

Namibia 122, 125, 126, 155, 187
Naon, Alejandro Ezcurra 122n
Natali 182n, 184
National Commitee of Negro Churchmen (NCBC) 66-67
National Council of Churches (USA) 24, 66
National Forum 100, 215, 232
National Party 12n, 217, 223-225, 235
Naudé, Beyers 75, 82, 92n, 97, 232
necklace murders 100, 144n, 185n, 233
Nefolovhodwe, Pandelini 216
Neuhaus, Richard 201
New African 188, 190
New Nation 93n, 147, 148n, 189
Ngubane 202n, 228n
Nicaragua 89, 155, 162-65
Nolan, Albert 52n, 55n, 56, 60n, 81, 83, 90, 97n
Norman, Edward 43n
Novak, Michael 57n
Ntwaso, Sabelo 74
Nujuma, Sam 122
Nyatsumba, Kaizer 234n

PAIGC 29, 48, 240-41
Pan Africanist Congress (PAC) 36, 84, 118, 122, 123, 127, 160, 166, 175, 177, 188, 192, 199, 210, 213, 225-227, 238, 240-41
Patriotic Front 29, 31, 36, 226
Peace Accord 205, 210, 217, 218, 220, 227
people's theology 59
Phakamani 142, 143, 144n, 146n
Phillips, Channing 22
Pityana, Barney 72, 121n, 161
PLO 207
political prisoners 204
political theology 58n
political violence 3, 100, 108-9, 112-13, 123-4, 128n, 177-78, 193, 209-10, 212-13, 233
Poqo 226
Porzgen, Gemma 203
post-exilic theology 160
Potter, Philip 33, 41
Pretoria Minute 204
Pro Veritate 76 82n, 137n
Programme to Combat Racism (PCR) 29-52, 72n, 76, 118, 121, 176;

Church of England and 30n, 32n; Conference on racism 1980 33-35; criteria for grants 38-39, 41; educational work 48-49; initial grants 29; Kairos Document and 118; Lusaka Statement and 121; programmatic work 49-50; row over grant to Patriotic Front 31-33; source of funds 28, 37n; total grant allocations 36, 192, 240-41
Prophetic theology 104, 173

Radio Freedom 124
Radu, Michael 201n, 202n, 232n, 233n
reconciliation 22-23, 148; ANC and 144-45; Chikane and 104; *Evangelical Witness in South Africa* and 117; Lusaka Statement and 126; Kairos Document and 104
Rees, John 177
Reformed Independent Churches Association (RICA) 152
Returned Exiles Coordinating Committee (RECOC) 207
Rhema Bible Church 151
Right Wing Christian Groups 151-153, 156
Road to Damascus 155-57, 172, 192
Rodriguez, Rodriguez Y 61
Rossouw, Rehana 187
Roux, Helene 113n, 216n

Rowntree Trust 48
Rustenburg conference (National Conference of Churches) 7n, 161-62

Salvation Army (South Africa) 77, 167
Safro, Wayne 209
Sandinistas (FSLN) 89, 163-65
Schlemmer, Lawrence 209n
Scholtz, Adelbert 80n
SCIAF 189
Sechaba 138n, 146n, 147n
See-Judge-Act 92
Sharpeville 200
Shaull, Richard 14-17
Signposts Magazine 151n
Sisulu, Walter 198, 200, 203
Sjollema, Baldwin 46
Slack, Kenneth 20n
Slovo, Joe 228n, 230-31
Sobukwe, Robert 225
social analysis 90, 102, 132, 244
Solidarity 227
Sompetha, Mbulelo 210n
South 187, 189
South African Communist Party (SACP) 135, 137n, 143, 154n, 201, 203, 206, 225, 228-232; ANC and 228-29, 231; programme 230; membership 230
South African Congress of Deputies 199, 228
South African Congress of Trade Unions (SACTU) 36, 199, 240-41
South African Council of Churches (SACC) 4, 25-26, 76, 77, 80, 81, 82n,

93, 97, 118, 120, 122, 149, 151; aims 166; Asingeni Fund and 177-180; civil disobedience and 107-8, 128-133; EC and 181-190, 196; expenditure 172-80, 194-95, 256-57; income 168-71, 194-95, 256-57, 258-264; Lusaka Statement and 126-29; members 167; mission and evangelism and 172-74; political violence and 127-28, 130-31
South African Indian Congress 199, 228
South African Institute of Race Relations (SAIRR) 3, 4, 5, 109, 202n, 204n, 209n, 215n
South African Students' Organisation (SASO) 72, 73, 75, 213-14
South African Youth Congress (SAYCO) 185
Southern African Catholic Bishops' Conference, (SACBC) 81, 91, 132, 149, 173; EC and 181-190, 196
Soviet Union 5, 201, 202, 203, 243, 228, 230, 231
Sowell, Thomas 21n
Stanbridge, Roland 202
Standing for the Truth campaign 131-32, 145, 149n, 160, 176
State of Emergency 101, 216, 233, 238
State theology 103
Storey, Peter 5, 127n
Suttner, Raymond 206

SWAPO 29, 36, 122, 125

Tambo, Oliver 21, 22, 34, 122, 123, 141, 198, 200, 202
Tanzania 201, 204, 206
Terre-Blanche, Eugene 212-13
Theological Education Fund 52, 242
Thomas, David 77n, 168
Timothy Training Institute 96
Tingle, Rachel 180n
Tissong, Mike 216
Tlhagale, Buti 62n, 72n, 73n, 74n, 84n
Torres 58n, 243n, 245n
Tradition Family Property (TFP) 61n, 91n, 122n, 189
Transformation Resource Centre 129n
Treurnicht, Andries 217
Trocaire 82, 83, 189, 246
Tutu, Desmond 5, 72n, 127, 128n, 152n, 170, 182, 195

Umafrika 188
Umkhonto we Sizwe (MK) 140, 200, 201, 205, 210; SACP and 228-229n
Umsebenzi 135, 201n, 203n
United Christian Action 151n
United Democratic Front (UDF) 80, 81, 84, 85, 95, 100, 108, 131, 177, 182, 184, 185, 202, 206, 215, 232-234
University Christian Movement 62, 75
University of Cape Town,

Department of Religious Studies 82n, 97n, 148n, 149, 153
University of the Western Cape 80
urban theology 59
Utley T. E. 43n

Van der Brent 26n
Van Hoven, Lynette 95n
Vietnam 202, 243
Villa Vicencio, Charles 76n, 82n, 89, 97n, 154n, 155n
Vincent, John 22n, 23n, 25n, 59n
Visser 't Hooft, W. A. 11n
Vos, Suzanne 221n
Vrye Weekblad 188

Walshe, Peter 10n, 13n, 76n
Wanamaker, C. 149, 150n
Wendland, H. D. 17
Western Cape Council of Churhces 152
Western Province Council of Churches 116, 151, 174
Wilmore, Gayraud 63n, 66n, 67n
Wink, Walter 129, 176
Wing, Joe 170
Woods, Gavin 222n
World Bank 45n
World Council of Churches (WCC) 10-52; Central Committee meeting Canterbury 1969 26-27; Church and Society Conference 1966 13-19, 75, 192; Ecumenical Decade for Women 173; Evanston Assembly 11; Harare consultation 1985 and 118-121; Harare consultation 1990 and 147; Kairos Document and 97; liberation movements and 29, 36-37, 43-48; New Dehli Assembly 13; Notting Hill Consultation 20-25, 67; reparations and 25, 26, 27; revolutionary violence and 15, 17-19, 20, 25, 38-44; South Africa, early policy towards, 10-13; Uppsala Assembly, 19-20, 38, 52; *see also Programme to Combat Racism*
World Day of Prayer to End Unjust Rule in South Africa 120

Young Lee, Jung 59n

Xuma, Alfred 198

Youth With A Mission 151

Zambia, 201 206
Zille, Helen 213n
Zimbabwe 226
Zion Christian Church 95

Page 28. C. Aid 26, 27, 29.
PCR p 29
Murder of Missaries & children 78
+ grant $85,000
Main Brit Donor. Meth Ch P 37
41. Buy Arms. & 42
44 & 45. Refloared by M-L
54, 55. Bible Selection
56. THE Cross & re promise
Contextual theology assault on
teaching of the church.
69. Kill white Jesus

82 & 83 Hidden achievemts in IRELAND
87. Violence & the Bible
90, 91. Teaching politicial action
BCC. 88-89, 90. Anglican.
94, s freding Communism.
103 Futile to remain Neutral
101 Kairos. means.
112 & 113 result. 113 & 114
116, 117
119 church & violence
120 & 121

122-123, 125, 127. Violence
& failure to condemn 129., 131
135, 136, 137, 141, 142 144,
145, 150 153. 156, 157,
158, 159 160, 161, 163 167
169. 173, 174, 175, 180, 181,
184, 185, 186, 187, 188, 189,
190, 191

|195|

(135)